Stolen Moments

Ann —
Best Wishes
always —
Barbara Jeanne John

Other Books by
Barbara Jeanne Fisher

I Will Never Forget

How Much Can Teddy Bear?

Nobody's Lion

Stolen Moments

Barbara Jeanne Fisher

Epic Press

Belleville, Ontario, Canada

Stolen Moments

Copyright © 1999, Barbara Jeanne Fisher

This book is a work of fiction. Names, characters, places or incidents are a product of the author's imagination and are used fictitiously. Any resemblance to actual events, locals or persons, living or dead, is entirely coincidental.

2nd Printing, January 2000

Canadian Cataloguing in Publication Data

Fisher, Barbara Jeanne
    Stolen moments

ISBN 1-894169-77-8

    I. Title.
PS3556.I796S76 1999   C813'.54   C99-900212-0

**For more information or
to order additional copies, please contact:**

Stolen Moments
P.O Box 563, Fremont, OH 43420 USA
mentorsfriend@yahoo.com

Printed in Canada
by

Dedication

To all the Dons and Julies of the world, and for the Stolen Moments they have shared... and in a very special way to all the people who have known lupus in their life....

I once read that "the best way to love something is to realize that it might soon be gone forever." Perhaps this is why we were able to love and share so much. How does one begin to thank people who have always been there for her?

I will be eternally thankful for the times we had together. Whenever you feel down, think of some crazy moment we shared, when our friendship brought a smile to my face, then, I beg you, remember me that way. A special thanks to Theresa, Joseph, and Jude....

Know that I care, all my love, forever and for always....

Barbara Jeanne Fisher

My deepest thanks to Dr. Matt Morrow, M.D., who edited the lupus material for me, to Bill Greenleaf and Carolyn Hopwood Blick, for all their encouragement and support, to my husband, Joe, and all those whose lives and love have touched my heart enabling me to write this book....

"Once I picked up *Stolen Moments,* I couldn't put it down. A love story not soon to be forgotten. It's exuberant, inspirational, breathtaking, and heart warming... all at once. A book to be read over and over again."

—Rosemary Farrar Pocock
Terra Community College

"For those of us who cried for both love and sorrow through *Love Story, Stolen Moments* is yet another chance to see some of the love and grief of two older people, meeting too late in life. The unlikely meeting, accompanied by the strong emotions, brought tears to my eyes. It is indeed the most beautiful love story I have every read."

—Anonymous

"*Stolen Moments* is captivating and packed with emotion. Barbara is a true inspiration."

—Brooke Benoit
Author

"From the very beginning, I was fully caught up in the heart-wrenching account of Julie Hunter's battle with lupus and her growing love for Don Lipton. Julie's story will remind your readers that life and love are precious and not to be taken for granted."

—Bill Greenleaf
Writer's Digest Associate and published author

"A 'can't put down' kind of book. A book written with knowlege, filled with emotions, and a wonderful story line.

—Anonymous

Prologue

It had been raining off and on for the past few days, but the sun was out and the sky was a brilliant blue on that day in late April when Don Lipton returned down the wooded path to the gazebo. The small wooden structure sat amid a resplendent cover of wildflowers: mellow gold poppies, brilliant yellow buttercups, dainty scarlet columbines, and deep purple violets.

Don clutched two books together in his hands as he climbed the steps and sat down on the wood-slatted bench. He remembered his first walk to this gazebo with Julie, and how she had smiled when he picked a bouquet of those beautiful flowers for her.

It wasn't until the scene before him blurred and fragmented that he realized he was crying. He leaned back and closed his eyes, taking in all the scents and sounds while tears trickled down his cheeks. The air was fresh, clean, cool, just as it had been the last time he had sat on this bench with Julie. Birds called to one another from the canopy of trees overhead, and farther away he could hear the murmuring brook that flowed under the planked footbridge. He could believe that angels lived here.

With his eyes still closed, his mind ran over every feature of her: The clean simplicity of her face framed by dark brown curls; her large brown eyes above a delicate nose; the small, determined chin that lifted slightly when she was angry.

The sunshine slanted in under the eaves of the gazebo, warming his upturned face. On days when he was feeling down, Julie had often told him that if he kept his face to the sun, he would never be able to see life's shadows. She had taught him so much about the beauty of life. She had awakened in him all this love he now felt for his beautiful, natural surroundings.

"Don," she used to say, "life isn't always fair. But you have to remember that one of God's most beautiful creations is the rainbow, and it wouldn't be possible without the clouds and rain."

She had certainly been the sunshine in his life.... God, how he missed her.

He opened his eyes and looked down at the hardcover book in his hands. *To Touch a Heart* read the title, above a pencil sketch of the gazebo. She'd finished the book only a few days before he saw her for the last time. It had come out two weeks ago, and was already getting wonderful reviews.

He moved the book aside and looked at the spiral-bound composition notebook beneath it. Her daily journal — hand-written notes and thoughts and heartfelt feelings she had recorded during the few months they had known each other.

This was all he had left of her. These two books and a million precious memories. Such beautiful memories....

Forcing his fingers beneath the cover of the notebook, he opened it to a tear-stained page. Carefully, he ran his fingers across it as if trying to *feel* her love in the words she had written to him. He knew them by heart:

My Forever Friend,

I once read that the best way to love something is to realize that it might soon be gone forever. Perhaps this is why we were able to love and share so much. How does one begin to thank an individual who has always been there for her?

I wish I could have stayed longer, but I will be eternally thankful for the time we did have together. Whenever you feel down, think of some crazy moment we shared, perhaps a time when I was happiest because you told me that I have "antsy eyes," or that my smile was beautiful. Then, love, I beg you, remember me that way.

My love, know that I care, forever and for always,

Julie

Don closed the book gently and leaned back. Remember her love? How could he ever forget the lady? Her too-brief presence in his life had certainly been a gift from Heaven. She had showed him how to love and give and care again. Julie had spent her days looking for ways to make the most of every second of life.

The ache returned, thick in his throat, hot in his chest and in his eyes. Don lowered his face into his hands, blocking out the sunny day and the wildflowers and all the other sights that reminded him so much of Julie.

Somehow, he had known from the beginning that she wasn't meant to be in his life forever. She had come when he needed her most. Her love and caring helped him dispel the ghosts and terrors of his own past — a past that had haunted him for twenty years.

She had been a part of his life just long enough to help him live again. But how, he wondered, could he ever live without her?

Chapter One

MONDAY, JANUARY 13 — Two years earlier

Dear Diary,

Today I am finally going after my lifelong dream. I am so excited! My daughter is grown up and married, and now, finally, it is time for me. Robert thinks I'm crazy for going to college at age forty-five.

Of course, sometimes I have my own doubts. My chest still hurts much of the time from this illness. I wonder when Dr. Cole will get the results from my latest blood tests....

One by one, the students filed into the classroom, shrugging out of coats and jackets. Looking around, Julie Hunter could see that most of them were in their late teens or early twenties.

She had been nervous all morning, and now a knot twisted in her stomach as she thought about how she must look to these young students. Many of them probably had *mothers* younger than her. What if she looked really dumb in front of them?

She drew in a deep, calming breath and tried to put that thought out of her mind. For better or worse, she was here. If anyone had a problem with that — well, that was *their* problem, not hers.

For some reason, the first students to enter had taken the back row seats, and she had no choice but to sit directly in front of the instructor's large wooden desk. The student desks, modern wood-laminate seats with writing platforms attached to the right side, were surprisingly comfortable.

As Julie sat down, two young girls in denim jeans and sweatshirts crowded toward the back. It appeared to Julie that they were having a contest to see who could blow the biggest bubble with their gum. Suddenly, they noticed an interesting-looking male on the opposite side of the room, and picked up their belongings and shuffled over to sit next to him. Handsome and broad-shouldered, the youth's green sweater displayed an athletic letter with two footballs.

The blinds on the windows lining the outer wall were open to allow the morning sunlight into the room. Julie wondered briefly why she was sitting in a classroom when she would love to be outside taking a walk. As she carefully arranged her papers and checked to make sure that her pencils were sharpened, she reminded herself that this was, after all, *her* choice.

She gathered in her self-confidence and sat up a little straighter in her chair. *Okay, world, I'm ready!*

Julie had waited a lifetime to go to college. She and Robert had been married soon after she graduated from high school, and their only daughter, Cheryl, was born a year later. Julie had spent most of the last twenty-five years being a full-time mother and wife.

Not that she minded. Thinking about Cheryl now made her smile, and she again looked around, wondering if Cheryl might have had a class in this very room while she was attending Claremont Community College. Cheryl had graduated four years ago with a degree in early childhood education, and had been teaching kindergarten at an elementary school across town. Unlike Julie, Cheryl had not met her soulmate and fallen in love until well after she had finished college.

Now she and Tom were expecting their first baby in early April, and Cheryl was looking forward to quitting work and devoting herself to her family. It was ironic, in a way; Julie had given all her time to her family and was now determined to get a college degree, while Cheryl had her degree and wanted only to devote herself to her family.

Not for the first time, Julie thanked God for giving Cheryl to her. They were as close as a mother and daughter could be. Actually, they were more than mother and daughter; they were also best friends. They lived only fifteen minutes' driving time away from each other, and on days when they didn't see each other, they almost always spoke on the telephone. Julie felt closer to Cheryl than to any other person in the world.

Over the years, as their relationship developed, Julie had felt especially thankful for that. Robert certainly wasn't someone with whom she felt comfortable sharing intimate feelings. She loved Robert dearly, and she knew he loved her too, in his way. But he was a man who didn't express feelings well — or receive them from others, for that matter.

It was a trait he'd either been born with, or had acquired as a young boy. Julie had long ago given up trying to change him, although talking to him was often maddeningly frustrating. A conversation about his work or his classic car collection or politics or the weather was fine, but if Julie came even close to expressing something she felt deeply, it was a sure bet that Robert would find a way to escape and hide away in his office or workshop.

If anything, it was even worse now that Robert was having problems with the business they owned. She knew he was more concerned than he'd let on to her — but of course, that was typical. She knew little of the business, and he seemed determined to keep it that way. She knew only that she'd seen the worried expressions on his face, and she'd caught glimpses of the financial projections he'd been putting together for the bank.

She also knew that at this time, with a threat to their very livelihood hanging over their heads, Robert felt that he needed her support more than ever. Not support in making decisions or sorting out the business problems, of course — support in terms of making sure the evening meal was always on the table at the prescribed time, and making sure the shirt he wanted to wear was pressed and hanging in his closet.

He resented her decision to go to college, and he hadn't been subtle about voicing that resentment. He wanted her at home, where he needed her. But she had decided it was time to be someone besides *Robert's wife* or *Cheryl's mother.* She wanted to be herself... Julie Anne Hunter. Robert had problems accepting that, but he would just have to learn to live with it.

She looked around at the young faces again. She might feel a little out of place, but so what? She knew she was bright, and she was certainly willing to work hard. She could keep up with them.

Looking across the room, she saw someone she recognized. She had met Rick Marston the week before at orientation. He was a friendly, outgoing boy, and they had chatted for several minutes in the auditorium while waiting for the school's president to make her appearance.

When Rick spotted her, he waved and came over to sit at the desk beside her. He looked well-scrubbed, his dark hair neatly combed. He was wearing Reeboks, jeans, and a sweat-shirt emblazoned with the name of a rock group Julie had never heard of.

"Hi, Julie!" He sounded genuinely pleased to see her. "I didn't know you were signing up for this class."

"I wasn't really planning to," Julie told him, glad to have someone to talk to. "It was in the right time slot for this semester, and I was told it was a requirement."

Rick nodded. "I've heard that the president of the college feels strongly that students should take at least one writing class. Maybe she thinks it's becoming a lost art."

The boy in front of Rick turned around. "Have either of you ever had Lipton for a class?" He was a slender boy with fine blond hair curling like golden smoke around his head.

Rick and Julie both shook their heads.

"No, but...." Rick hesitated, as if he'd been on the verge of saying something else. Finally, he just shook his head.

"Not me," Julie said. "This is my first semester here."

"Well, my sister had him two years ago." The blond-haired boy glanced around, then leaned a little closer and lowered his voice. "She said the guy is a real jackass."

The girl sitting on the other side of him spoke up. "I had him last semester. He's more than a jackass. He's an egotistical, super-cilious jerk who takes perverse pleasure in belittling students."

Rick Marston spoke up again. "From what I understand, the best way to survive his class is to lay low and try to skate through without drawing his attention."

As others around them chimed in, Julie began to realize that most of them were taking Lipton's class only because it was required in order to get a degree from Claremont Community College. Nobody had anything good to say about him.

Great, she thought. *My first class, and it sounds as if it's taught by a real jerk.*

Then she gave herself a firm shake of the head. She would not let the doubts and insecurities creep back in. And she would not allow herself to be intimidated by Donald Lipton or anyone else. She would do her best to slide through his class without making waves. After all, she had no real interest in this class. Her goal was a degree in mathematics. She loved working with numbers and was intrigued by the fact that in math, everything always had a correct answer. It was so unlike life, where sometimes there were no answers at all.

"Hi!"

Julie looked up, and realized that someone had taken the desk on her right side. The woman looked to be in her late thirties, trim and attractive, with shaggy blonde hair and expressive brown eyes.

"I'm Patricia Davis." She gave Julie a winning smile. "I didn't think students were supposed to start daydreaming until the instructor started his lesson!"

Julie returned the smile. "I'm Julie Hunter. I guess I was just trying to get in the right mood."

"Well, it's nice to see someone else from my generation." Patricia looked around the room. "I wonder if these kids have permission notes from their parents to be here."

Julie laughed, immediately feeling better. "You aren't nervous about coming back to school after so many years?"

"Nervous? Me?" Patricia glanced around the room again, then leaned closer and whispered, "I'm scared stiff. I'm just trying to hide it."

Julie laughed again. "You're doing a good job of that."

"What's your major?"

"Mathematics."

"Ah... a right-brainer. Logical, organized. I'm about as organized as a...." She flipped a hand, unable to come up with something to make her point. "Well, my husband says 'chaos' ought to be my middle name. I'm a communications major."

Julie couldn't help smiling. "I think you should do well at that."

"I sure don't have any trouble talking," Patricia agreed. "You planning on being a math teacher?"

For a moment, Julie didn't know how to answer. The aching pain in her chest was always there to remind her that she was probably being foolish to make any long-term plans at all. She had gone to see Dr. Cole at the end of the previous week, and was waiting to hear the results of numerous blood tests and x-rays. She had given so much blood in the past few weeks that Robert had teased her about it, telling her that the doctors should just put a spigot in her veins so they could turn it on when they needed another sample.

There was no way she could tell this friendly, outgoing woman about all the uncertainty in her future. "We'll just have to wait and see how it works out," she said at last.

Before Patricia could respond, the door swung open suddenly and thumped against the wall as a giant of a man strode into the room with a bundle of papers thrust under one arm. He stepped to the desk, dropped the papers onto it with a heavy *thunk,* and looked around the room.

Julie found herself staring. This was Professor Donald Lipton? He looked more like a lumberjack: tall, broad-shouldered, and rough, with a medium-length salt and pepper beard. Julie thought he looked to be a few years older than her. His graying hair, shot through with streaks of lighter gray that was almost white, might have given him a distinguished look if it hadn't been paired with a face that looked so haughty. He wore dark slacks and a blue plaid shirt that looked a size too small. No tie, and no jacket. Dr. Lipton was not, Julie decided, a man who cared much about his appearance.

After surveying the class — and giving no indication at all that he liked what he saw — Lipton opened a folder on his desk and began to call roll. After marking several names as the students answered, he stopped at one and looked out at a girl sitting several rows over from Julie.

"So, Miss Deemer, I see they haven't thrown you out yet. I did hear that we have a shortage of students again this semester, but I'm surprised you'd have the courage to try this class again." The girl shrank down into her chair and remained silent. Lipton's gaze moved to a young man behind her. "Mr. Joseph, I see that the D I gave you last semester hasn't dampened your enthusiasm. Did you come back to see if you could earn another one?" Lipton issued a harsh bark of laughter. "Earn! Poor choice of words."

My God, Julie thought, *is this guy for real?*

She answered when he called her name, and felt her heart sink when he paused and gave her a condescending smile.

"Well, Ms. Hunter, I'm glad to see we have at least one older student in the class. What brings you to college so late in life?"

She felt the blood rush to her face as his eyes focused on her. *What a pain,* she thought. Her flush deepened when he winked at her, then went on to complete the roll call.

"Good thing he didn't pull that crap on me," Patricia whispered, leaning closer to Julie. "I'd have given him a piece of my mind!"

Julie had no doubt of that. But she was remembering what Rick Marston had said. If she could lie low, maybe she could get through this class with a minimum amount of fuss.

Lipton leaned his rump against the front of the desk and folded his large arms across his expansive chest. "As I'm sure you all know, my name is Lipton. Some of you who have had me in the past know me as Don. I have also been called a variety of other names, but I would suggest before you try any of those, you remember who's holding the pen that grades your papers." He paused, and there was no hint of a smile on his face. It was as if he wanted to make sure the threat was taken seriously. "I have the power at all times to go back and make changes on your permanent records."

Julie noticed that the bottom of Lipton's shirt was pulled apart where it stretched across his stomach, and despite the harsh tone of his voice, she had to suppress a giggle. She found herself thinking that he might make a great department store Santa Claus. *Well, not exactly*, she corrected herself. *Santa was nice.*

She also noticed that he wore a simple wedding band, and couldn't help but wonder who would ever consent to marrying such a jerk.

Professor Lipton went on to give the class a spiel about class objectives, class attendance, and the writing assignments that he would be giving them every week.

"Those assignments have to be turned in on time, folks!" he said, thumping his fist on the desk for emphasis. "I could stand up here and plead with you, I can appeal to your good or bad nature as the case may be, and still a certain number of you will ignore the deadlines. So I warn you that for every day you are late with any assignment, I will deduct one-half point from your grade. Two days, and your A becomes a *B*. Eight days, and you will save your time and mine by not bothering to turn it in at all."

A hand went up from the boy with the curly blond hair. "What if we're sick on the day it's due?"

"Bring a note from the surgeon who did your quadruple bypass," Lipton said with a straight face. "Now, each of these assignments—" He stopped abruptly, staring at someone near the back. "Excuse me. I didn't mean to interrupt your chat back there. Did you have a question?"

"Well... actually, yes," came a timid female voice from behind Julie. "If we turn in all of the assignments on time, does that mean we'll get an *A* in the class?"

Lipton brushed her off coldly. "Why are you so concerned about your grade? It's what you *learn* that counts, isn't it?"

"Well...." The girl was obviously hesitant to go on in the face of Lipton's reaction.

"Well, what?" he demanded. "You have something else to say that might enlighten the class?"

With an obvious effort, the girl summoned up some courage. "I'm attending college on a scholarship, Dr. Lipton. I have to get good grades to keep it, and I just wanted to make sure I knew what would be required in this class."

"Ah, I see." Lipton nodded. "If this class is going to be too hard, you'll just drop it, right?" He didn't give the girl time to formulate an answer. "I'll tell you what. If you're looking for an easy class, why don't you sign up for Ms. Barnett's home economics class. I understand you'll get an *A* in that class if you don't burn the cookies."

Julie glanced around at the poor girl, inwardly fuming at Lipton's attack on her. By now, the girl looked as if she were on the verge of tears. Lipton had a smug look on his face, as if he were enjoying being the class bully. Julie couldn't take it anymore.

"Professor Lipton," she spoke up, working hard to keep her voice coolly polite, "I think her question is reasonable. I'm sure most of us are interested in knowing how we can do well in any class. Will all the writing assignments be weighted equally?"

Lipton turned slowly and gave her a hostile stare. "You're...." He paused to glance down at his class roster. "Ms. Hunter, right?"

"*Mrs.* Hunter will be fine," Julie corrected.

Lipton nodded. His face had flushed slightly, and for the first time, Julie noticed a small, curved scar above his left eyebrow, standing out white against the pink skin. "Do you have a scholarship to worry about too, Mrs. Hunter? Perhaps something for older students returning to college?"

Once again, Julie felt the blood rush to her face. "No, Professor Lipton. I don't have a scholarship. But I want to do as well as I can. It would help if we knew how your grading system works and how much weight you give to each assignment."

The flush in his face had deepened. Clearly, he wasn't accustomed to being faced down by a student. "You'll have ten assignments in this class," he said tightly. "I may give more weight to the final assignment, but I haven't decided about that yet. The others will all be weighted equally. Does that answer your question?"

Since she had gone this far, Julie decided to press on. "Not completely. When will we know about the weighting of the final assignment?"

"Probably not before I give it out," he snapped.

That seemed absurd to Julie. Surely, he had taught this class enough times to know how he would rank the assignments. But she decided to let that drop for now. "How much do you count off for punctuation and spelling?"

He stared at her silently for a long moment. Around her, Julie could hear other students shifting uneasily in their seats, obviously uncomfortable with this confrontation.

But Julie kept her eyes firmly on Lipton, refusing to let him stare her down. She thought she knew how he was feeling. He was accustomed to intimidating young students who were too afraid to confront him. Now he had come up against someone who wouldn't back down so easily.

"Mrs. Hunter," he said at last, his words dripping with acid, "I grade on effort. If you work hard to do the best you can, you'll get an *A* on every assignment. If you don't, you'll get less. It's as simple as that."

"So you don't care about punctuation and grammar?"

"I thought I just told you what matters to me," he said. "Effort."

That still didn't really answer the question, but Julie decided she'd pressed her luck far enough. "Thank you."

Lipton drew in air and let it out in a long sigh as he moved his eyes to take in the rest of the class. "Now, let me tell you what I expect to see in your writing assignments. I expect to see *people.* People who *do* things, *feel* things, *think* about things. People who confront fears and suffer pain and celebrate joys and—" Lipton stopped suddenly, and his mouth dropped open in utter disbelief. "Hold on! There's something very wrong here." His large body, moving at an astounding speed for its bulk, rushed to the middle of the classroom. Before anyone could have even an inkling of his thoughts, Lipton reached down and grabbed the pencil out of a student's hand, held it up over his head and, with two hands, broke it in two.

SNAP!

"We do *not* take notes in this class!"

While the young man whose pencil had been broken stared at him in disbelief, Lipton dropped the pieces onto the desk and repeated the astonishing declaration.

"I have a rule, folks. No taking notes in my class. Can anyone guess why I have that rule?"

Nobody dared offer an opinion.

"We're going to be talking about *writing,* folks. There are no chemical elements to remember, no equations, no rules and regulations." Pointing at his head, he said, "I need your attention right here. How can you keep your brain clear enough to listen if you're making hen scratches on those white sheets?"

Nobody had an answer to that. Silently, everyone put away their notebooks, including Julie. She wondered how she could possibly put up with this man for an entire semester.

Lipton returned to his desk and rambled on about writing, and about the accomplishments of some of the world's great writers. He poked fun at many popular American writers, asserting that "they wouldn't know what talent was if it kicked them in the butt." Julie wanted to ask how all these writers continued turning out bestsellers if they had no talent, but decided to keep her thoughts to herself.

When finally the class was ending, Lipton strode to the blackboard, shoved his rolled up shirt sleeves further up his hairy arms, and began writing. "Before the next class, I expect all of you to read chapter one in your *Beaman Guide for College Writers*. For those of you who haven't a clue what I'm talking about, that's the assigned text for this class. This chapter is about using your memory to generate writing ideas. I'm sure most of you can remember some important happenings in your life." Lipton turned to stare at Julie. "In fact, some of you have been around long enough to have an entire *warehouse* of memories. Wouldn't you agree, Mrs. Hunter?"

Again, Julie didn't speak. But she felt the blood rush to her face when the eyes of her classmates turned toward her. *Who does he think he is?*

When his jab did not evoke a response, Lipton gave up on her and continued. "After you read this chapter, I want you to write about a personal experience that changed how you acted, thought, or felt from that moment on. Your purpose is not merely to tell an interesting story, but to show your reader the importance that experience had for you. I suggest you pick an encounter with a person who for some reason greatly influenced you, or a person who presented you with a challenge or obstacle."

That should be easy, thought Julie. *Dr. Donald Lipton has already changed my view of college professors.*

"Excuse me," she said. "How long should it be?"

Once again, Lipton turned his stare on her. "You're asking me? I thought *you* were going to write the paper."

That was supposed to be an answer? "Well, of course I'm going to write it. But shouldn't we know how long to make it?"

"Yes, you should," he agreed. Now a grin was twitching at the corners of his mouth, and that made her angrier.

"Then why don't you tell us what the length should be?"

He issued another heavy sigh, as if Julie had asked the dumbest question in the history of mankind. "Mrs. Hunter, *you* are the writer of this piece. *You* are the one who needs to decide how long it should be. Make it no shorter or no longer than it *needs* to be. It's as simple as that."

Julie gave up. If he didn't care how long it was, then why should she? It would be easy to crank out one or two pages, and that was exactly what she intended to do.

"I might add," Lipton went on, "that the main purpose of this class is to teach you to write from your heart. Don't worry too much if I fail you. This class will be offered again next semester." Throwing his material together in a haphazard bundle, he turned toward the class and grumbled, "Now go be a nuisance to somebody else," before striding from the room.

After the door closed behind him, Rick Marston leaned over to Julie and said, "You're one brave lady. I've never heard of anyone standing up to Dr. Lipton like that before."

"That's probably one reason he's such a jerk," Julie said, still smoldering. "Everyone lets him get away with it."

"Good thing you didn't have a gun with you," Patricia said from the other side. "I think you might've shot him! Not that I would've cared. At least, that would've shut him up."

Julie had to laugh at that. "I'd better get to my next class, Patricia. See you later."

As Julie gathered up her books and headed for the door, her eyes caught the words Dr. Lipton had scrawled in heavy block letters on the blackboard. *WRITING IS HARD WORK.*

I'm not afraid of hard work, she told herself. *I'll show that pompous, egotistical idiot that even an old woman of forty-five can keep up with him!*

Chapter Two

Outside, Julie paused to study her map of the campus, then crossed the central courtyard toward her next class. Claremont Community College, at the west edge of the town of Freeborn, was small by big-city standards — fewer than 7,000 students. Freeborn had only about 60,000 residents, but the college had a good reputation that drew students from as far away as Sacramento, more than a hundred miles to the north.

The campus was attractively landscaped, and the structure itself was red-brick of contemporary design. Julie paused to admire the fountain at the center of the courtyard. It was surrounded by benches constructed of brick, wrought iron, and light oak. The constant ticking patter as the spray fell back into the pool was very soothing, and Julie thought this would be a good place to come and study on warm days.

Her next class was general psychology. Mrs. Cramer, a middle-aged, bespectacled woman who was clearly enthusiastic about the subject she was teaching, was pleasant as she went briskly through the requirements and objectives of the class. She even had time to get into the first chapter of the textbook.

"Carl Roger's theory is that we are not merely a bundle of moldable responses," she told the class. "Rather, we are creative beings capable of free choice, all in control of our own lives. We have a choice in everything we do in life."

Julie thought to herself, *Sure, then why are they making me take Professor Lipton's creative writing class for a degree in math?*

Mrs. Cramer briefly summarized the chapters of the class text, and Julie was surprised when she realized how much material the book would cover. Her interest perked up even more as she read the chapter title *Health, Stress, and Coping,* and she was amazed as she looked at the large, colored photos showing the inside of the human brain.

The class passed quickly, and she found her own enthusiasm growing. The world was full of knowledge, and this new learning adventure was opening it up for her. The college atmosphere made her feel alive, part of the real world that stretched far beyond the boundaries of the universe she had inhabited for so long as a mother and wife.

Her final class for the day was business math. A few of the younger students frowned as Mr. Neuman explained that in this class they would have to learn how to keep a checkbook, figure interest on savings accounts, and learn all about life and health insurance.

Julie had already done all those things in caring for her family. Her spirits were lifted when Mr. Neuman smiled at her and said, "Young lady, I'll bet you could teach me a few things."

Yes, Julie thought, *there are some advantages in going to college later in life.*

She smiled as she compared Mr. Neuman's friendly approach with Miss Peabody's algebra class she'd taken so long ago in high school. Miss Peabody would nod her ancient head as she pecked at the blackboard with a long pointer, reciting a boring litany about algebra with the enthusiasm of a zombie.

Julie had always wondered why Miss Peabody even bothered. The formulas and problems etched in chalk exactly duplicated those in the textbook. Even her words copied the book. For Julie, the biggest challenge during Miss Peabody's class became the development of an adeptness for sneaking in other reading materials. She lay them open on her lap so her eyes could slip off the textbook and onto the magazine or novel.

She could see that she was going to enjoy Mr. Neuman's math class, though. In fact, so far it looked as if her only problem with college was going to be Dr. Donald Lipton. If she could only tolerate him, she felt sure that she would enjoy this semester.

～

Julie was exhausted but pleased with herself by the time she pulled into her driveway at a little past four o'clock that afternoon.

She got out of the car, slung her backpack over a shoulder, and started up the flagstoned walkway to the front door. She and Robert had lived in this house, in a wooded, rural area well beyond the city limits of Freeborn, for only a few months. It was a two-story structure with bleached-wood walls, a cedar-shingled roof, and massive stone chimneys on both the north and south sides. It boasted front and rear porches on the east and west, and either vantage point offered a view of wooded slopes.

Everyone thought they'd been crazy for building their home so far away from the main road and other people, but it was their dream house, and they both loved it. Robert had a large shop built behind the house and equipped it with all kinds of tools that he used for his hobby of rebuilding cars. Next to the shop was a garage which held six of his most prized classic automobiles. His current project was a 1958 Thunderbird convertible. To Julie, it looked like a piece of junk. But she knew that when Robert looked at it, he saw it in all its gleaming, showroom glory.

He'd also had a special room built on the back side of the house for Julie's study, and after trying to decide between a swimming pool and a pond, they'd hired a landscape service to dig a pond that she could see outside the large picture window in her study.

Besides the pond, most of the enormous lot was devoted to open expanses of lawn. A score of trees stood in artfully placed groups, and there were beds of azaleas, California lilac bushes, and cape honeysuckles. Beyond the house were wooded hills and, dimly on the horizon, a broken line of mountains that were part of the Sierra Nevada range.

After taking a deep breath of the cool, fresh air, Julie unlocked the front door and stepped inside. The living room was large and airy, with cream-colored walls and carpet, dark oak end tables, and earth-tone chairs and sofas. Big plate-glass windows provided views of the lawn and surrounding wooded areas.

Dropping her backpack into a chair, she walked briskly into the kitchen for a cold glass of water. Her eyes went automatically to the answering machine on the counter and its blinking red light. After pouring a glass of water from the pitcher she always kept in the refrigerator, she stepped across to the answering machine and pressed the button. The first message was from Cheryl.

"Hi, Mom! How did you do in school today? Call me back when you get home. I still can't believe you're going to college!"

Hearing her daughter's voice always cheered her up, and Julie couldn't wait to tell her all the details about her first day of class. She pressed the *pause* button on the answering machine, then picked up the phone and dialed Cheryl's number.

"Hi!" Julie said when Cheryl answered. "How are you feeling today?"

"Hi, Mom!" Cheryl sounded as perky and cheerful as ever. "I'm feeling great. The baby's kicking a little, just to let me know he's there. I had a checkup two days ago, and everything's looking fine. The only problem I'm having is with impatience. I can't wait to see little Matthew."

Cheryl and Tom had decided on the name two weeks ago, after an ultrasound revealed that the baby she was carrying was a boy. "That impatience must come from your father's side of the family," Julie teased.

"Yeah, right, Mom."

They both laughed. Julie was the one who was always in a hurry, always itching to get things done.

It delighted Julie to hear her daughter so enthused over becoming a mother herself. Her morning sickness had passed, and her doctor was very pleased that she hadn't gained too much weight.

"How'd your first day at school go?" Cheryl asked.

"Not bad... actually, not bad at all."

"Good! So the jitters went away?"

Julie smiled. She had called Cheryl the night before and told her about the butterflies in her stomach. "I was a nervous wreck at first. But as the day went on and I began to meet my instructors and the other students in my classes, I started feeling a lot better. I met a very nice lady who's not much younger than me. Her name's Patricia. I was glad to see that I wasn't the only older student."

"Do you have any of the same instructors that I had? You don't have old Mrs. Koleski, do you? She was such a sweet lady, but older than the hills."

Julie laughed at her daughter's description. "No, I don't

have her. Old, huh? What is she... forty?"

Cheryl giggled. "No, Mom. *Really* old. Fifty, at least. But she taught American history. You aren't taking that, are you?"

"Not this semester."

"But you liked your classes?"

"Well... two of them, anyway. I like the professors in math and psychology. They went out of their way to make me feel welcome."

"And the third one?"

Julie hesitated. "I shouldn't make a judgment after only one day. But I have to say that I do already have some uneasy feelings about my creative writing teacher. I don't know why I even have to take that class, anyhow."

"Who's the instructor?"

"Donald Lipton. Do you know him?"

"No... at least, I don't think I ever met him. I didn't have to take that class when I went to school there."

"Too bad they changed the policy."

"What's the problem with Professor Lipton?"

Julie paused for a moment. She didn't want to come across as being too negative about her first day of college. And in truth, now that she was home, she began to believe that Donald Lipton couldn't possibly be as bad as her first impression of him suggested. "He just came across as kind of a grump," she said at last. "I think he must have been having a bad day."

"Well, don't let him get you down, Mom. You'll do fine in college. Keep the faith. Remember how much I hated my English teacher, Mr. Carlton? He used to make me so mad. He kept telling us we couldn't use the word 'it' or any contractions or pronouns in our assignments, and that really seemed ridiculous. But one day, about halfway through the semester, he explained that someday we might get a boss who would tell us to do something differently than we're accustomed to doing, or even in a way we totally disagree with. If that happened, Mr. Carlton said we'd better know that the boss's way is the right way. All of a sudden, in a crazy way, the guy made sense."

"Yes, I remember all the complaining you did about Mr. Carlton." It wasn't the same, though. Donald Lipton seemed to get a kick out of putting the students down and picking on them. Mr. Carlton, at least, had been fair.

"So Mom, how are you feeling today?" With the change in subject, Cheryl's tone had lost some of its vivacious brightness and had become somewhat cautious. She knew Julie didn't like talking about her health. "Any more headaches or dizziness lately?"

Ever since Julie had been diagnosed with lupus and had gone through a few bad spells, Cheryl always asked how she was feeling whenever they talked. Julie knew it wasn't just a polite question; Cheryl was concerned for Julie's health, and had made it known that she wanted to keep current on how things were going.

"Not really. I'm pretty tired today, but this has been a big day in my life." Julie glanced at the clock on the wall. "I'd better get off the phone. I'd like to get a bath and rest a bit. Then I'll have to see about dinner. Your dad will be home before long, and you know how he likes to have it ready when he walks in the door. He's been under a lot of stress at work lately, and I don't want to do anything to get him riled up."

Cheryl didn't say anything for a moment, and Julie knew she was trying to decide whether or not to press her about her health.

She apparently decided to let it drop. "Dad's a typical man, Mom. He wants his woman to wait on him hand and foot. Why don't you surprise him some night and have McDonald's hamburgers waiting for him, served up in your best China?"

It was Julie's turn to laugh. She could hardly imagine how Robert would react to that. "I don't think I want to try that one, Cheryl."

"Any news about the company? I know Dad has been worried."

"Nothing new as far as I know," Julie said. "But then, your father never confides in me about how the business is going. He'll take care of the problem, I suppose. He always has in the past."

"You're probably right. Okay, I'll let you go, Mom. I love you."

"I love you, too, babe. Talk to you later."

Chapter Three

After the conversation with her mother, Cheryl returned the telephone to its cradle, then sat there for a moment in the comfortable recliner, looking out through the partly opened curtains at the street outside. She and Tom lived in a quiet neighborhood just a mile or so from downtown Freeborn. They had both fallen in love with the small, gabled house when they first saw it, and although it had required a little fixing up, they didn't mind. The house was within their budget, and there was a second bedroom for the baby when it came.

Unconsciously, she ran a hand over her swollen abdomen, and smiled.

Cheryl had had a wonderful childhood, with a mother who gave her all the love and support she needed, and a father who worked hard to provide well for his family. But never in Cheryl's life had she felt more satisfied and content than now. She was married to a wonderful man, and now she was looking forward to starting a family.

She and Tom were both excited and eager to have their new baby, and they had agreed not to wait too long before trying for a second one. Being an only child, Cheryl was often envious when she went to Tom's parents' home on holidays. He was the oldest of six children, and his family's home always seemed so full of life and people caring for each other. She had always wanted two, or maybe even three children.

How lucky she was to have Tom. She had met him while she was recovering from a broken engagement. Looking back now, she realized that she might easily have fallen for *anyone* who showed her the slightest bit of love and attention. She had lucked out. Tom Merrow was certainly everything a woman could hope for in a husband. He was district manager of a large department store chain and, like her father, he was a dedicated employee. But he was also attentive to her every need.

Still gazing out the window, Cheryl found her thoughts returning to her parents. Her father had always had the need to focus on problems at the corrugated box plant he and Julie owned. While he could make important business decisions without any problem, he had always left the tough decisions about family matters to Julie. He preferred to concentrate on his work, and until lately his business had always done well.

Cheryl had only a vague idea of the problems that had settled on Hunter Container Corporation. Crown Paper Products, a large international company, was moving into the area, and they had plans to build a huge corrugated box plant with state-of-the-art equipment. They were already sending people around to talk to Hunter Container's largest customers, and Cheryl's father had said that there was no way he would be able to compete with them on prices unless he modernized his plant. The problem was, the modernization would cost millions.

For the past several weeks, Robert Hunter had been putting together financial projections and talking to banks, trying to line up the money for the modernization. He had always hated fussing with financial matters, and Cheryl knew that the stress and worries were eating at him.

She knew all of this not because her father had told her, but only because she'd read about the Crown plant in the newspapers, and from little scraps of conversation she'd over-heard from her parents.

With this threat looming over them, her father was immersed even more than usual in the running of the family business. But even when Cheryl was a little girl, he had always turned to his work when the going got tough emo-tionally. Whenever Cheryl was upset over some childhood problem, she always went to her mother. Her father would try to listen, but within seconds after she started telling him about her problem, his foot would start tapping and his eyes would stray away from her. She soon learned not to bother trying to talk to him.

She also remembered when Grandma Hunter went into the hospital with chest pains and was kept for several days for tests. Her father started working fourteen-hour days, just com-ing home long enough to get something to eat, to shower, and to grab a few hours' sleep.

Lately, ever since Julie began feeling sick, he had again started the routine of long work days. Most of the time when Cheryl dropped in to visit, Julie was at home alone. Cheryl felt sorry for her mother. She could tell how lonely she was, and eager for someone to talk to her.

Cheryl glanced at her wristwatch. She knew she should be following her mother's example and start fixing dinner. But she just didn't feel like cooking tonight, and she wasn't quite as well disciplined as her mother when it came to being the perfect wife.

What she felt like having tonight was pizza from Gambi-no's downtown. They had the spiciest sausage around, and Cheryl's mouth watered just thinking about it. She was pretty sure that if she gave Tom a hug and a kiss and a pleading look when he came in the door, he would be only too happy to take her out.

~

In her kitchen a few miles away, Julie frowned as she pressed the button on the answering machine to replay the brief message that had come in after Cheryl's.

"Julie, this is Kim from Dr. Cole's office. Dr. Cole would like to see you as soon as possible. Please call back to set up an appointment. Have a good day."

Julie's frown of worry deepened as she erased the message. She had been halfway expecting a call from Dr. Cole's office, since they had promised to let her know the results of the recent blood tests and x-rays. But she hadn't expected to hear the sound of urgency from Kim.

She tried not to let it get her down, but she couldn't help being worried. She had been diagnosed with lupus two years ago, and until recently the pain in her muscles and joints had been somewhat controlled by medicine. Although she had occasional flare-ups, she also had experienced long periods of remission, when no signs of the disease were present.

A few weeks ago, the medication seemed to stop working. New blood tests showed that her immune system had ceased to function properly and had lost its ability to distinguish between its own body cells and bacteria and viruses. That was the way Dr. Cole explained it, anyway. Instead of fighting these antigens, the antibodies were mistakenly fighting their own body cells.

She knew Dr. Cole was worried too, and that was why he'd ordered more tests. Julie had known from the start that lupus was serious. When she'd first been diagnosed, Dr. Cole had told her that there was no way to accurately predict its course. It had been devastating news... but at the time, it had seemed distant to her. She'd gotten the impression that she could keep an uneasy truce with the disease for many years.

But now, after only two years, it was already causing problems. Dr. Cole made it clear that if they were unable to get it under control, she would be facing extremely serious difficulties.

Julie hadn't asked what he meant by "extremely serious difficulties." She was pretty sure she could figure that out for herself.

Over the past two weeks, the pain had become much worse. Her chest hurt constantly. Most of the time, it was a dull ache that only flared if she took a deep breath. But some nights, the pain seemed to blaze inside her, keeping her awake despite the best efforts of modern medications.

She knew this would be a problem for her if she carried a full load of college classes. Dr. Cole had told her to get as much rest as possible. Robert had been much more blunt, telling her she was crazy for going back to college. At the same time, though, she knew that he had never really accepted the diagnosis. Either he was in a state of denial, or he was just too stubborn to agree with the doctors. He refused to believe that she had a serious illness.

She glanced at the clock. She had been home nearly an hour, and hadn't even looked at her homework assignments. By now, in addition to her exhaustion, her head was aching. Dr. Cole's office was closed for the day, so she would have to call him first thing in the morning. Right now, all she wanted to do was take a warm bath and freshen up before Robert got home from work. She couldn't wait to tell him about her first day at college — about her psychology teacher, her math teacher... and that beast who called himself a creative writing instructor.

Julie shook her head as if she might be able to shake off the shroud of despair that had settled over her, then pushed back the chair and got to her feet. Somehow, she would have to keep a positive attitude, and she vowed to work on that in the whirlpool as the warm bubbles caressed her tired, sore body. She often teased her husband by telling him that if the whirlpool could only carry in the groceries and take out the garbage, she wouldn't even need him.

As she began to undress, she glanced over at the full-length mirror. Her own face stared back: a face too narrow, thin nose, eyes and mouth too large. Men had called her attractive — even beautiful. But that was before she had started losing weight. If she had been trying to lose weight, she might have been pleased with herself, but lately she just hadn't had an appetite. In the past few months, she had dropped almost twenty pounds, and she was starting to get scared. Maybe that was why Dr. Cole wanted to see her. Perhaps he wanted to give her some pills to make her hungry. Wouldn't that be a switch?

Her hand lingered over one of several new bruises on her body. They seemed to be appearing from nowhere, in places she couldn't possibly have bumped. She reached up and ran her hand through her hair, then suddenly gave it a yank as if trying to pull it out. She released her hand, opened it, and looked, half expecting to see several of her brown curls. But there was nothing.

Yes! maybe Dr. Cole was wrong after all about her getting worse. He had said that one of the most frequent symptoms of her illness was hair falling out.

Julie spent the next hour in the whirlpool, letting her mind go wherever it wanted, avoiding any serious thoughts. This was *her* time... her daily treat to herself. Sometimes she sang, but more often she would simply lie back quietly and savor the fact that she was alive. Oh, how she loved life.

After her bath, she got dressed and went to her study overlooking the pond. She glanced through the wide window just in time to see a doe and her little fawn drinking from the water. She would have to remember to tell Robert....

No, she realized. He would just blink at her as if he didn't understand the point. So what would be the use?

She sat down at her desk and began writing in her diary. Just as she was getting ready to look over her homework assignments, she heard the crunch of tires on gravel, and knew that Robert's blue Ford pickup was pulling into the driveway.

She sighed and got up, heading toward the kitchen to prepare dinner. Homework would have to wait.

Chapter Four

Monday, January 13

I am so tired. What a long day! I think I might like college, if I can just survive Professor Donald Lipton. In this case, "if" is a big word. I can't forget to ask Dr. Cole for a new prescription for my pain pills. I have to call him tomorrow anyway. What news will he have for me?

"Hi, honey."

Robert came into the kitchen as she was peering into the pantry, trying to decide what to have for dinner. She turned in time to catch his critical look around the kitchen. She could read the disappointment in his face that dinner wasn't ready to be dished up.

"Hi, Robert. Dinner will ready in a half hour or so."

He nodded without comment, then draped his jacket over a straight-backed wooden chair and came over to give her a peck on the cheek. "I called earlier, but you weren't home yet."

"I stayed for a while after class to check out the library," Julie told him. "My classes went pretty well. Not as scary as I thought they'd be."

"That's good," he said absently, already turning his attention to the newspaper lying folded on the kitchen table. He was still handsome for his age — a fair-skinned man with sharp features and dark brown eyes. He always prided himself for receiving the award at his class reunions for the person who had changed the least. He wore his thick hair short, and except for a white shirt, almost always dressed in various shades of brown. Today he wore a brown linen jacket, tan trousers, and brown cordovan shoes. Even now, a stone's throw from fifty, he had the body of a trim thirty-year-old.

Everything about Robert was neat. Julie had never thought she could have considered neatness a fault, but Robert stretched it right to its definable limit. He was the first to admit that he was an "everything in its place" kind of guy. He even organized the mail into neat stacks before opening it. He always had the same thing for breakfast: Cheerios, Wheaties, All-Bran and a chunky granola mixed in a bowl with half a spoon of sugar and one cup of one-percent milk. Robert had calculated that this concoction provided a maximum of nutrients and roughage, and a minimum of calories and animal fat.

He liked to keep his thoughts in perfect order, too. For Robert, everything was black or white; there were no confusing shades of gray to worry about.

He had been a business major in college when Julie met him at a friend's house. She had soon learned that his father, Albert Hunter, owned Hunter Container Corporation and that Robert expected to eventually take over the company. Hunter Container made heavy-duty boxes used by manufacturers to ship their products, and they were the only corrugated container plant in the area.

It was a pretty boring business as far as Julie was concerned, but she'd been attracted to Robert's self-confidence and his sense of duty and responsibility. It was obvious that he would be able to give her a safe and secure life, which was something her mother had always stressed.

He had certainly not failed in that. By age thirty, he was plant manager, and ten years later he took over the reins when his father retired. The business had prospered well under his guidance — until now, at least.

Flipping back the newspaper, Robert grunted and pointed at something about a scandal in the governor's office. "Can you believe that? That guy just bought himself a world of trouble." He picked up the newspaper and began reading, then wandered off toward the living room.

Julie knew from experience that at least right now, Robert had no real interest in how her day had gone. Sighing again, she began to prepare the evening meal.

She had never been fond of cooking, because she had spent so many years catering to Robert and making what he liked. Just like tonight. She loved mashed potatoes, but Robert insisted that she bake them... so she would. Rather than argue over salad dressing, she always used the creamy Italian his mother had used for years. As she was pouring his coffee, she was thinking about how great a cup of tea would taste right then.

Although Robert never actually interfered with what she fixed for dinner, some of the comments he made when she chose something other than what he wanted were enough to make her lose her appetite. So she always planned the meals around him. It was so much simpler that way. When Cheryl was still at home, it had been even more complicated. Cheryl seemed to love all the foods that Robert hated, and they fought constantly, both telling Julie how and what to cook.

Looking back now, she realized that the past twenty-five years of her life had been spent trying to please everyone else.

Maybe that was why going to college had become so important to her. Her daughter had "left the nest," and Julie had finally realized that she would never totally please Robert. She wasn't getting any younger, and her health was deteriorating. For once in her life, she had decided to do something to please herself.

Thinking about college brought her thoughts back to Donald Lipton. She would do her best on the writing assignments, and try to ignore his insulting remarks. Maybe he would at least try to be decent. And if he didn't, she wasn't about to let him ruin her lifelong dream. The semester would pass, and soon he would be part of history as far as she was concerned.

"Not soon enough," she muttered.

~

With a sigh, Robert settled into the big brown recliner near the front windows. He shifted back, drawing up the footrest and moving the large back of the chair into a more comfortable position.

For a moment he just sat there, letting the cushions of the chair soak up the stiffness that had gathered in his muscles and joints over the long afternoon. This old chair was his favorite piece of furniture in the house. It fit him perfectly, and he liked the welcoming softness of the brown corduroy fabric.

He'd had the chair nearly ten years, and it was starting to show its age in the seat and arms, where the corduroy had worn smooth and to a lighter shade. Julie had pleaded with him to replace it, or at least to have it recovered before they moved into their new house a few months ago, but he'd flatly refused. Twenty years ago she'd talked him into having his favorite chair reupholstered, and it had never been the same. The cushions, which had once molded perfectly to his body, became tight and unyielding with the new fabric. No way would he let the same thing happen to this one.

He opened the newspaper and began running his eyes over the headlines. He always looked forward to reading the newspaper in the evenings after a hard day's work. It was one of life's little pleasures. Robert had a wide-ranging interest in the news. Somehow, after dealing with the daily stresses of running a company with more than two hundred employees and ten million dollars in sales, reading an article about a street-widening project in downtown Freeborn or about political turmoil in China helped him relax.

He knew Julie couldn't understand that. She had no interest in world affairs, and she'd often commented that reading about all the world's troubles probably only added to his stress. She couldn't grasp that after dealing with his own problems all day, he needed to read about problems that didn't concern him. The problems now facing the state's governor, for example, had nothing to do with Robert or Hunter Container Corporation. They were the governor's problems. He'd brought them on himself, and he was the one who would have to deal with it.

As he scanned the newspaper now, though, he realized that his heart really wasn't in it this time. As much as he wanted to, he couldn't get his mind off the threat that had come out of nowhere like an unexpected natural disaster to wreak havoc on his life.

His father had founded Hunter Container Corporation more than forty years ago, when Robert was a small boy. Sinking every dime he had into the business, Albert Hunter had worked sixteen-hour days to build a successful business selling corrugated containers to manufacturing businesses in the area.

All his hard work paid off, and when Robert took over the business, it had prospered even more, continuing its reputation for quality, customer support, and fairness. That had been a huge source of pride for Robert. When Albert died several years ago, it was with the knowledge that the business he'd worked so hard to build was in safe hands.

Now it seemed possible — likely, even — that everything would be lost. Crown Paper Products, a massive conglomerate with more than three billion dollars in annual sales, was stretching its tentacles toward Hunter Container's sales area. The company had announced plans to build a corrugated box plant near the town of Ellsworth, ten miles away on the Grand River. It would be huge and modern, and Robert knew he would never be able to compete with it on price. Crown had a policy of undercutting local competitors long enough to put them out of business so they could have the local market to themselves.

The new container plant would be up and running in nine months, and Crown sales representatives were already talking to Robert's biggest customers about long-term contracts. If he tried to match Crown's prices, he would lose money on every box he sold. His only hope was to modernize his plant so he could cut costs and stay in line with Crown's prices.

He would need close to three million dollars to do that, and right now his challenge was to convince a bank that he was a good risk for such a loan. Howard Simmons, president of Freeborn's California National Bank, had agreed to look at his proposal, but he hadn't even come close to making any promises. It would take about six months for the modernization work, and Robert knew that he had to get the financing immediately in order to secure crucial sales contracts.

Sighing, he folded the newspaper and laid it on the floor beside his chair. Through the door behind him, he could hear Julie bustling about in the kitchen, preparing dinner.

Why, he wondered irritably, couldn't she have it ready when he came home? She knew he liked to eat as early as possible. But she often kept him waiting, and he felt sure that this nonsense about college would make things even worse. Why was she so determined to go to college? She was forty-five, for God's sake! What could she possibly do with a college degree, even if she was able to stick it out and get one?

Not that he expected her to. Julie had performed her role as wife and mother admirably through the years. She had dedicated herself to her home, husband, and daughter, and had never complained. But none of Julie's other ventures had worked out. When Cheryl was in high school, Julie enrolled in a correspondence course in floral design, and for a year or so she worked with dried flowers and silk plants to make arrangements that she sold at local bazaars. She didn't make any money to speak of from that, and Robert had finally convinced her to give it up.

For a while she did volunteer work at the library, and had even helped out in home economics classes at Cheryl's school. She hadn't stayed with any of it, though. Robert knew she blamed him for putting too much stress on her, although she'd never come right out and said it. The fact was, he did expect her to have time to do certain things like keeping the house clean, cooking meals, doing the laundry, and shopping for groceries. He gave his time to making money so his family could afford to have the things they needed and wanted, and it was the least she could do to give him the support he needed.

He knew this wasn't fashionable thinking for the '90s. The roles of the sexes had gotten all screwed up; men were doing household chores, and women were becoming corporate executives. In his heart, Robert knew that wasn't right. From the very beginnings of mankind, it had always been the man who went out to provide for the family while the woman took care of their children. Robert saw this as *duty* and *responsibility,* although he knew others called it *male chauvinism.*

He'd given up trying to discuss it with today's "modern thinkers."

But never in his wildest thoughts had he imagined that his own wife would get a wild hair and decide to go to college — and well into middle age, yet. Worse, she'd done it even though she knew he didn't like the idea. Now, when he needed her most to help him get through this crisis, she would be spending hours at the college and even more hours huddled in her study working on homework.

"Robert?" Julie called from the doorway. "Dinner's ready."

It's about damned time, he thought sourly, getting to his feet.

~

Preparing dinner had taken longer than usual because Julie was so tired. Robert looked like he was in a bad mood, but when he sat down at the table he seemed to make an effort to shake it off. He commented on Julie's special touches that made each meal a little unique. Julie didn't believe in saving things for another generation to savor. She liked to use her beautiful things, believing that they were made to enjoy, not to pack away to pass on to posterity.

This night, she was serving Robert's favorite bread pudding in dishes manufactured by the Jewel Tea Company at the turn of the century. They had belonged to Grandmother Hunter. The beautiful old dining room table, polished to a high gloss, was covered with a hand-crocheted cloth that had been one of her own parents' wedding presents, and she and Robert both loved to drink out of the crystal wine goblets that had once belonged to his Great Aunt Katherine.

As they ate, she started to tell him more about her first day of classes, but it became obvious that he wasn't interested. She knew he was preoccupied with the problems at the office, so she decided to take the conversation to his turf.

"Have you had any luck with the bank?"

He offered a shrug. "Not sure, yet. Mr. Simmons asked me for some updated operating statements."

When she realized he considered that to be a complete answer to her question, she pressed onward. "Did you give those to him?"

"Not yet. Baxter's putting them together."

She knew that Dave Baxter was the plant accountant. "When does Mr. Simmons expect to make a decision about the loan?"

"How am I supposed to know?" he said, his voice sharper now, reflecting the frustration he was feeling.

She decided to drop the subject. She didn't want to get him upset, and she knew too well that he didn't take her questions seriously, anyway. She had nothing to do with the company, and he had never made the slightest effort to include her in any of the decisions about it.

Robert cleared his throat and spoke with a more conciliatory tone. "Honey, did you get hold of the contractor and tell him that the front door still isn't quite right? You just can't trust anyone to do a good job these days." Before Julie could answer, he stood up, walked over to her side of the table, and put his arms around her. "You look so young, Julie. How have you been feeling lately? Have you heard from Dr. Cole yet?"

She hadn't expected that. Like the family business, Dr. Cole was usually a taboo subject at the dinner table. "As a matter of fact, he left a message for me to call him."

"Do that," Robert said, nodding. "I'm going out to my shop and work on the T-bird for a little while. If you need me, just yell. Thanks for the supper."

Robert disappeared, and Julie sat there alone at the table, wondering how they had stayed together for so many years. She knew that they loved each other. That wasn't a problem. But outside of Cheryl, they really had nothing in common.

She couldn't even remember the last time they'd had a meaningful conversation.

She sighed, pushed back her chair and got to her feet to begin clearing the table.

~

After cleaning up the kitchen, Julie lay down for a brief nap. That was something Dr. Cole had told her to do, although she rarely did. Today, though, she was exhausted, and the rest was welcome.

Robert still had not returned from his shop when she went down the hall to her study to do her homework.

The room represented all that she cherished in life. A border ran along the top edge of the wall that was a Victorian repeated pattern of books, piano music, an old-fashioned feather quill with an ink jar, and flowers. The windows were extra large, going from ceiling to floor, allowing her to have a full view of the pond and the acres of open countryside. Around the room were scattered family photographs — most of them depicting Cheryl at various ages.

Often, Julie would come here to think about life... or in other instances to read and forget about it. Either way, it was the perfect place to escape.

With a feeling of satisfaction, she lay out her books and began to do her homework. As she'd expected, the math was elementary to her, and it took less than fifteen minutes to complete the assignment. The psychology was interesting, and took a little longer. She read the chapter Dr. Lipton had assigned from the writing book, and decided to take a stab at writing her first paper.

She swivelled her chair around to her desktop computer and flipped the switch, drumming her fingers on the desk while the software booted. Then she clicked on the icon to bring up her word processing program.

"I want you to write about a personal experience that changed

how you acted, thought, or felt from that moment on," Lipton had said.

Julie stared at the blank screen while allowing her mind to sift through the possibilities. She certainly had plenty of experiences that had changed her life. The day she'd met Robert. The day they were married. The day Cheryl was born.

But every time she thought about one of those touching moments, her mind brought up the image of Professor Lipton standing there before the class, arms folded, chin out thrust as he looked around with that supercilious expression, verbally jabbing his victims and grinning at their discomfort. How could she share one of the most important moments of her life with that man?

Well, she had no choice. She resolutely placed her fingers on the keyboard and began recounting the day Cheryl was born. After a few paragraphs, she realized that it was sounding more like a newspaper account than a heartfelt event. She cleared the screen and started over.

This time it seemed too mushy.

She cleared the screen again and sat staring at it. She could feel tension growing in her arms and shoulders.

For Pete's sake! she scolded herself. *It's just a college writing assignment.* There was no need to let it get to her this way.

WRITING IS HARD WORK! Lipton had written on the blackboard. In her mind's eye, she could almost see him leering at her. *"I told you so."*

She shook her head vigorously. She was already letting him play mind games with her. She couldn't let that happen.

But an hour later, she still hadn't written a single sentence that she was happy with. Frustrated, she jabbed the switch to turn off her computer. The assignment wasn't due until Wednesday, anyway. She was too tired, and too distracted with worry about the message from Dr. Cole's office.

Surely, tomorrow would be better. She would do Lipton's damned writing assignment then.

Chapter Five

Tuesday, January 14

I had no idea that a simple writing assignment could cause me so much grief. When you know somebody else is going to be reading it, it's a lot harder to come up with the right words to get across what you want to say. I usually write in my diary each day, and that's always been easy. But this is a lot different....

When the alarm beeped at seven-thirty the next morning, Julie reached across to the night stand and pushed the switch on the radio sideways, cutting off the annoying sound and turning on music — a light rock station that had thus far escaped the trend toward the early-morning double-deejay fruitcake shows that drove her crazy.

Robert, who was always an early riser, had already left for the plant. Julie's only class that day was at ten o'clock, and she didn't want to be late. She planned to leave a little after nine-thirty. Dr. Cole's office opened at nine, though, and she wanted to make that call first.

She threw back the covers and got out of bed, instantly shivering with the early-morning chill, and padded over to the thermostat to turn up the heat a few degrees. Yawning, she went into the bathroom and started the shower water. Then she pulled off her nightgown and let the wisp of pink silk fall across the bed.

For a moment, she studied the contrast of the pink silk lying on the off-white eyelet lace of the comforter. Julie had always been fond of pretty things. That was something she had picked up from her mother. It was expressed in her preference for exquisite lingerie, and in the harmonious colors that she gathered around her. The bed and bed covers were off-white, trimmed with blue and gold. Robert had grumbled a little about that, but didn't complain too much. She always bought bath towels that were thick and lush because she enjoyed the feel of them on her skin.

She thought back to the bedroom she'd had as a girl: the blue and white floral curtains and bedspread, the canopy on the off-white four-poster bed, and the window seat upholstered in the same floral pattern. She smiled as she recalled how she used to sit on that window seat and dream her adolescent dreams.

Still smiling, she stepped into the shower. After drying off with a huge terry-cloth towel, she applied minimal make-up, then went out to the kitchen where she poured herself a glass of grapefruit juice. She knew Dr. Cole wanted her to eat a large breakfast, but even the thought of food made her stomach close up in rejection. Seated at the breakfast bar, Sony remote in hand, she casually clicked on CNN for a concise rundown on the world-at-large: Terrorist attack... Louisiana manhunt... Middle East rigmarole... A major Las Vegas jackpot winner....

Same as yesterday. Same as the day before. Same as tomorrow. She couldn't imagine why Robert got so much out of perusing the newspaper every night. Five minutes of CNN was more than enough for her.

She used the remote to turn off the television, and took the grapefruit juice into the family room where she could look out over the pond. The sun was above the trees now, turning the water to liquid fire. She sighed at the unabashed beauty of it all. This was why she had fallen in love with this area the moment she saw it.

Finally, at a few minutes after nine, she rinsed out her glass in the sink, then picked up the kitchen phone and dialed.

"Good morning, Dr. Cole's office," said the receptionist.

"Hi, Kim, this is Julie Hunter. I got a message from your office yesterday to call back, but I didn't get home until after office hours."

"Hi, Julie. Dr. Cole hasn't arrived yet, but I know why he wanted to talk to you. He has the results of your most recent blood tests, and he wants to talk to you and Robert about them."

"Robert?" Julie repeated. Although Dr. Cole was also Robert's doctor, Robert almost never went with Julie for her appointments. He didn't like doctors to begin with, and he was having an especially hard time accepting the fact that Julie was seriously ill. He was always such a pain at the doctor's office, she didn't press him to go with her. "Why does he need to see us both?"

"I can't really answer that, but I know he was serious when he suggested that both of you come. Would you like to make an appointment now?"

Dumb choice of words, Julie thought. *Who would want to make a doctor's appointment just to hear bad news?*

"Julie, are you still there?"

"Yeah, I'm sorry. Do you have any time open for late Friday afternoon? I might be able to get Robert to take off work early that day, but don't count on it. He thinks that plant can't run without him."

"I have an opening at four o'clock Friday afternoon."

"That sounds good."

"Okay, Julie. We'll see you then."

~

Julie's only class on Tuesdays and Thursdays was humanities. Her instructor, Mrs. Reed, was a smartly dressed woman in middle age. Her manner was competent and brisk, yet very friendly. She told the students to feel free at any time to ask for help with anything they didn't understand.

Best of all, Patricia Davis, Julie's new friend from Professor Lipton's class, was in this one too. Mrs. Reed seemed more than pleased to see these two non-traditional students in her class, and complimented them for taking time to do the important things in their lives.

When she said this, Julie glanced over at Patricia, who was smiling back. The two of them shared a secret understanding. Julie felt sure that they would be comfortable and confident in this class.

The other students, although much younger than she and Patricia, were pleasant to them, and the morning passed quickly. Two things kept nagging at her mind, though. One was her concern about what would be in store for her at Dr. Cole's office on Friday. She wished now that she'd made an earlier appointment so she could get it behind her.

She also found herself thinking frequently about her writing assignment for Professor Lipton's class. She had been up for hours the night before trying to get it done, but so far she had been unsuccessful.

Before she left the classroom, Patricia once again told her how pleased she was to have met her. "Well, Julie, what do you think? Do you think we can keep from making these young kids feel too bad because they can't keep up with us?"

Julie smiled. "We can sure give it a try."

"Want to get a cup of coffee? We could go to the cafeteria, or there's a machine in the breeze way leading to the courtyard."

Julie hesitated. She did want to get to know Patricia better. "Let's try the machine. I can't take too long. I still haven't written Lipton's assignment."

Patricia gave her a wry smile as they picked up their books and headed for the door. "You had to remind me of that jerk?"

"Sorry. Have you done the assignment?"

Patricia nodded. "Yep! Did it last night. Spent all of twenty minutes on it."

Julie issued a silent sigh. Apparently, Patricia had done exactly what Julie had intended to do with Lipton's assignment: whip through it as quickly as possible and get on to more important things. For some reason, Julie hadn't been able to do that. She just hadn't been able to get it right.

They carried their Styrofoam cups of coffee to a bench near the courtyard. After more conversation, Julie and Patricia realized they had a lot in common. Julie was surprised to learn that Patricia had undergone open heart surgery three years earlier. She had not one but five grown children, and was holding down a part-time job at a local clothing store.

Julie was impressed. It also helped her to put her own situation in perspective. If this lady could do all that she was and still go to college, it should be easy for Julie.

~

Her feeling of confidence was badly shaken that evening when she glanced at the digital clock beside her computer. It was already past ten o'clock, and she was still struggling with Professor Lipton's writing assignment. Robert had stopped by a few minutes earlier to tell her goodnight on his way to the bedroom down the hall, and gave her his usual admonition about getting enough rest, as Dr. Cole had ordered.

Her eyes moved back to the blank computer screen. She had been sitting here for nearly two hours, wasting time with many false starts and stops as she struggled to find a starting point for Lipton's assignment. The tension had tightened up the muscles in her back and shoulders, running up her neck to give her a dull headache.

Why was this simple assignment causing her so much aggravation? Julie had planned only to spend a half hour on the assignment, or perhaps an hour at the most. She no longer cared about pleasing Lipton, and intended only to do a minimal job on the paper.

It should be easy to write about the birth of her daughter. It had been one of the happiest times in her life, and it was certainly a very personal experience that had affected her ever since.

But for two hours, she had been grappling with word choices and phrases that didn't sound right to her. When she tried to write informally, she failed to capture the emotions she had felt. When she tried to bring in too many details, they seemed to overpower the emotions.

Frustrated, she decided to take a break and call Cheryl to find out how she was feeling. Julie couldn't wait to be a grandma, but her feelings were bittersweet since she knew that she might not be around to see her grandchild grow up.

"Hi, Mom!" Cheryl said cheerfully. "How are you feeling today?"

"Pretty well," Julie answered. "A little chest pain, but no more than usual." She knew from experience that if she told Cheryl she was feeling fine, Cheryl wouldn't believe her anyway and would only fish for more information. Instead, Julie had learned to downplay the pain she was feeling.

"Dad says you're going to see Dr. Cole again on Friday. Any developments?"

Apparently, Robert had already talked to Cheryl. For some reason, it annoyed Julie. He wouldn't even talk to her for more than five seconds about her illness, and yet he freely blabbed to Cheryl.

"Dr. Cole wants to talk to us about some blood tests and x-rays I had last week," Julie answered lightly. "Just the usual stuff. Have you been feeling okay today?"

"Never better! How come you're up so late? Dad said Dr. Cole has been telling you to get more rest."

I wonder how Robert manages to find so much time to talk to Cheryl about this, Julie fumed. "I'm about ready to go to bed. Just finishing up some homework. Speaking of which, I'd better get back to it."

"Oh, yeah... homework!" Cheryl laughed. "Boy, do I remember that college homework. You were always after me to get it done early so I wouldn't have to stay up all night. Remember?"

"Yes, I remember." Julie found herself smiling. "You really didn't put off doing it until the last minute, like a lot of kids. You were just so much of a perfectionist, you'd spend hours getting every little detail just right."

"Well, maybe I'm a chip off the old block. Speaking of which, why are you still up so late, hmm? Getting all those details just right?"

Julie sighed. "Not exactly. I can't even get that far."

"What class is it?"

"Creative writing. I don't know why it's giving me so much trouble."

"What are you writing about? With that creative mind of yours, you shouldn't have any problem coming up with something." Cheryl loved teasing her mother. "Have you thought of any ideas yet?"

"Well, actually I have. I'm supposed to write about a personal experience that changed how I acted, thought, or felt from that moment on. I can think of many personal experiences that qualify, but I really don't want to share them with strangers — and especially not with someone as heartless as Donald Lipton. No way!"

"Oh, come on, Mom. Are you going to let that man get you down? Think positive. Tell me, what are some of your ideas?"

"Well, honey, I was thinking of writing about the day you were born."

"Really? Cool! Wish I could help you, Mom, but I can't remember much about it."

"Okay, young lady, don't be so smart," Julie scolded her daughter with pride. "Cherrie, that was one of the most precious days of my life. I will never forget that day, or how it felt to finally hold you after carrying you inside me for nine months."

"I think I can understand that," Cheryl said. "Each time I feel little Matthew move or kick me, I get more anxious than ever to hold him. I spend hours wondering what he will be like. I have to admit I'm a little nervous, though. How will I know how to take care of him?"

"Oh, that'll all come to you as you need to know it," Julie assured her. "No one can tell you everything you'll need to know. But it will come naturally."

"Well, I can hardly wait. And I can't wait to see Tom in the delivery room with me. He was so devoted to me during the Lamaze classes. I was so proud of him."

"When I had you, the fathers had to stay away." Julie laughed as she remembered. "Back then, the babies were only brought to the mothers a few times a day for feeding, and even during those times the fathers were kicked out of the rooms."

"Are you kidding me, Mom?"

"No, not at all. I remember so well the day we brought you home. Your father helped me into the house, then he grabbed you out of my arms and said, 'Let me hold her, damn it! She's my kid, too!'" Julie had lowered her voice, trying to mimic Robert's masculine tone. "That was the first he complained about any of it, but he made sure I knew that he thought the hospital's policy was unfair."

Cheryl laughed. "Mom, can you imagine Dad in the delivery room?"

"Ha! Not without a cup of coffee and the latest newspaper."

That brought more laughter from Cheryl, and Julie realized she was already feeling a lot better than she'd felt before making the call.

For the next fifteen minutes, they joked back and forth about how things had changed over the years, and agreed that for the most part, things were better. Cheryl and Tom had already taken parenting classes, and they planned to take more classes as their child got older, at various ages. Julie was touched by how devoted they already were to this child that hadn't even been born yet.

As she and Cheryl talked and shared their feelings about this beautiful life-giving experience, it all came back to Julie... what it had been like to be a young mother, the awesome responsibility of taking a little life in her hands. Feelings of anticipation, attachment, anxiety, and love overflowed from deep within....

It was almost enough to take her breath away, and for a long moment she sat there gripping the telephone, her memories ranging back —

"Mom?"

Julie realized Cheryl was still there on the other end of the line. This was the grown-up Cheryl, not the little pink baby of so many years ago.

Julie cleared her throat. "Sorry, babe. My mind was wandering. I'd better make it wander right back to this assignment. I've put off writing it long enough. Thanks so much for helping me, honey. I'll let you know how I do. Wish me luck."

"All right, Mom. Glad you called. Love you."

"Love you too, Cheryl." On the verge of saying goodbye, she remembered something else. "Oh, hey! Don't forget that you and Tom are coming over for dinner tomorrow night."

Cheryl laughed. "Tom isn't likely to forget, Mom. He loves your cooking. The only problem is, you're spoiling him. He's starting to expect the same from me."

"I'll try to make something terrible, so he won't be spoiled," Julie promised. "Six-thirty, okay?"

"We'll be there. See you then."

After hanging up, Julie leaned back in her chair, smiling. Cheryl had that rare quality of extruding enough cheerfulness for both her and her receptor. The extrusion immediately placed you at ease; she was a crowning extrovert, no pretense of any kind. She never seemed to have any "down" days. Even in high school, through the years that were notoriously rough on girls and their growing hormones, Cheryl had always been pleasant.

Images came to Julie: Cheryl laughing and teasing one minute, then the next minute all serious about her studies or some club activity. She'd been involved in so many extracurricular activities, Robert and Julie had at first worried that her academic work would suffer. It soon became clear that Cheryl could balance it all out perfectly.

There was no doubt that the birth of their daughter had changed Julie's life forever. Now, after talking to Cheryl, it was all there inside her, crystal clear and as real as the love she felt for her daughter.

She opened a desk drawer and pulled out Cheryl's baby book. She unlaced the pink ribbon holding it together and began looking through the pages. Each photograph stirred more memories within her. Here was the one Robert had taken the day they had brought Cheryl home. She'd been so tiny! And... in this one, Julie was holding Cheryl at her christening. And... Cheryl's first Christmas, and her first tooth, and her little legs climbing those big school bus steps on the first day of kindergarten.

Where had all the time gone? If Julie had known earlier that her own life might be shortened by illness, would she have spent more time with her beautiful daughter? How much time did she have left to share with her now?

She turned another page and found Cheryl's birth announcement. She remembered how excited she and Robert had been that night. She had called Dr. Devoe at midnight to tell him that her water had broken, but she was experiencing no pain. He had told her that as long as she was comfortable, she should go back to bed and rest, that he would see her the following morning.

At 1:30 a.m., Julie had her first contraction, and from then on, they were regular and close. Robert had quickly grabbed the small suitcase she had prepared, and moments later they were on their way to Tyler General Hospital.

Robert had been a nervous wreck. In spite of Julie's begging him to slow down and assuring him that first babies take a long time to arrive, he continued the nighttime ride full speed ahead, careening down side streets and blasting through stop signs with horn blaring.

Although she was upset with him at the time, as it turned out, Robert had done the proper thing. Cheryl Lynn Hunter was born only moments after their arrival at the hospital... just twenty-six minutes after Julie's first contraction. What a night!

Julie had experienced severe morning sickness during the entire nine months of pregnancy, and had even been hospitalized for dehydration at one point. So even though she was two weeks overdue, Cheryl weighed only four pounds, three ounces.

Julie would never forget the ultimate joy she had felt the moment she held that tiny bit of life for the first time. She remembered counting each finger, each toe, and softly patting the top of that itsy bitsy head. Cheryl was smaller than many dolls, and Julie's grandmother had made Cheryl's Baptism gown from a sixteen-inch doll clothes pattern.

Still deep in thought, Julie closed the baby book and swivelled her chair back to the computer. This time when her fingers went to the keyboard, they moved with confidence and started producing the words that her heart was feeling. For the first time, they seemed to flow effortlessly from her fingertips.

The first draft took less than twenty minutes, and she spent another fifteen minutes going over it carefully to correct any spelling and punctuation errors. It was only two and a half pages, and she heaved a sigh of relief as the last sheet fell into the printer tray.

She read it over one more time, and was thrilled with it. This was good! And it had been so easy. Was this what it was supposed to be like for writers? In a way, she thought with a smile, it wasn't too different from giving birth: A lot of waiting and fussing, a few moments of sudden activity, then the delightful final product.

Still smiling at that thought, she saved the file onto a disk and shut down the computer. She glanced at the clock. It was just past 3:00 a.m.

Both legs had gone to sleep, and pins and needles tingled up from the balls of her feet as she pushed herself away from the computer and stood. A few minutes later, she was slipping into bed beside the sleeping Robert. The crisp, clean linens were pure pleasure. She lay there for a long time, feeling wired, her mind still going over the piece she'd written.

It was ironic. The night before, she'd lain awake worrying because she couldn't get it written. Now that she'd written it, the damned thing was still keeping her awake.

Chapter Six

Donald Lipton came strolling through the door five minutes late. The classroom quieted instantly; his presence alone was enough to intimidate the students into silence.

Patricia and Julie had been chatting, and now Patricia slipped a note to her. *Well, my friend, are you ready for this guy?*

Julie smiled and wrote back: *Is anyone ever ready for him?*

Julie's hand rested on her writing assignment, which lay flat on the desktop in front of her. She had been feeling upbeat and confident, but that began to give way to irritation when she saw Lipton take his place behind the desk and cast a quick, arrogant glance around the room.

With no greeting and no apology for being late, he began sorting through a pile of mail he had carried in with him. It apparently didn't matter that twenty-three students were waiting for him to begin the class.

Finally he stood up, walked over and pulled the door closed, and went back to lean against his desk. He looked around the room again, stroking his beard with one hand. "Shall we take roll call... or just assume you're all here?"

Nobody seemed to know how to reply to that, so they all kept quiet.

"Let's do it the easy way," he said in a flat tone. "If you aren't here, speak up so I can mark you absent." Offering a lopsided grin, he looked around the room. "That was a joke, kids! My God, let's hope your writing skills are better than your sense of humor."

What a clown, Julie thought.

"Ms. Hunter, you should be honored that I didn't exclude you when I used the word *kids.* Can you remember what it was like to be one?"

A dozen possible replies fought to get out, but Julie pushed them all down and sat in silence, gritting her teeth. She had vowed that she would not allow herself to be baited by this man. If he wanted to make a fool out of himself, that was fine with her.

"No sense of humor, I see," Lipton said at last. "Okay, folks, pass your assignments to the front of the class." He waited until they had all reached the front row, then scooped them up and tossed them in a careless heap on the desk. "I'll have these back to you next Monday. That, by the way, is when the second paper is due. For this one, I want you to write a short piece describing a place that's special to you. Bring the reader right to the place with descriptions of physical settings, and make sure that description reflects the emotion you felt when you were there." Again came the lopsided grin. "I would prefer that you don't write about being in the back seat of a parked car with your girlfriend or boyfriend. Although the physical settings and emotions there might fit the criteria, at least one of your classmates is from the dark ages and might be embarrassed to hear what you have to say."

Julie glared at him, wondering what she had done to deserve this much unwelcome attention from him. Patricia was almost as old as she was, yet he hadn't been picking on her at all.

Was it because she'd stood up to him when he harassed that poor girl who asked about his grading system? That had to be it. She still wasn't sorry she'd done that. Even when she was a young girl, she'd always felt compelled to speak her mind to the class bully. She only hoped that he would eventually let it drop.

Lipton went on to talk about the chapter they had read in the book, and assigned another chapter for the following class period. Nobody took notes — not after the little scene he'd performed on Monday. Not that there was anything worth writing down. He was not a dynamic lecturer, and Julie found herself wondering why he bothered to teach a college class if it meant so little to him. Obviously, he took no joy in it. His only pleasure seemed to come from intimidating students.

A few students ventured questions about the material he was covering, and his sarcastic responses only reinforced her opinion of him. A typical reply was, "That should be obvious, Miss Reid," or "You must not have read the chapter, Mr. Wolford. Otherwise, you wouldn't have to ask a question like that."

On several occasions, Julie had to bite her tongue to keep from telling Professor Lipton exactly what she thought of him. By an act of sheer will, she managed to keep silent. It wouldn't have done any good, anyway.

When the class period was over, Lipton simply gathered up the assignments and left the room.

Julie stared at the doorway as the sharp sounds of his footsteps receded down the concrete walkway. *What could have produced such a jerk?* she wondered. Overbearing mother? Bad genes? Some lethal combination of both? She remembered the wedding band on his finger, and wondered again what kind of woman could have possibly been attracted to him. *Certainly no one could love him... and he is definitely incapable of reciprocating.*

Maybe the short piece she had turned in today would give him a glimpse of what he'd been missing.

~

The rest of the day went smoothly, and Julie hurried home after her last class so she could start getting everything ready for dinner that night with Cheryl and Tom.

She was adding seasoning to the pot roast when Robert got home a few minutes past six. After the obligatory kiss on the cheek, he gathered up the newspaper and went to his chair in the living room.

The doorbell rang at 6:15, and the door opened as Julie wiped her hands on a paper towel and stepped out of the kitchen. Tom and Cheryl came through the door. Robert put down his newspaper and got to his feet.

"Hi, Dad!" Cheryl came over and gave Robert a hug, then turned to hug Julie. Julie thought she had never seen Cheryl looking prettier. Her long, dark hair was tied behind her with a bright green silk scarf that matched one of the colors in her maternity top. Her brown eyes, so much like Julie's, sparkled as she made a point of sniffing the air. "Mmm... smells good."

"Sure does," Tom agreed. He was a tall, slender man with an easy smile and blue eyes. His light brown hair was neatly combed, giving him a look that Julie secretly thought of as Mr. Young Executive.

This was not in a negative sense, though. Julie loved Tom almost as much as she could have loved her own son. He was ambitious and wanted to do well, but he also had his priorities straight. Cheryl was the most important thing in his life; that came through in every gesture and intimate look they shared — even when they were around other people.

Tom came across the room to give Julie a hug and to shake Robert's hand. Tom had correctly assessed long ago that Robert was not a man who expected or wanted hugs from other men. Then he sniffed again. "Meat loaf?"

"Close," Julie said, laughing. "Pot roast."

"I sure hope you two are hungry." Robert rolled his eyes and looked at Julie. "These days, your mother only cooks when we have company, and then she doesn't know when to stop."

"Don't listen to your father, Cheryl," Julie interrupted in a halfway teasing manner. "Typical male... never happy. Besides, I cook almost every night."

"Now you two behave yourselves," Cheryl scolded with a grin. "Mom, do you need any help?"

"Well...." Julie hesitated for a moment, then glanced toward the table. "Maybe you could fill the water glasses, honey. And you two men might as well go ahead and sit down. Everything is ready."

The conversation was lively during dinner, first about Cheryl's pregnancy and Tom's work, then Robert's business — which Robert brushed aside quickly — and Julie's classes. Although Julie and Cheryl saw each other or at least talked on the phone almost daily, the men were seldom in touch with each other.

Tom, trying to show interest in his mother-in-law, questioned Julie about going to college. "Isn't that tough at your age?" he teased.

Julie pretended to be offended by the remark. "Just a minute, young man. You'd better apologize, or I'll bypass you when I serve your favorite Dutch apple pie."

Tom's blue eyes sparkled as he grinned. "I apologize! I was only giving you a hard time. Am I forgiven?"

Julie accepted the apology, and for a few minutes she described her classes and teachers. When she came to her creative writing class, she shook her head and said, "I'm not sure about that one. I don't know how anyone can tolerate the teacher, but I'm going to give that class a try. Sooner or later, he'll surely run out of ways of putting students down."

After dinner, Robert and Tom moved into the living room while the women cleaned the kitchen.

"This Professor Lipton is really getting under your skin, Mom," Cheryl said as she stacked dishes on the counter next to the sink. "Don't take it so personally. It's obvious the guy's a jerk. You've been wanting to go to college for years. Relax. Don't take that guy so seriously. Don't let him spoil it for you."

"You're right, hon." Julie cleaned the table top with a sponge, then wiped her hands on a towel. "I'm not going to let him or anyone else get in my way." She glanced at the stacked dishes. "I'll put those in the dishwasher later. Let's go to the study and I'll show you some cute baby pictures of you that I ran across the other day." She gave a motherly smile to her daughter. "I wonder if your little one will look like you or Tom. Either way, the baby will be beautiful."

"Spoken like a proud grandmother to be."

"I think it was more like a proud *mother*," Julie corrected. "I'm so proud of both you and Tom, babe. You will make great parents."

While Robert and Tom were still talking in the living room, Julie and Cheryl went down the hall to her study, where they spent most of the evening looking at family albums and baby pictures, laughing and trying to imagine which of the family traits the newest family member would have.

"Dang it, Mom. What if my baby has Uncle Charlie's big nose... or Aunt Helen's high forehead and square jaw... or all three?"

Julie laughed. "*Nobody* could be that unlucky! Don't worry, Cheryl. He'll be the cutest little boy that hospital has ever seen."

~

It was past ten when Julie waved goodbye to Tom and Cheryl, and closed the door. Already, the house seemed empty again.

"That was nice," she said, turning back into the living room. Robert was already settling back down on the sofa with the newspaper. "Did you and Tom have a nice visit?"

"Sure," he said.

She had no doubt that Robert and Tom had talked about the crisis facing Hunter Containers, and she resented the fact that Robert would open up to his son-in-law, but not to his own wife. She wanted to ask him how things were going with the financial projections the bank had requested. She wanted to talk to him about the contracts he was trying to negotiate with his large customers.

But he'd already turned his attention back to the news, and she knew that prying him away from that would take an act of God. She also knew that he would never seriously consider any thoughts or opinions she might have, anyway. That was man's talk. Women knew nothing about running a company.

Without speaking, she crossed to the hallway and went down to her study.

Chapter Seven

Friday, January 17

*I didn't sleep again last night. I have so much on my mind.
Robert has finally agreed to go to the doctor with me today, but
he doesn't pretend to be happy about it. I know he thinks I'm making a big deal over nothing, but my pain keeps getting worse, and
I am so scared....*

"Damn!" Robert fought the car out of a skid as they
turned into the parking lot for Dr. Cole's office. It had been
raining all day, and the rain-slicked streets were treacherous.

Julie hardly noticed. Her mind was on the news that might
be waiting for her inside the old brick structure they were
approaching. Over the past few days, she'd tried to put it out
of her mind, but now it was staring her in the face. She almost
wanted to tell Robert to turn the car around and take them
back home. But she couldn't do that, of course.

Robert brought the car to a cautious stop in front of the
entrance overhang. Julie sighed and reached for the door
handle.

"Do you want me to come in with you, or should I just

wait out here?" He patted the brown leather briefcase on the seat between them. "I could work on those financial projections Mr. Simmons at the bank asked for."

Julie turned and stared at him incredulously. If he had seriously thought he had a choice before, there was no doubt now.

"I'll park the car and be right there," he grumped. "Get in out of the rain."

Julie pushed open the door, and with two steps was under the protective overhang. She went ahead through the double glass doors as Robert pulled the car down the nearest aisle, looking for a parking space.

Once inside, Julie gave her name to the receptionist and sat down in a chair against the back wall. Dr. Cole's waiting room was bright and cheerful, with colorful prints on the walls and several potted plants. It was a welcome contrast to the gloomy day.

Robert came in a few minutes later, shaking water off his brown jacket before hanging it on the rack near the door. He took the seat beside her and sighed noisily. On the other side of Julie, a heavy-set, elderly woman was reading a three-month-old *Reader's Digest.*

"I still think you should see somebody else," Robert said, shifting uncomfortably in the armless chair. "I'm not sure this guy knows what he's talking about. My mother had all the same problems you've got. Arthritis, her doctor said. Told her to take aspirin. She had a touch of pleurisy in her chest, too."

She looked over at him. "You've been seeing Dr. Cole for twenty years, Robert. He's the one who got you back on your feet after you wrenched your back, remember? He's the one who showed you how to keep your blood pressure under control without medication. He also—"

"All right, all right," he muttered. "I get the point."

They had been through all of this before. The pain in her chest wasn't pleurisy, and the pain in her joints wasn't just regular arthritis. It was the lupus flaring up, but Robert didn't want to believe it. Dr. Cole had diagnosed Julie's lupus two years ago, and he'd sent her to a specialist in Sacramento to confirm it. Dr. Cole, frequently consulting with the specialist, had been treating her condition ever since — the same length of time that Robert had been denying it.

Robert leaned forward and plucked an *Outdoor Living* magazine from the stack on the low wooden table in front of them. He was soon immersed in an article about bass fishing.

Julie knew he would never admit the seriousness of her illness, and at that moment she could have used his understanding more than ever before. She felt sure that Dr. Cole would be giving her bad news today, and as she thought about this, the positive feelings she had gotten from her first week of classes were washed away by feelings of depression and despair. The pain in her chest was a constant reminder of the disease that was slowly taking her life, and in this harsh light of reality, she knew that attending college was an empty gesture. Most likely, she wouldn't live even long enough to get the degree in mathematics she'd dreamed of for so long, let alone ever put it to use.

By sheer willpower, Julie began to shake off the self-pity. She told herself that she had no choice but to live one day at a time, and get through it the best that she could. She had spent the last twenty years trying to convince Cheryl of this, and she felt that giving up now would in a way be letting her daughter down.

Besides, it was always possible that she was entirely wrong about Dr. Cole's reasons for wanting to see her and Robert. Maybe this would turn out to be *good* news.

Julie had brought her notebook with her, knowing that Dr. Cole usually ran behind schedule. Now she opened it on her lap and glanced at the assignment Mr. Neuman, her business math professor, had given the class. So far, most of what they had been doing was review, and this homework didn't look too difficult. With luck, she would be able to get it completed before she went in to see the doctor.

But while she tried to focus on Mr. Neuman's homework, her mind kept thinking about Lipton's writing assignment. He wanted them to describe a place that was special to them, and she'd already picked out what she wanted to write about: a cabin she and Robert owned at Dawley Lake, in the foothills of the Sierras only two hours' drive from their home. They went there several times a year.

As she started to write about it, she brought it back into her mind. Secluded, peaceful, surrounded by nature on all sides... some of her most treasured moments had been there. Away from the world and all of its modern conveniences, she and Robert had actually had a few intimate conversations there. They continued to go up to the cabin frequently after Cheryl was born, and as Cheryl grew, she also loved the place.

Julie fondly remembered those years, and she missed the intimacy that she and Robert had once shared. With the problem facing his plant, he was spending more and more time at work. And when he was home, he was usually working on the Thunderbird in his shop or reading the newspaper or watching a sporting event on television — all activities that effectively excluded her.

Although she felt neglected, she also knew that he was immersing himself in other activities in order to avoid facing the truth about her illness. She had no doubt that he truly loved her. It was just difficult for Robert to face some of the tougher things in life.

"Mrs. Hunter?"

Julie looked up to see Dr. Cole's nurse standing in the doorway leading to the back office.

"The doctor is ready to see you."

Julie nodded and closed her notebook, then got to her

feet. Robert turned a page of the magazine and continued reading about bass fishing.

"Mr. Hunter, I think Dr. Cole would also like you to come in with your wife today," said the nurse. "Do you mind?"

"Would it matter if I did?" Robert muttered. He tossed the magazine onto the low table and reluctantly followed Julie.

Dr. Cole rose briefly to shake their hands and waved them to two wooden armchairs flanking his desk. He was a large, kindly-looking man with tidy gray hair, a double chin, and half-moon spectacles.

Still grumbling under his breath, Robert sat down next to Julie. Dr. Cole's office was furnished much like the waiting room, but was a great deal more cluttered. The lacquered wooden furniture looked as strong and serviceable as it must have been half a century ago when new. It made Julie suddenly aware of time passing, steady and ruthlessly — that she was also running a race with time, and that these stout chairs, which had already outlasted scores of users, would almost certainly outlast her.

"I'm glad to see that you came along today," Dr. Cole said to Robert.

"So what's all the panic about?" Robert asked gruffly. "The way my wife is acting, you would think she's dying or something."

Dr. Cole stared at Robert, seemingly taken aback by the frontal attack. Robert stared back in a manner that was almost defiant.

Finally, Dr. Cole cleared his throat and said, "Your wife is a very sick lady, Robert. I want to go over the results of the most recent blood tests." He cleared his throat again, and his eyes remained on Robert. "I hope you realize that this is very difficult for me, too. Julie is not only a patient of mine, but a very good friend. I'm human too, and it hurts to see people I care about sick."

"So what are you trying to say?" Robert asked.

Dr. Cole issued a quiet sigh and turned to Julie. "Your blood tests from last week confirm what I feared. Your lupus is getting much worse. Much more of your body is affected now. Your red blood count is very low, which could be why you've complained of weakness and being short of breath."

Julie felt a cold comber of fear wash over her. "This is what you've been afraid would happen, isn't it?"

He nodded solemnly, his face reflecting compassion. "I'm afraid so. The most recent x-rays show that the lining around your heart and lungs are inflamed. With this pulmonary involvement, we have to be particularly careful that you don't contract pneumonia or, as in rare cases, start hemorrhaging in your lungs. So far, the heart looks good, but the kidney function tests are questionable. I think we need to repeat the urinalysis. Down the road, we may consider doing a biopsy of the kidney."

Robert had leaned forward, finally looking as if he were interested. "So what does this all mean?"

For a moment, Dr. Cole looked down at his hands, which were clasped in front of him. He finally looked up and met Robert's eyes. "It means the lupus has progressed to an extremely serious stage. I had hoped we wouldn't face this until much later. In some patients, lupus can remain fairly inactive for many years. I'm afraid Julie isn't one of the lucky ones."

"But...." Robert shook his head, seemingly unable to formulate his next question. "When you say serious...."

"I mean 'serious' in every sense of the word," Dr. Cole said when Robert's words trailed off. "Your wife is going to have to fight like hell to stay alive until a cure is found for this disease. I'm hoping that with the proper rest, diet, and exercise, along with her stubborn disposition...." He offered Julie a faint smile. "...she can be around to pester us for quite some time yet. But I have to be honest with you. The test results scare me. I thought you both should be aware of that."

Julie had remained quiet. Now she forced herself to ask the question they had all been skirting. "How much time do I have?"

Dr. Cole was visibly uncomfortable with the question, but he didn't flinch away from her eyes. "Lupus is so unpredictable, Julie. There's no way to know for sure what route it might take. If it slows down and decides to give your body a rest, you might have...." He faltered briefly, then continued. "Well, maybe four or five years."

Julie could only stare at him.

"C'mon, Doc," Robert protested. "You're scaring her."

Dr. Cole's eyes moved to Robert. "I'm afraid that four or five years is the *best* we can hope for. If the lupus continues to progress at the rate we've seen over the past few weeks, the time may be much shorter." He looked back at Julie. "I'm sorry for having to give you this news, Julie—"

"Shorter?" The word came out of her in a barely audible whisper. She forced a little more strength into her voice. "How much shorter?"

"Well... as I said, it isn't easy to predict—"

"Doctor, I want to know!" She was leaning forward now, hands fisted in her lap, back rigid. "Just tell me. Please!"

Dr. Cole nodded slowly. "I'm not trying to be coy with you, Julie. Believe me, I'm being as honest as I can be. The lupus has been attacking your body fairly vigorously recently. If it doesn't let up... well, it's possible you could die within a matter of months. We'll keep tracking it, of course—"

"But it might ease up?" Robert asked quickly.

"Yes. That's what we're hoping for—"

"Can't you give her something that will help?"

"We can treat the symptoms. Pain medication will help. If she contracts pneumonia, we can fight that with antibiotics. If the kidneys are affected, she may eventually have to go on dialysis—"

"Well, then—"

"But you have to understand," Dr. Cole pressed on, "that none of these measures will help the underlying problem of lupus. There's no cure for that disease. If it progresses to the point where the kidneys are seriously involved, I'm afraid that will mean it has reached—" He stopped abruptly, his eyes returning to Julie. "Well...."

"Terminal?" Julie managed to say. "Is that the word you're looking for?"

He nodded. "Yes, Julie." He cleared his throat again and looked down at the file that lay open on his desk. "Now, I want to make sure we keep a good record of the progression of the disease. To do that, I'll need to ask you a few questions. Have you been sleeping all right lately?"

The shock was beginning to recede a little. She forced herself to focus on his question. "Not always. My chest aches most of the time."

He jotted a note. "How has your appetite been?"

"About the same as always. Maybe a little less."

"She eats like a damn bird," Robert interrupted.

"Have you had any soreness in your mouth?"

"Yes, as a matter of fact I noticed that for the first time this morning. Today my mouth has been sore around the base of my tongue. What does that mean?"

"There are several main symptoms of lupus," he explained. "I can better follow the illness by keeping track of those that you are experiencing. Have you noticed your hands or face being extra sensitive to the cold? Have you noticed them turning bluish in color?"

Julie thought about that. "I'm not sure, Dr. Cole. I've never liked the cold, but I haven't noticed them looking bluish."

"What about the sun, Julie? Are you sensitive to the sun?"

She nodded slowly. "I mentioned that to Robert just the other day. I sometimes feel dizzy or faint when I'm out in the sun for too long at a time. A few weeks ago, I took a long walk in the sun, and I got a slight fever and broke out in a rash."

Dr. Cole jotted more notes. "Make sure you call my office to let me know if you experience anything like that again. For now, I'm not going to tell you to stay out of the sun completely, but make certain you wear a hat and the proper sunscreen. Okay?"

"Okay."

"Have you been avoiding stress as I suggested the last time?"

Robert had been fidgeting in his chair. "Hell, no!" he burst out. "You should see her, Doc. She signed up for some classes at Claremont Community College, and it's driving her crazy. She stays up half the night working on homework."

"Come on, Robert," Julie said. "That isn't true—"

"Like hell! It was after three when you came to bed the other night. You thought I was asleep, but I saw the clock. I told her she's too old to be playing this kid's game, Doc, but she won't listen."

Julie could feel the tears filling her eyes. She wondered if Dr. Cole noticed. He had become a great friend, but she knew that if he went to her defense, he would make Robert even more angry.

"So you're going to college, Julie?"

Julie responded by nodding her head.

"Well, I personally think that's great. I remember how often in the past you've mentioned your dream of some day getting a college degree." He reached across the desk and took her hand. "But my friend, you've got to remember that you're dealing with a chronic illness. You'll have to follow all my instructions to the letter, or I'm afraid you won't be able to keep taking classes. You'll need to start taking two or three naps each day, or at least lie down and rest. You have to avoid stress and fatigue. It's important to do the exercises I gave you." He squeezed her hand. "And, Ms. Julie, eating like a bird isn't quite good enough!"

He switched her medication to Azathioprine, and informed her that due to the nature of the drug, she would have to have regular blood tests performed because the drug could interfere with the proper formation of blood cells. The development of an infection was more likely because the drug reduced the activity of the immune system. He warned both Julie and Robert to notify him immediately if she developed a fever or any new symptoms while taking the drug. He said he would order an MRI and several other tests to rule out additional complications, and said he wanted to see her again in two weeks.

As she stood up to leave, Dr. Cole put his arms around her and gave her a hug. "Hang in there, Julie. I'm rooting for you. Good luck in school... but don't overdo it." He grabbed Robert's hand and shook it. As their eyes met, Dr. Cole added in an undertone, "Take care of her, Robert. She's going to need your love now more than ever."

Robert's eyes were downcast as he followed Julie out the door.

The rain had stopped, but the sky was still dark with swollen clouds. The breeze was fresh and cool, prompting Julie to pull her jacket more tightly around her shoulders.

"I still think this guy's a quack," Robert said as they got into the car. "If you're really as sick as he says you are, then he should just put you in the hospital and take care of the problem."

Julie, fighting to hold back tears, didn't reply. That was always Robert's answer: A quick fix for everything. He didn't realize — or wouldn't admit — that some things just can't be fixed.

Robert knew that Julie was upset with him, but he had to speak his mind. He felt sure that Dr. Cole was making too much out of Julie's illness.

They spoke little during the ride home, and the uneasy silence was maintained through dinner. Afterward, Robert got to work on the financial projections for Mr. Simmons at the bank while Julie cleaned up the kitchen, then went to her study.

He was still hassling with the numbers at 10:30, hunched uncomfortably over papers spread out across the dining room table. His eyes burned from staring at them for so long.

Mr. Simmons had asked him to put together detailed financial projections to show how much he expected Hunter Container to earn after the modernization project. It was a reasonable enough request, Robert knew. After all, if the bank was going to loan him three million dollars, Mr. Simmons would want to make sure he would be able to repay it.

But knowing it was a reasonable request didn't make it any easier. For one thing, he had an internal resistance to working with numbers. They never added up the way they were supposed to, and he lacked the patience to work out all the little errors that inevitably crept into any financial statements.

Robert felt at home on the floor of the plant itself, helping his employees coax more production out of stubborn machines, handling all the little day-to-day problems that were part of any manufacturing operation. He thrived on that challenge. He loved working with machinery.

But numbers were entirely different. Numbers were slippery. They could trick and deceive you if you weren't careful. Machines either worked or they didn't work. If they didn't work, you could tinker with them until they did, or you could throw them out and buy new ones. But numbers could *seem* to work while in fact they weren't. They gave Robert headaches.

He'd tried to get Dave Baxter, the plant accountant, to put together the profit and cash flow projections, but it soon became clear that Dave wasn't up to the job. The projections required dozens of assumptions about things ranging from the cost of wages in five years to the price Robert would have to pay for raw materials. Factoring the effects of the modernization into the process made it even more complicated.

Muttering under his breath, he tossed his half-eaten pencil onto the table and leaned back, easing the crick out of his back. He glanced toward the kitchen, thinking to ask Julie to bring him a cup of coffee — then remembered that she was in her study with the door closed, working on homework.

He drew in a breath, heaved it out in a long sigh, then got up and went into the kitchen to fix himself some instant decaf. He spooned granules into a cup and put on some water to boil.

From down the hall, he could hear the faint tapping of the computer keyboard in Julie's study. He knew that she had been staying up all hours to do homework, and he also knew that if she had that much energy, she couldn't be as sick as Dr. Cole had said. Dr. Cole was fine for things like back sprains and high blood pressure, but this lupus was something else. Even Dr. Cole had admitted that he hadn't seen many cases.

The teakettle shrieked, and Robert poured boiling water into the cup. After he stirred in some powdered creamer, he carried it back to the table — back to the nightmare of scattered papers and unanswered questions.

He had little doubt that Julie's health problems would clear up eventually, and then Dr. Cole would smile and shrug and say she was very lucky. But in the meantime, it was one more distraction that Robert did not need.

He sighed and sat back down, then picked up his pencil and got to work.

Chapter Eight

Monday, January 20

Is Professor Donald Lipton really a human being, or is he a demon sent to Earth to torment and frustrate college students? This morning as I arrived at school, I thought I saw another side of Dr. Lipton. Warmth, possibly. Caring. But later, I wondered if I'd just imagined it. When I talked to him after class, he was as cold and unfriendly as one person can be to another....

The new medicine Dr. Cole had prescribed helped with the soreness in Julie's mouth, but chest and joint pain continued through the weekend. She felt tired and depressed. Even though bed was exactly where she wanted to be, Julie knew she couldn't let the pain keep her there. She had several homework assignments to do, including the piece she still had to write for Dr. Lipton's Monday morning class.

Robert was no help. As usual, he had an easy answer for her problems: "If you just lie around feeling sorry for yourself, you'll never start feeling better."

She did stay in bed until a little after noon on Saturday. When Cheryl stopped by to show her mother the new maternity top she had just bought, she was surprised to find Julie still in a nightgown.

"Gosh, Mom," she said, lifting an eyebrow as she surveyed Julie's frazzled appearance. "What's with you?"

Julie felt her spirits lifted immediately by Cheryl's visit. "Don't worry, babe, I'm just being lazy today. All I need is a little rest, and I'll be as good as new. You know, I'm twenty-some years older than you were when you did this college thing."

"According to Dad, it's a little more than just being tired." Cheryl took her mother's hand and led her over to the beige sofa under the large front window. After they sat down together, she added, "He says the doctor is worried about you."

Julie lifted an eyebrow. "Did he say *he's* worried about me?"

Cheryl's eyes flickered slightly. "Well... Dad doesn't really believe there's anything to worry about. That's what he says, anyway." She took Julie's hand. "But if Dr. Cole's concerned, then so am I, Mom."

Julie felt a flash of irritation at Robert. How could he downplay her illness so much to her face, then talk to Cheryl about how worried Dr. Cole was? The last thing she wanted to do was cause Cheryl too much worry. "Dr. Cole didn't like the results of the most recent tests," she said, trying to make her voice sound casual. "But it was no big deal. You know your father. He overreacts to everything."

"Dad? Overreact? Not likely, Mom—"

"Well, he was too busy arguing with Dr. Cole to listen as carefully as he should have. Dr. Cole says the lupus may become inactive and won't bother me again for years. It's just acting up now to be a nuisance."

"But what if it doesn't become inactive?" Cheryl pressed.

"Then we'll just have to wait and see what happens." Julie

forced herself to hold eye contact with her daughter. "I'm going to be fine, Cheryl."

"Well... okay, if you say so." Cheryl shifted to a more comfortable position on the sofa. Julie smiled, remembering what it was like to carry all that extra weight, and to forever be trying to ease the strain. "How did your writing assignment work out?"

"Pretty well, thanks to your input," Julie said. "You really helped bring back to me what it's like to have a baby."

"Good! Did you get a good grade on it?"

"Professor Lipton hasn't given them back yet. But I'm not too worried about it." Julie realized that was the truth. Even though she'd been nervous when she turned in the assignment, she was confident that Dr. Lipton would find it acceptable. She'd certainly worked hard enough on it. "Now we've got another one to do."

"Wow! Sounds like Dr. Lipton is going to keep you busy. What's this one about?"

"We're supposed to write about a place that's special to us. I've decided to write about our cabin."

Cheryl's smile brightened at the thought of the place in the mountains that she, too, loved so much. "Oh, that's a good idea. Lots of nice memories up there."

"That's what I'm hoping."

"And what about Professor Lipton? Is he still giving you fits?"

Julie sighed. "Cheryl, that man is a walking, talking fit! But like you said, I'm not going to let him get to me. He's just a mean-spirited, egotistical blow-hard, and he's not worth any concern at all on my part."

Cheryl grinned. "That's the spirit, Mom."

"Enough about all that. Let's talk about Junior." Julie reached across and patted Cheryl's abdomen. "How's he doing in there?"

"He's doing fine. That reminds me, I have something for you." Cheryl reached into her purse and handed Julie the picture taken at her most recent ultrasound. "According to Dr. Weaver, this is your soon-to-be grandson, Matthew Thomas Merrow!"

Julie took the picture from Cheryl and stared at it. Then her eyes, brimming with tears, moved up to Cheryl. "I love you, honey."

"I love you too, Mom." Cheryl leaned over and put her arms around Julie and hugged her for the longest time.

Suddenly, the reality of her own fate overcame her, and Julie reached up and put her arms around her daughter's neck and pulled her close.

"Do you really know how much I love you?"

Cheryl seemed taken aback by this unfamiliar, weakened side of her mother. "Of course, Mom. I know how much you care. How can you even ask?"

Julie continued to hold her close, as if trying to gather every last bit of love that she could... as if letting go now would cause her to lose her forever. Again, she whispered, "I do love you so, Cheryl. Forever and for always, I will love you."

Before she left, Cheryl gathered the pillows from her mother's bed and propped them up behind her on the sofa, then covered her with an afghan. Julie also asked for her notebook and pen so she could work on her writing assignment.

She sat there for a long time after Cheryl had gone, looking out the window at the front lawn and the trees beyond. It was all so beautiful.

Finally, she opened the notebook and started thinking about Professor Lipton's assignment. How did one begin to put into words the feelings that come from being in a special place?

She tossed the words around in her head... *tranquil... isolated... sheltered....*

But before she could write a single word, she lay her head back against the pillow and drifted off to sleep.

~

The rest of the day and all of the evening was wasted because Julie felt too weak to even think about working.

On Sunday morning, she did manage to get dressed, but church was out of the question. She took a mid-morning nap, and then forced herself to sit in front of her computer long enough to complete Professor Lipton's writing assignment. It was a struggle to the end.

Somewhere in the middle of a woods, sitting at the edge of Lake Dawley, is a little.... No — she backed up and made a change: *...tiny cabin.* She could visualize it. *It is indeed the most beautiful place on Earth. I have been there many times with my husband....* No — *Robert. Each time has been more special than the time before....* No — *previously!*

Damn! What did words really matter? This entire writing thing was a giant pain.

Word by word, she struggled through it. When she was finally satisfied with the piece, she finished her math homework.

~

Even though it was only 7:30 p.m., she was exhausted and wanted to go to bed.

But as tired as she was, when she got into bed, she lay there staring up at the ceiling, unable to get to sleep. She felt strung out... "wired," as Cheryl would have called it.

Maybe Cheryl was right — maybe she was being too much of a perfectionist. What else could account for her struggling so with Professor Lipton's writing assignment? She didn't even care about this class. It wasn't part of her major course of study, and in fact, she knew she wouldn't learn anything useful from it even if she worked hard. It would make a lot more sense to skate through.

And that, she decided firmly, was what she would do.

But even making that decision didn't make her feel much better. She knew her body was weakening as the lupus waged war against her defense system. If her current physical state was any clue, the disease had won the battle today. And if it continued to win, she wondered seriously if she would even be able to finish this semester, let alone another three and a half years of college.

Robert snored softly beside her, oblivious of the mental turmoil she was going through.

If she was unable to finish college, she knew that Robert would see it as one more failure. According to him, she had never been successful at anything — other than being his wife and a mother to Cheryl. She had "failed" at everything else she had attempted to do. At least, that was how he saw it.

Julie had never felt physically or mentally worse, and suddenly all of her insecurities were coming out. She knew she wouldn't get any support from Robert, and talking to him about the way she felt would accomplish nothing but an "I told you so" from him.

"I give up," she murmured to herself under her breath. "I don't think I can take it anymore."

At the same time, she knew that life didn't offer her any options. She had to take life and accept it exactly the way it was. She was losing control, and there wasn't a damn thing she could do about it.

Groaning, Julie rolled over onto her side, fluffing up the pillow and burying her face in it. The tears she had been holding back came spilling out then, and her chest ached with the sobs that followed.

Chapter Nine

When Monday morning rolled around, Julie was still both physically and mentally depleted, and the last thing she wanted to do was face more of Donald Lipton's cutting remarks and haughty looks. What she *did* want, though, was to see his reaction to her first assignment — the one about the birth of her daughter. The anticipation of that was enough to drag her out of bed and into the shower.

An hour later, she pulled into the school's parking lot. As she went up the steps toward the courtyard and the walkway that would take her around to Lipton's classroom, she heard the cry of a small child. Turning, she was surprised to see Donald Lipton across the courtyard, squatting near a small boy who was crying.

My God, she thought. *What's he done to that child?*

She knew there was a day care center on campus for the convenience of students who had young children, and assumed that the boy had wandered away from there. *Too bad he had to wander right into the troll of the school*, she thought.

She instinctively started around the inner walkway, but stopped when she saw Lipton take the boy's hand in his own big hands and brush it gently. Partly concealed behind some shrubbery, she knew Lipton hadn't seen her.

"Skinned up your hand pretty good there," he was saying, squatting so that his own eyes were level with the boy's. "I know what it's like. When I was a little older than you, I tripped over my own feet and went down right in front of a bunch of girls in my class. They all laughed at me. Can you imagine that?"

The boy brushed away the last of his tears, and Julie saw a half-smile form.

"*Ker-splat!*" Lipton went on, now releasing the boy's hand and waving his arms expansively. "That was me, all right. Right on my face. That's why I'm so ugly. Lucky you! You landed on your hands!"

The boy laughed then and said something Julie couldn't hear.

"Yeah, maybe you're right," Lipton agreed. "Think you're gonna be okay now?"

The boy nodded, and now Julie heard his timid voice: "Yes, sir."

"Good!" Lipton got to his feet and brushed off the knees of his dark slacks. "Now, let's go see if we can find your mom. I'll bet she's wondering where you are. With any kind of luck, we might find a pop machine. Feel like a root beer?"

Dumbfounded, Julie watched as Lipton and the boy headed toward the registration office, hand in hand. Was that some humanity she had seen in the man? Was it really Donald Lipton she'd seen, or was it possible he had a twin brother who was a nice man?

A few minutes later, still puzzling over what she'd seen, she took her seat next to Patricia. On the other side, Rick Marston said hi to her, then went back to his conversation with the blond-haired boy in front of him.

"What a weekend!" Patricia said, slumping at her desk as

if under a heavy burden. "I'm beat from all this homework — and it's only the second week."

Julie smiled and reached across to pat her arm. "Cheer up, Patricia... we only have nineteen more weeks after this one."

Patricia groaned just as Professor Lipton arrived carrying a large folder under his arm. Julie's heart began to race as she recognized the stack of papers he removed from it — the writing assignments they had turned in the previous week.

Lipton wasted no time with roll call this time. He turned to the class and assumed his customary position leaning against the desk with his arms folded. Any hint of humanity she might have seen on his face in the courtyard was gone.

"Well, kids, it's like this. After reading your first papers over the weekend, I can already see who's going to put in the effort here, and who's thinking they can take it easy. Some of these papers were so bad I didn't know whether to return them or just do us all a favor and burn them."

The students sat in stunned silence.

"This time I was easy on you, though." He reached for the stack and began handing them back. "Don't expect me to be Mr. Nice Guy next time."

As the students received their papers, Julie heard mixed reactions — usually either groans or sighs of relief. She glanced over at Patricia when her paper was returned. Patricia looked at it nervously, then grinned and gave Julie a thumb's up and flashed her paper with a big *B* at the top.

On the other side, Julie heard Rick lean forward to the blond-haired boy and say, "Wow! I got a *B*, and I didn't even try! I think this class is going to be okay, after all."

"Only a *B,* Rick?" the boy said with a smile. "I got an *A* on mine."

"Teacher's pet," Rick teased.

Julie began to relax. If Professor Lipton was handing out *A*'s and *B*'s this easily, all her worry had been for nothing. She knew she had done a good job on that assignment.

Her thoughts were interrupted by Lipton's voice at the desk behind hers. "Jennifer, I want to ask you a question about your paper. Were you intentionally trying to imitate e e Cummings in your writing, or is your total lack of punctuation and capitalization merely a sign of poor education?"

Without waiting for a response, Lipton walked up to Julie and slowly placed her paper face down on the desk before her. Instead of moving on to the next student, he remained beside her.

She left the paper untouched. No way would she pick it up with those piercing eyes staring down at her like a predator looking for its next meal.

"Ms. Hunter, aren't you going to look at your paper?" he prodded.

Julie felt the blood rush to her face. The class had gone quiet, and Julie knew that all the other students were watching this tableau play out in front of them.

She couldn't let it draw out any longer. She reached out and flipped over the paper, and froze when she saw the red *C* scrawled at the top. There were no corrections in grammar, no misspelled words, no explanations whatsoever. Just that huge, glaring *C*.

Lipton made a clucking sound and moved on to finish handing out the papers.

The shock that held Julie paralyzed gradually gave way to rage. She could feel the blood thudding in her ears, and the sick sensation of stress-caused dizziness. This was her first graded assignment in college — and she'd gotten a *C*.

She drew a steadying breath. There had to be a mistake. She had done a good job with this assignment. There was no way she deserved a *C*.

Just a mistake. She resolved to talk to Professor Lipton after class, and once that decision was made, she felt the emotions inside her begin to calm down. *He screwed up somehow in his grading*, she told herself. *He'll fix it.*

Lipton had held back a few of the assignments, and now he read excerpts from them, pausing now and then to offer criticism and, occasionally, even a rare comment that almost bordered on praise.

Finally, he asked for the current assignment, and while they were being passed forward, he gave the class another reading assignment from the textbook.

"I do hope your moaning, class, isn't a sign of your inability to read. You must know how to do *something*. Heaven knows we haven't any real writers in here. You're dismissed. Go be a nuisance to somebody else."

Julie had intended to follow him outside and confront him there, since he usually bolted from the class the moment it was over. This time, though, he sat down at his desk and began jotting some notes on a yellow pad.

She waited until most of the students had left the room, then slowly approached Lipton's desk.

He looked up, his face expressionless. "Yes?"

She met his gaze unflinchingly. In a voice she hoped did not betray her nervousness, she said, "Dr. Lipton, can we talk about my grade on this paper? You gave me a *C*. Can you explain why?"

"My job is to grade, Ms. Hunter, not to explain."

She drew a deep breath, trying to hold onto her temper — which was difficult when what she wanted to do was slap his arrogant face. "You didn't even make one correction on this. All of my words are spelled correctly, and my grammar is perfect. Why did I get a *C*?"

Donald Lipton issued a heavy sigh. "Ms. Hunter, there is more to writing than memorizing a dictionary and knowing all the proper grammar. Of course those things help, but there's a lot more to a piece of writing than the mechanics."

He turned back to the notes on his yellow pad, as if he expected that explanation to satisfy her. But it didn't. Not by a long shot. What he'd said was that the *C* was no mistake, that she'd gotten what she deserved. But she still didn't understand why.

"Can you be more specific?" she asked. "What did my writing lack?"

With another sigh, he tossed his pencil down and leaned back in his chair, facing her. The curved scar she'd noticed earlier showed pale white against his forehead. "The subject of motherhood should be warm, but your description was cold and lifeless. It was more like a textbook. You've got to learn to write from your heart as well as from your head. I think I did you justice by giving you the *C*. That is average, you know."

Cold and lifeless? She couldn't believe he was saying that about her writing. This cold fish? What could he possibly know about warmth? He was about as remote a man as she'd ever met.

"I'm well aware of the grading system," she said with acid politeness. "What I don't understand is why you would say that my writing was cold and lifeless. Can you give me some examples?"

"Look," he said. "I would suggest that from now on, you try harder. Keep trying, and you may just figure it out." He picked up the yellow legal pad muttering, "Guess I'll have to do this in the office," laid it on top of the stack of assignments that had just been turned in, and thrust the whole bundle under his arm. He got to his feet and started for the door, then turned back for a parting shot. "Of course, if you can't do it, you can always drop the class." Without giving her time to respond, he turned and strode out the door.

Julie felt the hot blood of fury rush to her face as she stood there staring at the closed door. Did he want her to drop the class? Was that why he was being so hard on her? But why? Maybe he just had something against older students. Or women.

But that didn't make sense. He wasn't exactly cordial to Patricia, but he wasn't going out of his way to torment her. Was it possible that he was still carrying a grudge because of the way she had stood up to him during that first day of class?

She shook her head firmly. Whatever the reason, she wouldn't let him get to her. And she wouldn't drop this class. If he thought he could get rid of her that easily, he was crazy.

~

A slight grimace crossed Don Lipton's face as he stepped into the sanctuary of his cluttered office and closed the door behind him. He snatched the white mug from the corner of his desk, glanced inside and decided it wasn't grungy enough to kill him, and poured himself a cup of coffee from the thermos that stood on the low credenza.

As he sat down behind his desk, his mind went back over the conversation he'd just had with Julie Hunter. Older students were always a pain. Always thought they knew everything. She was a helluva writer, though. The piece she'd turned in for her first assignment was one of the best he'd ever seen.

He also had to admit that she was attractive when she was angry. She was slim, but with a good figure, and he liked the way her brown hair was feathered about her face. Her brown eyes and long, dark lashes would have given her a look of dewy innocence if not for the determined chin and the sharp intelligence in those eyes. Very little make-up. And that small gathering of freckles across her cheeks and over the bridge of her nose had really flared when her anger built up.

He offered himself a slight shrug and sipped the lukewarm coffee as he reached for the stack of assignments. He had more important things to do than sit here thinking about an overaged student who couldn't take a little heat.

But as he sorted through the assignments, his eyes immediately fell on her name: *Julie Hunter.* He slipped her paper out of the stack and, leaning back in his chair, began to read.

Damn, he thought after a moment. *The first one wasn't a fluke. She's good!*

Chapter Ten

Sunday, February 2

Life used to be so simple. I'm not sure which pain is the worst — the pain from my illness, or Dr. Donald Lipton. It's funny how unfit the doctorate degree seems with his name. Doctors are supposed to help people feel better. Not this guy!

Robert spends more time than ever at work lately. Sometimes I get so lonely and afraid. I try to tell him, but he listens with his ears closed....

Over the next several weeks, Julie struggled almost daily with the weakness and pain of her disease. Based on the results of her MRI and most recent blood tests, Dr. Cole had told her that the new medicine seemed to be helping some, but when she pressed him, he admitted that the overall outlook still didn't look good.

She kept busy with school work, which usually helped her focus on something more positive than her illness. She had gotten a solid *A* on her first business math test, and had even helped some of the younger students with their homework. She had always handled the family finances, and the homework in this class was almost simpler to her than what she had done before in real life. She'd also gotten an *A* and several compliments from her psychology professor for a short research paper. Mrs. Cramer had used her first written assignment as an example for the rest of the class to follow.

Even the weather was cooperative, with sunny days and unseasonably warm temperatures that helped make her feel a little better.

Professor Donald Lipton kept giving her fits, though. She had wanted to maintain a straight *A* average for the semester, but had given up on that goal because of his class. Now her grades had become more of a personal battle with Lipton. She kept trying to please him, but to no avail. She rushed through her homework assignments from the other classes with little effort, and then began her nightly battle with the writing assignment from Mr. Impossible.

However, in spite of her hard work and unremitting efforts, she continued to get *C's* on every paper. Patricia and Rick and other students in the class had shared their papers with Julie, and even they readily agreed that their papers weren't any better than hers even though they were getting *A's* and *B's*.

She knew that her own writing had improved, so why didn't Lipton see this? Why was he being so hard on her?

Another worry that nagged at Julie was Robert's continuing business problems. Although he made no effort to keep her informed or to ask her opinion about them, she knew he was still under a lot of strain. She heard telephone conversations when he was at home, and she'd seen some of the documents as he labored over them at the dining room table.

She knew that Mr. Simmons at the bank had given tentative approval for the modernization loan. But there was a catch. Two of them, actually. Mr. Simmons had agreed to provide only $2.6 million for the modernization, not the three million Robert had asked for. That meant Robert would have to find some corners to cut in order to keep costs down, and Julie knew he'd been struggling with that for the past week.

In addition, before finalizing the loan, Mr. Simmons wanted to see some long-term sales contracts with major customers. Julie had overheard Robert complaining bitterly about that to Tom one Sunday afternoon when Tom and Cheryl had come over for lunch. How, Robert wondered, was he supposed to secure long-term contracts from major customers without knowing for sure that he would be able to go ahead with the modernization? If he promised low prices, then was unable to modernize the plant and cut production costs, the operating losses he would suffer fulfilling the contracts would put him out of business. But if he quoted prices that were higher than those of Crown Paper Products, he would never get the contracts in the first place.

"Damned if I do, and damned if I don't," he said to Tom, who was sympathetic but unable to offer any solid advice.

Never before had Julie seen Robert so upset by anything, and it worried her. If Hunter Container was forced into bankruptcy, she and Robert would face financial ruin.

~

One evening when Julie was struggling with one of her papers, Cheryl stopped by for a visit.

Professor Lipton had told the class to write about a time in their life when they had to make a choice between two equally attractive or dismal alternatives.

While Cheryl and Robert sat at the kitchen table having coffee, Julie retreated to one of the chairs in the adjoining family room where she could sit with her notebook and draft out the assignment.

Her first thought was to write about her decision to drop Lipton's class and forfeit her degree, or stay there and be treated so unfairly. Some choice — definitely *dismal*. She was certain that her feelings would be enough to fill up several pages, and there would be no doubt in anyone's mind that she was feeling what she wrote.

But somehow, she doubted if that would be the way to raise her grade. After giving it some more thought, she finally decided to write about the time a few months ago when she and Robert were trying to decide between having a swimming pool or a pond at their new house. Both were equally attractive to them, but they finally decided that the pond would be less work and would fit better into their rural landscape. Julie loved the pond, and in the end she was sure they had made the right choice.

She started jotting down notes about the feelings she'd had as she and Robert had been considering the decision, but she knew instinctively that she wasn't "capturing the moment," as Professor Lipton liked to say in class. After that first confrontation, she'd never again questioned any of the grades he had given her, and he had never written anything on any of her papers to give her guidance. But she still remembered what he'd said about the piece she'd written about being a mother. *Cold and lifeless.* That was how he'd put it.

Ever since then, she had tried to bring more emotion into her stories — but apparently, with no success. She knew she was having no better luck with this one. Even though it had been a difficult decision at the time, she felt that she wasn't bringing out the way she had truly felt about it. She had no doubt that Professor Lipton would feel the same way.

"That's it!" She threw her notebook and pen across the room where they clattered against the wall and fell to the floor. "I've had it! Why do I even try pleasing that bearded jerk?"

Robert turned to look through the doorway at her, his face reflecting genuine concern. "Julie, calm down! Why don't you drop that class? You said yourself that you didn't want to take it in the first place. You don't need that stress in your life." He turned back to Cheryl and added, "Neither do we."

Cheryl stood up and came over to her mother, leaning over to put her arms around her. "I didn't realize you were so upset about this, Mom."

Julie drew a breath that sounded more like a sob. "I don't know why I'm letting it get to me... I really don't."

Cheryl sat and hugged her for a long moment, then drew back and looked carefully at her. "Then let's talk about it, Mom. Maybe we can figure it out. Okay?"

Robert made a grunting sound as he got up and headed for the back door. "Good idea, Cheryl. You see if you can figure it out. Try knocking some sense into your mother while you're at it. I'm going to do some work in the shop." The door slammed behind him.

"Don't pay any attention to him, Mom," Cheryl said quietly. "He'll do better with that old Thunderbird." She paused for a moment, her eyes still on Julie. "Maybe we should talk about this writing class... and Professor Lipton—"

"I really don't see where there's anything to talk about. I tried to talk to him about my homework, and he makes it sound like I'm asking him to go out of his way to explain what I'm doing wrong."

"But that's what teachers are supposed to do, isn't it?" Cheryl asked. "Aren't they supposed to give you feedback so you can improve your work?"

"That's what I always thought. A simple explanation would have been enough. Instead, he tells me to drop the class. I wonder how much he gets paid for doing that." Julie threw up her hands. "I don't know why I don't just give up. No matter how hard I try, I'll never be able to please him."

Cheryl was silent for a moment as she thought about what her mother had said. Julie could see the love and compassion in her daughter's eyes.

"So what's the big deal, Mom?" she said at last. "Why is it so important for you to please him? Gosh, you seem almost *obsessed* with pleasing this man. It's obvious to me that he can't be pleased by *anything* from a student."

Julie drew a breath and released it in a long sigh. "Nobody understands. I wanted so badly to get an *A* in every class, and I'm doing great in all the others. But that damn class... I know no matter how hard I work, that class will keep me from doing it."

Cheryl nodded slowly. "I understand what you're saying, but not everyone is a great writer. Look at all the other things you do so well. The grades aren't the important thing, Mom. You're trying to get that degree you've waited so long for. That's the important thing. Maybe Dad's right. Why don't you drop that class?"

Without realizing it, Cheryl had touched upon the deepest reason for Julie's feelings of defeat. "You're right. My ultimate dream is to get my college degree, but I want to do well in the classes I'm taking... *all* of them. Dropping the creative writing class won't help. Thanks to the people who design the courses, I would have to take it again, anyway... and Professor Lipton is the only creative writing instructor."

"All right, you have to take the class. But Mom, don't you think you're causing yourself too much trouble with all of this? Didn't Dr. Cole tell you to avoid stress? Okay, so you're getting *C's* in this one class. That's still a passing grade. It'll give you the college credit you need. Then you can put it behind you and go on to more important classes. I'm sure lots of other students are getting *C's*—"

"And maybe they're satisfied with them," Julie said, her voice quivering. She was close to tears, and she looked away so Cheryl wouldn't see them. "But I wanted to do better. Getting straight *A's* was my personal goal."

Cheryl paused again before replying, and for a moment the two women looked out through the large front windows at the wooded slope across the road. It was a beautiful, peaceful scene which usually boosted Julie's spirits. Now it just seemed to add to her weariness.

Finally Cheryl spoke again, her voice soft. "Are you sure it isn't more than just the grade?"

This brought Julie's eyes back to her daughter's. "What do you mean?"

"I mean...." Cheryl waved a hand as if searching for the right words. "Well, it's the way you talk about this class, and Professor Lipton. I'm wondering if you're putting too much emphasis on what he thinks about you and your writing."

Julie frowned. "Why would I care what that jerk thinks or feels about me?"

Cheryl's eyes remained on Julie's. "That's what I was wondering. It's almost as if, deep down, you're determined to please him no matter what."

Julie couldn't help laughing, although even to her own ears it sounded a little strained. "That's the most ridiculous thing I've heard in a long time. Never in a million years would I care what that man thinks about me personally. I'm just upset about the grades he's giving me." She shook her head. "But you're right. It's silly to get so strung out over a class that isn't even important to me."

Even as she said it, though, she knew she was speaking more for Cheryl's benefit than her own. What was driving her to write an assignment acceptable to Donald Lipton wasn't just the desire for a better grade — although that was certainly part of it. And it definitely wasn't out of any misguided need to please him.

What was driving her was an almost overwhelming sense of frustration. Julie had always believed that a person could get over almost any obstacle if he or she worked hard enough at it. In Professor Donald Lipton, she had encountered an obstacle that was growing to monumental proportions — and something inside her saw it as a challenge that had to be overcome. As Cheryl pointed out, it was silly to devote so much time and energy to this problem. Logically, Julie could understand that and fully agree with it. But something inside her refused to give up, and that core of resolute determination would not listen to words of logic.

She gave herself a shake of the head. *Enough!*

She put her homework aside and spent the next hour or so visiting with her daughter — and they were both careful to avoid anything about Professor Lipton or his class. Cheryl's due date was only five weeks away now, and she and Tom already had a room ready for little Matthew when he decided to make his appearance.

Although the conversation didn't return to Julie's problem with Dr. Lipton, her mind continued to fret with it. By the time Cheryl left a little before ten o'clock, Julie had made a decision. Tomorrow she would go to Dr. Lipton's office and insist that he explain her grades to her. She'd had enough of his games. This time she wouldn't let him off the hook. She knew that what she was writing was good, and she wouldn't leave his office until he told her why she wasn't getting *A's* for her work.

Chapter Eleven

Classes the following day passed quickly and without too many problems. Even Professor Lipton managed to be on time, and limited his insults to only a few half-hearted jabs.

But Julie hadn't changed her mind. After her final class, she climbed the steps — all forty-four of them — to Professor Lipton's office. At the top she stopped to catch her breath. Her heart was racing, and she had to lean against the wall for support. She knew she should have taken the elevator, but for some reason that choice suggested weakness, and she wasn't ready to admit that yet.

She waited a few minutes longer, then walked down the hall looking at the signs on the doors. There it was: *DONALD LIPTON, Ph.D.*

Julie gave a perfunctory knock on the door, then pushed it open and walked in. Donald Lipton looked up from his desk, his face registering surprise. She saw something else there, too — and for a moment he almost seemed glad to see her. Then it was gone, and she was sure she'd only imagined it.

"What the hell?" he demanded.

The office was small, and brightly lighted with a row of standard fluorescent light strips recessed into the modern grid ceiling. A single bookcase stood against one wall, its shelves filled with an assortment of books leaning against one another like tired soldiers. Crooked stacks of papers occupied two of the shelves. The desk was small and cluttered, with a computer monitor perched dangerously close to one edge and a haphazard collection of papers and file folders strewn across the desktop.

As she dropped her backpack onto the floor and sat down in one of the uncomfortable armchairs in front of his desk, she realized how small and dreary the room looked. There were no personal touches of any kind: No certificates on the walls, no framed family photographs, no little knickknacks from home. The place had all the personality of a bank teller's cubicle.

Just like Dr. Lipton himself, she thought.

Lipton had been working at his computer, and she could see from the empty candy bar wrapper that he had been snacking. Several bottles of spring water were on top of his desk, and the waste can, full to the brim, had spilled over onto the floor.

"I want to know why you're being so hard on me," she demanded without preamble. She wanted to hold onto the anger inside her. She wanted to lean on it for support, and she wanted him to see it. "I've gotten a *C* on everything I've turned in—"

"Because it's average work," he said, his face taking on a ruddy glow. "And what gives you the right—"

"I know what's average, Professor Lipton. At least, I know what's average in your class. I've read many of the other students' papers." She reached into her backpack and grabbed the stack of papers he had returned to her, all marked *C*. As she pulled them out, her car keys fell out and clattered to the floor. Embarrassed, she reached down to pick them up and return them to the backpack. "And I know that some of your other students are getting *A's* for work that isn't half as good as mine."

A slow, infuriating grin spread across his face. "Well, at least you don't lack confidence in your own abilities—"

"No thanks to you!" she blazed back. "Do you know how much time I put into your assignments? Hours! I didn't even want to take this course. It was required, you know." Her chin rose a fraction of an inch. "I'm a math major, and I might add, I do very well at that. I do great in every one of my other classes."

"Good for you, Ms. Hunter," he said, his voice infuriatingly calm. "But you fail to remember that I am the instructor in the creative writing class, and it is up to me — not you, and certainly not the other students — to determine what grade you deserve. But if you're willing to give up so easily, if you can't deal with a little difficulty in your life, I would once again suggest that you drop the class."

"Damn you!" Julie didn't care anymore. "I'd like nothing better than to deck you."

His grin widened. "I didn't think you were the violent type."

She bolted from her chair, planting her hands on her hips. "You think a lot of things without much evidence, don't you?" Donald Lipton had hit a nerve. Who was he to tell her she couldn't handle a challenge when it was becoming a challenge just to deal with the pain of breathing? Of course, he had no way of knowing that. He most likely assumed that all was right in her world.

Then, to her horror, she felt hot tears well up in her eyes and roll down over her cheeks. She turned away, brushing at them with a hand, but more came instantly to take their place. She felt the emotion clutching at her chest now. She was trembling, and knew he could see it.

Standing, Lipton reached over to a box of tissues on his desk. With full force, he yanked two or three out at once and handed them to Julie. "Here, take these. I'm only charging fifty cents apiece today."

Julie snatched the tissues from him and wiped angrily at her eyes. This was absolutely the worst thing that could've happened, but she was powerless to stop it. She would have gotten up and fled the room, but she knew that her legs would never be able to carry her.

Lipton sat back down, and something in him became a little less stiff. "Julie... can I call you that?" Without waiting for a reply, he added, "You can call me Don. I see potential in your writing, but you never quite bring it out all the way. You're going to have to work harder to make your characters and prose come to life. You have the right ideas, but when I read your papers, I sense a heart full of emotions just fighting to escape... and so far, you haven't found the way to make that happen."

The tears had finally dried up as he talked. She blew her nose and straightened in her chair, determined to see this through. "I don't know *how* to make it happen. Aren't you the one who's supposed to help me? So far, you haven't written a single suggestion on any of my papers."

"That's because I want it to come from *you*, doll," he said quietly. "I want you to figure it out for yourself."

Doll? Surely she hadn't heard him right. Surely even Don Lipton, Mr. Personality himself, wouldn't dare to use such a familiar term with her.

"That's what writing is all about," he went on. "It comes from inside each one of us... at least, it does if we're any good. Of course, if a writer doesn't have that inner voice, it means he isn't any good. Then he goes to Hollywood and writes scripts for movies."

He grinned at his little joke, but Julie wouldn't give him

the satisfaction of sharing it. "Do you think I have that inner voice?"

"I *know* you do, doll. You just have to find it."

There it was again, and this time she knew she hadn't imagined it. She felt an instant flare of anger, but she put it down before it could burst out of her mouth. For now, she wanted to keep him on the track of the conversation. She would deal with his sexist attitudes later. "So how do I find it? Aren't you supposed to help me do that? As you like to point out, *you're* the instructor."

He sighed. "All right. I'll give it a try. In that first paper, you talked about the birth of your daughter, and you described how giving birth can change a woman's life. But Julie, you failed to make me understand how your daughter's birth changed *your* life. I mean, from reading your paper, someone wouldn't know if your daughter's birth really messed up your life's plans or brought you great joy.

"The same goes for that cabin you wrote about. I read *woods* and *trees* and *fireplace* and *lakes*, but I sensed underneath that you were trying to say it was a neat place for lovers to go to get away from the world." Suddenly he pushed himself out of his chair and began pacing back and forth in the small room, gesturing with his hands. "You omitted words like *touch* and *communication* and *sharing*. You used objects instead of feelings." He turned abruptly to face her. "And Julie, objects don't come from the heart."

Julie sat unmoving in her chair, struck dumb by the passion that had suddenly erupted from Don Lipton. It was as if a switch had been turned on inside him. He leaned toward her, his face expressing true enthusiasm for the first time. If he felt that much passion for writing, why didn't he let his students see it in the classroom?

"Do I make any sense?" he asked. "Maybe I've been harder on you because I know you're capable of doing so much more. Do you understand?"

Before she had time to formulate a reply, he reached out and took both of her hands, lifting her up from her chair to face him. He towered over her by at least eight inches.

"It's in there, Ms. Hunter!" he blurted, jabbing a finger at her chest. "All you have to do is dig a little deeper."

Still, she was unable to speak. This display was the last thing she would have expected from Professor Donald Lipton.

Finally he cleared his throat and stepped back, looking down at his watch. "Now, do you mind if I get to my next class? I'm already ten minutes late, thanks to you." He stepped around her briskly and, just before reaching the door, turned back. "If you can let your heart speak in your writing, Julie, you'll get the grade you want in my class. It's as simple as that."

Chapter Twelve

Thursday, March 20

It's hard to believe that two months have passed already. I'm really proud of how well I've been doing in college so far. Well, I'm still having fits with Dr. Lipton and his creative writing class, of course. After talking to him yesterday afternoon, I'm more confused than ever. He's been giving me C's because he thinks I'm a good writer? Go figure....

It was the height of the lunch hour, and the noise of cutlery, aluminum trays, and the loud braying at collegiate humor made conversation difficult when Julie and Patricia paid for their food and started looking for an empty table. They finally found one in a back corner, grabbing it only seconds after its former occupants had vacated. The noise was somewhat muted back here, and they were able to talk without raising their voices too much.

"I'm glad we finally had time to eat together, Julie," Patricia said. "I've been so busy this semester."

Julie stirred sugar into her iced tea. "Tell me about it!"

Patricia opened her chicken sandwich and removed the

large slice of tomato. "It's exciting to learn about new things. I just wish it wasn't so much work. I'm able to keep up with everything, though, and I'm getting mostly *A's* and *B's.* Allen and the kids sure are surprised that I'm doing so well."

"That's great, Patricia. I don't know how you do it with so much going on all the time." Julie took a bite of tuna sandwich and washed it down with iced tea. "My daughter is supportive, but Robert wants me to drop out of college and forget about it."

"Really? Why?"

Julie didn't want to tell Patricia about her illness, so she shrugged and said, "I suppose he thinks a woman's place is in the home. Besides, he's having some problems with his business right now, and that has put him under stress."

"Nothing too serious, I hope."

"Well... we don't know for sure yet." Julie really didn't want to go into all the details about the threat hanging over Hunter Container. Robert's mood had lifted a little over the last week or so, and he'd mentioned in passing that he'd been able to secure some key contracts from major customers. He wasn't sure if it would be enough to get the much-needed modernization loan from Mr. Simmons at the bank, but it was a big step in the right direction. Things were looking better, although Julie knew they weren't out of the woods yet.

"I hope everything works out okay," Patricia said.

"I'm sure it will. Robert has pulled miracles out of the hat before."

Julie suddenly remembered that it was time to take one of the pills Dr. Cole had prescribed. She swung her backpack around to set it on the floor next to her, then looked through the compartment where she usually kept them. The bottle wasn't there.

"Is something wrong, Julie?" Patricia asked.

She knew that she'd taken a pill out of this bottle at lunch time the day before, and she always left the bottle in the back-pack so she would have the pills at school. She had another bottle at home for morning and evening doses.

Then Julie remembered the previous afternoon in Professor Lipton's office, when the keys fell out of her backpack. Was it possible her bottle of pills had fallen out, too? If so, it might have rolled under his desk where she hadn't seen it.

"Julie?"

She closed the backpack and picked up her sandwich. She'd probably lost the bottle while she was getting the knap-sack out of the car. "I was just looking for some medication I'm supposed to take at lunch time. I must've misplaced it. It's no big deal, though. I've got more of them at home. I'll take one later."

Patricia was looking at her with concern. "Is it pain medication?"

"No, not at all." That was true; she took her pain medication mornings and evenings, although she often tried to skip the morning dose because it made her feel drowsy and sluggish. She wanted to be alert during her classes. "This is for... something else."

Patricia sipped her tea, then said, "Julie, forgive me if I'm prying into your business, but I've been worried about you. Are you all right? I noticed a few times in class that you appeared to be in pain—"

"I'm fine, Patricia," Julie interrupted. She didn't want Patricia or anyone else to know about the lupus. That would only add complications to her new friendships and classes. Besides that, she couldn't stand to hear one more person telling her that she needed to get more rest. "I've had a touch of something these last two weeks, and I haven't been able to shake it off." She gave Patricia a wry smile. "Maybe if I could rest after school instead of having a daily battle with my writing assignment, I could get better."

As she'd hoped, the change in topic derailed Patricia's questioning. The other woman grinned. "Dr. Lipton sure is a challenge, isn't he?"

"That's one of the nicer words you could use to describe him." Julie had already decided not to tell Patricia about the meeting she'd had with Lipton the day before. She had lain awake much of the night thinking about what he'd said, wondering if he really meant it or if he'd just said those things to get her off his back.

"I see potential in your writing."

Those words kept replaying in her mind like a looped audio tape. If he really thought she was a good writer, why hadn't he given her better grades on her assignments?

She'd also found herself thinking more about the enigma called Donald Lipton. During that brief meeting in his office, it was as if he'd undergone a transformation. He had certainly revealed a great deal of passion about writing — something she had seen no sign of in class. He had seemed genuinely eager to make her understand what he was saying, and she was sure she'd even detected some human warmth in there somewhere, radiating out with his words.

So who was Donald Lipton? Was he the cool, aloof professor who went out of his way to alienate his students, or was he the warm, caring man she'd seen helping a little boy with a skinned hand, or the passionate writing instructor she had seen for those few brief moments in his office?

"Julie?"

She realized suddenly that she had been staring down at the half-eaten sandwich on her plate. She looked up at Patricia.

"Earth to Julie," Patricia said with a smile. "You were gone there for a minute. Way out somewhere in the stratosphere."

"Sorry." Julie began to lift the sandwich for another bite, then decided she'd had enough. She pushed the plate away and moved her glass of iced tea closer. "Do you have any hobbies, Patricia? I mean, what do you do in your spare time?"

"Oh, I have a million things I would love to do someday," Patricia answered. "I would love to travel all over the world, and I've never learned how to swim. You're going to think I'm crazy, Julie, but I used to think someday, in a hundred years maybe, I would like to learn how to fly a plane. My heart surgery sort of messed that one up. Of course, right now, my primary goal is to walk up on that stage and get my college diploma. Doesn't that thought excite you?"

Julie nodded, but didn't trust herself to speak. Patricia had unknowingly touched on something that was extremely painful for Julie: The future. *A million things to do... all over the world... a hundred years from now... and saddest of all, get her college diploma.*

Excite her? God, how that idea had once excited her. But unless Dr. Cole was wrong about her prognosis, she knew that it was unlikely there would ever be a diploma for her. Her heart ached, and she wanted to escape.

Patricia reached across the table and gently touched the top of Julie's hand. "You can't tell me there isn't something wrong now. Can I help, Julie?"

Julie shook her head. "There's nothing anybody can do, Patricia. It's just something I'll have to work out on my own."

Patricia's eyes remained on hers. "Did I say something to upset you?"

Julie forced a smile. It felt stitched on. "No, Patricia. I've just been going through a slump lately. I'll get over it soon."

"Well...." Patricia clearly wasn't buying Julie's explanation. She glanced at her wristwatch. "Oh, my God! I'm going to be late for my next class! Professor Albertson is a real stickler for promptness, too." She hurriedly gathered up her books, then reached for her tray.

"I'll take care of that," Julie said. "I'm going to stick around here for a while, anyway. You go ahead."

Patricia stood there uncertainly for a moment, looking down at her. "Thanks, Julie. But are you sure you're all right?"

Julie nodded. "I'm fine. Now you take off. You don't want to get Professor Albertson all riled up."

"All right." Patricia reached out and touched her arm. "I'll see you later."

After Patricia had hurried away, Julie gathered up the paper plates and plastic utensils onto the trays and took them to the large disposal units, then returned to her table with a refilled glass of iced tea. She sat there for several minutes, her mind once again going back over the remarkable conversation she'd had with Professor Lipton the day before.

"I see potential in your writing...."

And why, she asked herself, was she even cluttering up her mind with all these thoughts about Professor Lipton? Cheryl had done her best to make her see that it was pointless, that Lipton wasn't worth the mental energy he was costing her.

Then another troubling thought worked its way into her mind. After yesterday's confrontation with Professor Lipton in his office, Julie had been anxious to get home so she could call Cheryl and tell her all about it... and about Lipton's comment that she had writing potential.

But when she'd picked up the telephone, something made her hesitate. She had found herself thinking about how Cheryl might react to Julie's news. She'd finally replaced the receiver without making the call, but it was still bothering her. During their last conversation about Professor Lipton, Julie had noticed more than a little concern on Cheryl's part. She remembered Cheryl's words perfectly: *"Are you sure it isn't more than just the grade?"*

What, exactly, had Cheryl meant by that? And why hadn't Julie simply asked her at the time what she meant?

She knew why. She hadn't wanted to face what might have been an uncomfortable answer. It was clear enough that Cheryl was worried about Julie. She thought Julie was taking Professor Lipton and his creative writing class much too seriously.

Julie knew she wouldn't be able to give Cheryl a satisfactory answer. Maybe she couldn't even give *herself* a satisfactory answer. She had set out to get all *A's* in her first semester of college, and now it seemed unlikely that she could reach that goal. But did it make sense for her to be so upset about it? Was it possible that Cheryl was right? Was she letting Don Lipton get to her on a personal level? If so, in what way? And for God's sake, why?

Julie shook her head. She wasn't a psychologist. Anyway, she felt sure that Cheryl was making too much out of her frustration over Lipton's class. But that earlier conversation with Cheryl had left her feeling reluctant to share anything else about Professor Lipton or his class with Cheryl. She didn't want Cheryl to be concerned, whether the concern was valid or not. And she didn't want to feel obligated to explain everything she was feeling inside.

Even these thoughts brought sadness. Julie didn't want to do anything that might damage the long-time treasured relationship she had with her daughter. She and Cheryl had always been able to talk about anything, and now she felt that she was keeping something from her.

Gosh, Julie thought, *this man is messing up my entire life — even my relationship with Cheryl.*

She gave herself another brief shake of the head. She would have to put that out of her mind. Another assignment was due in two days, and she hadn't even started it yet.

She got out her notebook and started sketching out the idea for the assignment. For this one, she was to write a vignette in which two characters discover for the first time that they are in love with each other.

She had no idea where to start, and Lipton had given the class nothing to go on. *Par for the course*, she thought bitterly.

She had come to dread these assignments because of the negative response she kept getting from Lipton. With the grades he'd given her so far, even if she were to get *A's* on every assignment from this point on, she wouldn't be able to pull an A for the class. That made her feel like a failure. For her first semester of college, she had already failed to reach one of her goals of straight *A's*.

Julie was still deep in thought and writing notes when Rick Marston brought his tray over and asked if he could join her. Julie closed her notebook, glad for the distraction.

"Sure, Rick. Have a seat."

"What are you so busy writing about?" he asked, sitting down across from her. On his tray was a hamburger that looked as if had been loaded with every condiment known to man. Surrounding it was a sea of greasy French fries.

"Oh, I'm working on a draft for our next writing class assignment," she replied. "Sometimes I draft it out in longhand, then type it on my computer later and print it out."

He carefully picked up the huge hamburger and somehow managed to get his mouth around a bite. Wiping his lips with a napkin, he swallowed and nodded. "You put a lot more effort into these things than I do. I just sit down and bang it out, then go over it once to fix up any punctuation errors. Sounds as if you're really making a project out of it."

"That's the way it is for me. If I sit in front of the computer with no idea of what I'm going to write about, I go blank. But Rick, I just get so frustrated and angry every time I work on one of these assignments. I know that even when I do my best, it isn't going to be good enough." She paused, wondering if she should tell him about the meeting she'd had with Professor Lipton. For some reason, she just couldn't. It would be like revealing something too personal about herself, but she wasn't even sure why she felt that way. "You saw my last two papers. You said they were very good. Lipton gave me a *C* on both, and even then he acted as if he was doing me a big favor."

Rick washed down some French fries with a swallow of Coke. "I don't know what to tell you, Julie. Your last two papers *were* very good. They deserved *A's* if anybody's did. From what I've seen, you're probably the best writer in class. Professor Lipton just has it in for you, for some reason. I certainly don't agree with the way he treats his students." He paused, his face taking on a pensive look. "But you know, on the other hand, I can at least halfway understand why he is this way, given what he's been through."

Julie lifted an inquisitive eyebrow. "What he's been through? What do you mean?"

Rick took a moment to finish his hamburger, then drank the last of his Coke.

Finally: "I shouldn't have said anything. I know for a fact that Dr. Lipton doesn't want people digging up his past."

That only succeeded in piquing Julie's curiosity even more. "Come on, Rick. Tell me what you know. I'm so mixed up over that class. If you know anything that might help me understand what makes Lipton tick, you'd be doing me a great favor by telling me. It won't go any further."

Rick sat quietly for a moment, then finally nodded. "Okay, Julie, but you have to promise not to tell anyone else. I only know about this because my girlfriend Betsy has some distant family connections with Professor Lipton. She'll skin me alive if she thinks I'm passing around the information."

"It'll go no farther. I promise."

"Okay. Twenty years ago, Dr. Lipton's wife and three-year-old daughter were killed in an automobile accident. Lipton survived the crash with just a minor head wound." Rick lifted a hand and touched his forehead above his left eye. "Maybe you've noticed the scar. Betsy said her mother told her that the deaths of his wife and daughter changed him dramatically. You probably aren't aware of this, but Lipton had been getting a lot of critical acclaim for his own writing before the accident. But he stopped writing immediately afterward, and as far as I know, he hasn't written a word since then. Nothing that's been published, anyway."

Julie hadn't expected anything like this. When Rick mentioned that Lipton had been through a lot, she'd imagined that he might have been a drug addict at some time, or that he had gotten in trouble because of an affair with a student. Something like that. "He wears a wedding band. Has he remarried?"

Rick shook his head. "As far as I know, he won't have anything to do with women. That wedding ring is from his marriage to Emily."

"That was his wife's name?"

"Yes. Their daughter was named Abigail." Rick still had a worried look on his face. "Julie, really, I shouldn't have told you any of this. Betsy made me promise—"

"I wheedled it out of you, Rick," Julie said, offering him a smile. "I really appreciate your telling me this. Believe me, it does help to know that Professor Lipton has a reason for being... well, for having such an attitude problem. But don't worry. As I said, it won't go any further."

"I hope not, because I really like Betsy." Rick glanced at his watch, then got hurriedly to his feet. "I've gotta get going, Julie. See you later."

She watched him as he took his tray to the disposal unit, then rushed out the door.

For several minutes, she sat there sipping her tea, thinking about what Rick had said. She remembered the scene she'd witnessed in the courtyard several weeks ago, when Lipton was comforting the little boy who'd fallen down. She had seen real warmth in him then, and he had exhibited both warmth and passion for writing when he'd spoken to her in his office the day before.

But those were only brief flashes of humanity. Maybe what Rick had told her did help explain the huge chip on Lipton's shoulder.

Then she shook her head. Lots of people suffered losses. Some of them were as great as the loss Donald Lipton had endured. But that didn't give them the right to take it out on everybody else.

Julie didn't believe that the accident that took his family was totally what had turned Lipton sour. In order to be that good at being a jerk, you had to be born with the talent.

Chapter Thirteen

Wednesday, April 9

Who is Donald Lipton? That's the question of the day. Is he the man who was so gentle with the boy in the courtyard, the writer who became so passionate when talking to me about the "potential" he saw in me, or the college professor who goes out of his way to alienate and frustrate his students?

I have to confess that I have no idea. He's all three, I suppose. Three men perversely wrapped up in one set of skin and bones....

Each breath was painful, but Julie hid the pain behind an expressionless face as Professor Lipton began handing back the assignments they had turned in the week before. This was the first assignment since their meeting in his office.

She'd been especially pleased with her vignette, and actually felt as if she'd done a good job of capturing the emotion of the moment when the man and woman in her story discovered that they were deeply in love with each other.

Lipton walked past her and flipped the paper-clipped pages onto her desk without comment. She stared at it for a moment, gripped by a trepidation so strong it nearly paralyzed her. Then, with a trembling hand, she reached out and turned it over. He'd given her a *C+*.

She drew a deep breath, and was rewarded with a sharp pain across her chest that made her wince. *I hate him*, she thought. She felt something snap inside her, and sat through the rest of the class in a cold silence.

It had already been a rough day, with a lot of chest pain that constantly reminded her of her disease, and it was probably that path of frustration that drove her to go to Lipton's office to confront him again after her last class.

But he wasn't there. His office door was closed and locked.

"He's probably in the cafeteria," another instructor offered as he passed by in the hallway. "Don usually gets a snack about this time of the day."

He was there, all right, sitting at a small corner table far away from anyone else. He was writing into a notebook that lay open on the table, seemingly paying no attention to the activity around him.

Julie went to the drinks counter and poured tea into a Styrofoam cup, then stirred in half a packet of sugar. Her hands were shaking, and she knew it wasn't the weakness caused by lupus this time. She was determined to confront Professor Lipton again, and she didn't care what he thought about it. She felt sure that talking with him wouldn't be pleasant. Don Lipton was a miserable man; his only joy in life seemed to come from spreading that misery around as much as possible.

She walked up to the table and sat down without invitation. Startled, he looked across at her. "Now what is it?"

She glanced at the open notebook, surprised by what she saw. "Is that poetry?"

He flipped the notebook closed as a flush crept up from his neck. "Ms. Hunter, if you need to talk to me, I suggest that you come to my office—"

"I just did," she interrupted. "You weren't there. Dr. Lipton, we need to talk. No matter how hard I work, I just can't seem to get it right."

"I already told you what you would have to do to improve your grades, Ms. Hunter," he said coldly. "If you can't—"

"Damn you!" she hissed. "You're no help to your students. You're too damned wrapped up in yourself. You can have your stupid class!"

Julie stood up, ready to run out of the room, but Lipton pointed toward the chair. "Sit down." Shocked by his firm command, she sat back down. "Calm down, doll—"

"And don't call me that!" She lowered her voice, aware that heads were turning their way. "I'm not your *doll!*"

"All right, all right," he said with a placating gesture that was far from an apology. "Try to pull yourself together." Lipton paused for a few seconds, then in a more considerate voice, he said, "I've worked with a lot of students who were talented, Julie. Invariably, they've failed to find success in writing because they weren't willing to put forth the effort it required. I believe this shows a lack of courage more than anything else."

Courage? What could he possibly know about courage? He had run away from his own writing because of an accident that happened twenty years ago.

"I want to pull the very best out of you, doll. So far, you've been holding back, as if you're afraid to go all the way with your emotions. I want to force your writing to mature so it can *live* and *breathe.*"

Julie sat in silence, trying to digest what Lipton was saying to her.

"I don't want you to be satisfied with just doing a mediocre job. That's why I've been grading you so harshly."

Julie finally found her voice. "But Dr. Lipton, my interest doesn't really lie in writing. I've given this a lot of thought after what you said the other day. I'm pursuing a degree in mathematics. You said I have writing potential, but that isn't really what I want to do."

He flicked a hand, as if what she'd said was unimportant. "Well, some people have a tendency to seek security in mathematics. They seem to feel that they are in control. No matter how you do it, two plus two will always be four. Writing, on the other hand, requires an individual to be unique. Some people hide behind numbers and never take a risk." He fixed her with a stare. "What are you hiding from, Ms. Hunter?"

Julie instantly felt her hackles rise. "I'm not hiding from anything. I like mathematics. You have no right to accuse me of hiding—"

"Have it your way, doll," Lipton said.

She gritted her teeth. "And don't call me—"

"But I can guarantee you that you'll continue to get *C's* in my class unless you work harder to bring real human feelings into your writing." He gave her an appraising look. "Maybe you don't have any feelings to bring in. Maybe that's the problem."

"What?" she sputtered. "How dare you—"

"The date for dropping classes is long past, but I have the authority to make an exception. If you really want out of my class, I'll let you drop it with no grade. You can't beat that."

Julie took a few calming breaths. She couldn't keep letting this guy get under her skin. "I don't want to drop your class. All I want is your help in improving my writing. You could do that by putting some comments on my assignments to explain specifically what you don't like about them."

"Well... I guess I could start pointing out some examples of where your weaknesses are. But you'll have to show me that you're learning from what I say." He sighed. "Look, doll, if it'll help you, I guess I can find time to spoon feed you. But don't forget this is college, and you're expected to do some of this on your own."

Julie forced herself to remain calm. "I wish you would stop calling me 'doll.' I do have a name, you know. But if you really think I have some talent as a writer, then I want to see what I can do with it." She realized, almost with surprise, that the statement was true. "I could use your help."

He stared at her for a moment while he seemed to consider that. Then he gave her a half-shrug of his shoulders. "All right, Ms. Hunter. Then we agree. I'll give you a few pointers on your assignments. If I see that you're doing better, I'll keep giving you feedback. If I don't see you working, then I won't either. Fair enough?"

Her lips were pressed together in anger, not so much at his words as his condescending manner. But she forced her voice to remain civil as she said, "Fair enough, Dr. Lipton." Rising from her chair, she turned her back on him and headed toward the door.

"Ms. Hunter?"

She jerked back around to him. "Yes?"

He pointed to the Styrofoam cup she'd left on the table. "Don't you think you should throw that away? Or do you expect the hired help to do your dirty work?"

Seething, she snatched up the cup and stalked away.

~

The smile faded from Don Lipton's face as he watched her go. The cold ache returned, filling his heart, his very soul, telling him how lonely he was. Sometimes it happened like this. But it was his own fault for letting this woman get to him.

Later, as he pulled into the driveway at his house, he realized how empty it looked. More than empty — it looked *abandoned.* Don wondered if passerbys noticed the unoccupied look. He parked the car at the beginning of his drive and got out to get the mail from the mailbox.

When he went into the kitchen, he checked the answering machine, but there was no blinking light. Nobody had called, which was the way it almost always was. He opened the sliding glass door to the patio and stepped outside. The weeds had long since taken over, crowding out the flower beds and filling the cracks between paving stones.

Summoning a little willpower, a resolution to clean things up, he crouched down and pulled a few of the largest weeds. The thought occurred to him that if these were not pulled, they would become giants, overgrowing the patio. He moved down the edge, pulling weeds and piling them on the paving stones.

The ground was packed hard and dry, holding the roots tightly. He became irritated when some of the tops pulled off, and he knew he would have to go back with a screwdriver and dig out the remains. Weeds were like that. If you let them go too long, they would take root and hold on for dear life.

Like the weeds inside his soul.

He could feel the beads of sweat soaking into his shirt back. This was hard work — harder than he'd imagined. His calves gradually became sore from the unaccustomed squatting position. He wondered if he shouldn't wait till he was in his old clothes. But he decided to at least finish one turn around the patio, just getting the biggest weeds. No way he could get all of them, but at least he could get a good start on them.

When he finished the loop and stood up, he stretched and bent back and forth. He felt old having to rest and relax the muscles, stiff from stooping, and sat down at the wooden picnic table in the center of the patio.

The umbrella over the old cedar table had turned dark from years of weather. Most of the benches were stained and wobbly. They had been pushed in underneath the table, unused for months. But resting on one, for an instant he could see Emily and Abby sitting at the table, the way they had for so many mealtimes. In this vision, they were talking and eating, passing the grilled hamburgers and pickles and salad that he and Emily had prepared and set out.

The scene was a composite of so many mealtimes that Don couldn't pin down what year it represented. His mind flashed from times when Abby was just a baby in a highchair, to times when she was wobbling around on unsteady feet, to times when she chased after butterflies in the back yard. He could hear her high-pitched voice, bubbling with enthusiasm and curiosity.

For Don, this vision was like a kaleidoscope, a video of his life and marriage, with a zoom lens going in and out, revealing a variety of scenes.

A hornet flew from under the folded umbrella, warning Don to get up, to move. The vision passed, and he was back inspecting the weedy, empty patio.

His weedy, empty life....

~

The week following their talk, Dr. Lipton deigned to jot a comment on one of Julie's assignments. For this assignment, Lipton had asked the class to give him a brief scene in which a young boy learned for the first time that his parents were going to be divorced.

Julie thought she'd done a good job with it. In her scene, a man named Jeff had taken his son Kevin on a fishing trip. At the lake, he told his son that he and Kevin's mother were ending their marriage.

Dr. Lipton had written, *This whole thing is too cut and dried, Ms. Hunter. Father tells son he and the boy's mother are splitting, boy is sad, father tries to console him. You need to dig deeper inside the soul of the man whose marriage is ending, and the heart of the little boy whose life as he has known it from birth has changed forever. Where are the boy's feelings of fear and sadness and insecurity? You have revealed none of these in your writing.*

The second assignment was to be from the perspective of a young girl traumatized by the sight of a cat killing a young bird that had fallen from its nest. Julie took her time with this assignment and came up with what she thought was a unique and insightful reaction from the little girl.

This time, Lipton commented on her paper that the character didn't come across as a little girl, that her reaction was far too mature. *Ms. Hunter, little girls don't understand death. This had to be a traumatic experience for one so young. You entirely forgot what it is like to be young, and to see life wiped out so harshly, so unexpectedly. Dig deeper, Ms. Hunter. You will have to dig into the very deepest part of your heart.*

Julie found herself almost as irritated by his condescending remarks, scrawled in heavy red ink on the margins of her papers, as she'd felt by the lack of them.

She wasn't going through a very good time in other ways, either. Her illness was giving her a great deal of pain, and had shown no signs of the remission that Dr. Cole had hoped for. If anything, things were looking worse every time she had blood drawn.

Dr. Cole said she would probably have to be hospitalized if her condition didn't improve soon. She couldn't stand the thought of missing a week or more of classes just as the semester was coming to a close.

In her moments of despair, she knew that all of what she was doing was in vain, anyway. She would never live long enough to get her college degree, much less find all that writing potential that Professor Lipton seemed to believe she had.

She felt the need to talk to Cheryl about it, but she didn't want to worry her daughter, especially since she was so close to delivering her first child. Robert wasn't much help. As always, his attempt to comfort her was something like, "I don't know why you don't just get out of that damned class, Julie. All it's doing is causing you a lot of pain and aggravation."

He was right, of course. But she couldn't make herself follow his advice. She just couldn't give up.

She kept thinking about the chameleon-like nature of Don Lipton. One moment he could be gently comforting a little boy, and the next he would be bringing students to the verge of tears with his scathing, sarcastic comments. In class, he acted as though it was a chore talking about writing, but in his office that one afternoon, he'd been more passionate about the subject than Julie would have believed possible.

She couldn't stop thinking about the accident that had killed his wife and little daughter. He had told her repeatedly to dig into the deepest part of her heart, but she sensed that he had suffocated his own inner feelings with sorrow and pain. Rick had said that Lipton used to be well known in the literary world, but hadn't been published since the accident.

Maybe something inside him had died with his wife and daughter. *No, that isn't quite right,* she corrected herself. Whatever was inside Don Lipton was still in there. She'd seen it displayed on at least two occasions, and there in the cafeteria, she was sure she'd seen him writing poetry. That spark was still there, even if just a faintly glowing coal.

What would it take, she wondered, to breathe that coal back into flaming life?

~

"This one is pretty good," Lipton said, leaning against the desk in his usual pose. "I'll read part of it."

It was a Wednesday morning in late April, and Julie's chest felt on fire. She kept shifting position in her desk, hoping she might somehow ease the pain. She had taken a pain pill before leaving the house this morning, but it seemed to have no effect.

Despite the pain, though, she felt hopeful about the assignment she'd turned in the past Friday. For this one, Lipton had asked them to write about an elderly man who was feeling overwhelmed with sickness and loneliness, and who was on the verge of suicide.

Despair and depression was something Julie thought she could handle, something she really understood, and she'd stayed up all night to finish the assignment.

The one Lipton was reading was well written, she had to admit. She felt a lump grow in her throat as she listened. He read another one, which he identified as Patricia's. It, too, was quite good, and Julie whispered some quick words of congratulations to Patricia.

Lipton put the manuscript down, removed his glasses, and gazed out at the class. "Let's have some comments."

An overweight girl in the front row ventured an opinion: "The characterization is good."

"Characterization," the professor repeated. "Yes. Characterization was handled pretty well. Anybody else?"

Several more hands showed, some raised quickly, others slower. Lipton pointed to the boy behind Julie. "Yes?"

"I liked the way the emotional tension built up. It held my interest really well right to the end."

Lipton nodded. "Structure was solid." His eyes went to Julie. "Ms. Hunter, would you like to contribute something to this discussion?"

Julie was reluctant to say anything. In the past, Lipton had always seemed eager to contradict or criticize her comments. "I liked it," she said. "I agree with what the others said."

Lipton nodded slowly, favoring her with that maddening half-smile. "So you have nothing original to offer?"

Julie felt the blood rising into her face. She had no idea what he was after, so she kept silent.

Lipton eventually read another piece, and said that it, too, showed some promise. In both cases, he had made some suggestions that he said would improve the stories, but noticeably absent were his usual sarcastic and biting remarks.

"Let's see what you think of this one," he said, reaching for another paper-clipped sheaf of papers from his desk. He began reading:

"I don't think I can go on another day. Every part of my body aches, and my heart is full of loneliness. I just want to die. Oh, God, where are you? The elderly man's legs weakened, and he fell into the chair behind him. If this was life, then he'd had enough of it."

Julie stiffened as she realized that Lipton was reading her own paper. Her heart rate picked up considerably. At last, she had pleased him. She could hardly believe it.

But when Lipton finished reading, he just shook his head. "This, class, could have been a great piece of writing. But while this writer has gotten off to a good start, she chickened out when it came to fully exploring the elderly man's feelings. She has led the reader to expect great insight, and instead gave him the usual trite Hollywood-style crap."

Julie stared at him, frozen into immobility by his words, her throat dry and tight. Pain clawed at her chest.

"You will notice that this writer started out in a way that made us want to see into the very heart of this elderly gentleman," Lipton went on, holding Julie's assignment by thumb and forefinger, as if fearing that he might catch something from it. "Then she fizzled away and let us down. What sort of pain did this man have? Why was he alone? Would he really consider killing himself? How? The writer gets us all excited, and then basically tells us to figure it out for ourselves." He shook his head. "This, kids, is an example of a lazy writer. She didn't dig deep enough. She didn't search the soul of the dying man. She has done only half the work."

Julie didn't even feel anger at Lipton for his cutting remarks. Her heart was breaking. Now she realized that she'd been a fool to think she would ever be able to please him. She should have known from the first day of class that for whatever reason, he had it in for her. He wasn't interested in any writing talent she might have. All he saw in her was a way to vent the bitterness that seemed to have consumed him twenty years ago.

How could she possibly tolerate another five weeks of this? She didn't think she could.

Chapter Fourteen

Friday, April 25

This has not been one of the better weeks in the life of Julie Hunter. Pain, despair, depression — it's like everything hit me at once. There have been a few surprises, though. A telephone call from Professor Lipton, for one. And some revealing information I found in the college library....

Something was holding her in its clutches. She couldn't see its face, couldn't even discern the shape of its body. But whatever it was, it was squeezing her around the chest, threatening to crush her ribs....

Julie shot upright in bed, still gripped by the terror of the nightmare, heart pounding against her rib cage like a wild animal. She reached out a trembling hand to turn on the lamp beside the bed, then forced herself to breathe slowly, trying to ease the constricting pain out of her chest as comforting light flooded the room. Gradually the fear began to recede, leaving only the reality of the pain.

She sighed, looking toward the window. Outside, the morning was gray against the lace curtains, and she could hear rain pounding against the window. Then she glanced at the clock on the night stand. It was past eight o'clock. She vaguely remembered turning off the alarm earlier.

Another bolt of pain went through her chest as she lay back down. She winced at the dead, cramped feeling inside her. She'd tossed and turned most of the night, unable to escape the vision of Don Lipton's smug face as he'd humiliated her in front of the entire class.

Everything seemed hopeless to her. She shuddered at the thought of what the future held.

For the first time, Julie couldn't work up the energy to drag herself out of bed and get ready for school. It wasn't just the rain. Pain seemed to have invaded every part of her body, and the medicine Dr. Cole had given her was no help. She had barely slept, and the thought of going to Lipton's class was more than she could bear.

She rolled over in bed, burying her face in the pillow as sobs wracked her body. What had she done to be cursed in this way? What god had she offended?

She skipped all her classes that day, and after a depressing visit with Dr. Cole, who was still trying to convince her to go into the hospital, she felt worse than ever. On Saturday morning, she was too sick and depressed to think about doing her homework assignments. What was the use? Even Cheryl couldn't cheer her up when she came over for a visit on Sunday afternoon. Cheryl's baby was due at any time, and for once, Julie felt no joy in the anticipation.

In fact, the only thing she was able to work up any energy or enthusiasm for was a terrible argument with Robert on Sunday night. He was packing for a trip to Omaha, taking the red-eye so he could get in a full day of meetings with the engineers who would be overseeing the plant modernization. He would be gone for three days, talking to the engineers and touring two corrugated container plants that their firm had recently modernized.

Robert had finally gotten the bank loan, and now he was facing a multitude of decisions about the kind of equipment to use and what structural work on the buildings would be needed to accommodate it. With new sales contracts in hand from major customers and the bank loan to pay for the modernization, it looked as if everything was going to work out. But it was still a major hassle, and Robert was busier than ever coordinating everything that needed to be done while still running the day-to-day operations of the plant.

Julie realized later that she didn't really mind seeing him go on this trip. It was more the notion that he *could* go that upset her so much. She was too sick to even go to church that morning. The pain was worse than it had ever been, and it was easy for her to imagine that the lupus was doing more damage with each passing day. She would never be taking another trip, yet here was Robert, busily packing his suitcase.

"Do you really have to go," Julie asked. "I would feel better if one of the other guys went so you could stay here with me."

"None of them have the experience for this, Ju. It's important to the company."

"What about what's important to me?" she asked, already close to tears. Her chest felt as if something with huge teeth was eating a hole through her. "You're always so concerned about the health of that damned company. What about *my* health?"

He stopped packing and turned to face her. "Why are you acting like such a baby about this, Ju?"

"Like a baby? Damn you!" Julie shouted. "Go ahead and go on your stupid trip. All I am to you anymore is a *sweet convenience.* Just get out of here. I don't need you! I don't need anyone!"

Without another word, Robert had picked up his luggage

and kissed her quickly on the cheek. "I'll call later to let you know that I've gotten there okay."

At that moment in time, she couldn't have cared less.

When her alarm clock began cheeping at her on Monday morning, she slapped it harder than necessary and rolled over in bed without even giving a second thought to getting up and getting ready for school. Although she was still physically capable of taking care of herself, mentally it seemed like such a chore to get up, take a shower, and get dressed.

It was nearly eleven o'clock by the time she dragged herself out of bed. It wasn't just the pain, she realized. Mostly, it was just that she had nothing to look forward to that day, no real reason to get up at all.

~

She was sitting at the kitchen table sipping tea and wondering if she could gag down a bowl of cold cereal when the telephone startled her.

She let the phone ring three times, then decided to answer it. Chances were it was Robert calling to see how she was doing. If she didn't answer, he might come home.

"Is this Ms. Hunter?" asked a male voice.

"Yes...."

"Julie, this is Don Lipton. Are you on vacation, or are you skipping class so you can spend more time playing with your numbers?"

Julie was too surprised to answer for a moment. The last thing in the world she'd expected was a phone call from Professor Lipton.

"Are you there, doll?" he prompted.

Julie forced herself to remain calm. "Dr. Lipton, I've decided to... to drop out of your class. This whole college thing was a big mistake."

"Drop out?" he repeated, as if the notion astonished him. "I didn't have you pegged as an out and out quitter."

That was too much. "I've had it with you!" She felt the words coming out of her before she could stop them. She didn't even *want* to stop them. This man was an incredible jerk, and somebody had to tell him. "Who do you think you are? No one should have to sit in your damned class, let alone take all the grief you dish out to me and everyone else in class. Nobody can stand you. Your attitude and cutting remarks have made you the most despised instructor on campus."

If Julie's remarks hurt, Lipton hid it well. "I know what people think about me, and I really don't care. I have very little regard or patience for people. But I have to confess, Julie, that I'm truly sorry you've decided to drop the class. I still say you could be a good writer. I mean *really* good. Most of the stuff being published nowadays is trash. You could've done better than that."

She didn't know what to say, so she clutched the phone to her ear and said nothing at all.

"If you've made up your mind, I suppose there isn't anything I can do to change it. See you later, doll." The phone clicked in her ear.

Julie held the receiver for several moments, then lowered it slowly into its cradle.

Why couldn't he just leave her alone? If he really felt that she was such a great writer, why didn't he encourage her instead of taking every opportunity to destroy her confidence?

She lowered her head and began to cry. Her life was falling apart. Why couldn't she find something good in it before it was too late?

~

The following morning, Julie got up and tried to decide what to do with her day. She kept thinking about Don Lipton and all the things he had told her on the phone the previous day. She was still confused about his comments regarding her writing talent. Did he really mean it, or was he just stringing her along for some perverse reason of his own?

By noon, she was feeling a little better and decided that she wouldn't let the problems with Donald Lipton force her out of school entirely. She still didn't know if she would ever go back to his class, but she had other classes she enjoyed, and she intended to see them through.

It was too late for her humanities class with Mrs. Reed, so she decided to go to the library to work on her research paper for her psychology class.

The library was crowded with students studying or doing research for term papers. Julie found a vacant spot at a table near the reference desk, and looked through her binder for her notes about the term paper in Mrs. Cramer's psychology class. Spending a couple of hours on it today would give her a better idea of where she was going and how much time she would have to devote to the project over the next few weeks until the semester was over.

Despite the constant harassment of Dr. Lipton, over the past three months she had become comfortable with the environs of the college. She no longer cared, or even thought about, what the other students might think about this middle-aged woman attending classes with them and waiting in lines at the cafeteria. She was usually able to sink into her own world of books and papers and magazine articles when she was working in the library, paying no mind to the quiet activity around her.

Today, though, was different. She couldn't focus on her research topic, and it seemed that every voice and every rustle of a paper was a distraction.

That wasn't really it, of course, and she knew it. What was on her mind was the same thing that had been distracting her since the first day of class: Professor Donald Lipton.

Finally, with frustration at her own compulsiveness, Julie

went to the reference desk and asked a librarian where she could find copies of old newspapers. She was directed to the microfiche area.

For the next two hours, she looked back through front pages of the *Freeborn Chronicle* before finally finding an article about the accident that killed Lipton's wife and daughter.

Two Killed in Auto Accident
A twenty-four-year-old mother and her three-year-old daughter were killed today when the car in which they were passengers skidded out of control during a thunderstorm and ran into the back of a gasoline tanker truck. The driver of the car, Donald Lipton, was knocked unconscious but was pulled out of the burning wreckage by the truck driver. The car was fully engulfed in flames before Lipton's wife, Emily Lipton, and daughter, Abby, could be saved.

There was more, but Julie's eyes were drawn to the two photographs of the wreckage that were included with the articles. The car's door had been wrenched open, and Julie could see the charred remains of the interior.

She was stunned by the horror of the tragedy. How terrible it must have been for Don Lipton to regain consciousness in the hospital, only to learn that his wife and young daughter were dead. Worse, she realized, he must have felt terribly guilty. He had been driving the car when it crashed, and he was the only survivor. How the blame must still be haunting him, even after all these years.

One of the newspaper articles mentioned some of Lipton's accomplishments as a writer. She saw that Rick Marston had been correct. In the years before the accident, Lipton had gotten a lot of critical acclaim for his short stories and poetry.

Unable to stop herself, Julie searched through old magazines until she located some of his writing, and was deeply touched by it, especially by his exquisite poetry about the beauty of love. It was hard to imagine that the man who berated her so viciously in class was the same man who could have written such moving poems.

After looking further, she discovered that not a single story or poem had been published after the accident. It was as if the misfortune had turned off some inner tap. A year after the deaths, he had accepted the teaching job at the college.

It was dark by the time she stepped outside. Her head was throbbing, and the pain in her chest prompted her to shift her books to her other arm. Sometimes, just changing position could ease the pain a little. Now she was also noticing a sharp pain in her neck. That was new, and she knew Dr. Cole would want to hear about it.

Sighing, she started down the library steps. The campus was lighted in a low-key way, with translucent globes set on ten-foot posts, leaving spots of brightness in otherwise unrelieved darkness.

She stopped suddenly. In the distance, she saw Donald Lipton striding along the sidewalk, his large figure moving in and out of the pools of light, heading toward the parking lot. She stood in shadowed darkness, watching him walk through this slow-motion strobe, bright one moment, dark the next until he passed out of sight.

When she was sure he'd had time to get in his car and leave, she walked slowly toward her own car. The air was cool, but her light jacket was adequate for the task. After a week of sporadic rain, the Channel 7 weatherman had said that the days would be turning gloriously warm and sunny.

But she kept seeing the photographs of that burned-out car, with the front door hanging open and the interior burned into an unrecognizable mess.

My God, she thought. *How terrible it must have been.*

Again, in her mind, she saw Donald Lipton walking through those pools of light on his way to the parking lot, his face illuminated one moment, and in dark shadow the next. But that wasn't the way life was for Donald Lipton, she realized. He'd passed through a shadow lasting twenty years.

Inexplicably, she felt like crying. This time, it wasn't for herself.

~

By the time Julie got home to the empty house, she was exhausted both mentally and physically. Her pain seemed to be increasing with every hour. Robert had left a message on the answering machine that the meetings were going well and that he was impressed with the engineers he planned to hire for the modernization project. Another message was from Cheryl.

"Just checking in, Mom. Nothing new from Matthew, I'm afraid. He must be asleep in there. Let me know if you need anything while Dad's gone."

She didn't have the energy to return Cheryl's call. Instead, she took double her usual dose of pain medicine and went to bed.

She had intended to return to school the next day, but she felt too awful to even think about getting out of bed until after noon. She and Patricia had exchanged phone numbers earlier in the semester, and Patricia had called twice to see how she was feeling. Julie had fended off serious questions, and instead blamed allergies.

Robert returned home later that day and talked to her just long enough to upset her.

"Don't you think it's about time you stop pretending you're a kid again and just drop out of college? This fast pace is killing you."

Julie didn't respond, but she was irritated by his know-it-all attitude. Why couldn't he grow up and start facing reality?

More importantly, why couldn't he give her the kind of support she needed?

She knew he was still under a lot of stress, too. The major work on the plant was to begin soon. Robert was heavily involved in that, and was still trying to cut costs in order to make sure everything would get done within the budget mandated by Mr. Simmons at the bank.

She was too tired to worry about that, though. She remained home on Wednesday and Thursday, but she was starting to feel a little better. Not normal, by any means, but less miserable. Friday afternoon, she called Patricia to find out what Professor Lipton had given them for their latest assignment. She still wasn't sure if she would be going back, but she wanted to know, just in case. She also called the college and spoke to her other instructors, apologizing for missing so many classes and getting the assignments she'd missed. Without exception, they expressed concern and sympathy, and said that they hoped to see her back in school soon.

~

Late Friday night, after Robert had gone to bed, Julie was still in her study. She put her completed business math homework into its folder and leaned back away from the desk, stretching the stiffness out of her muscles. She'd been sitting there for over an hour finishing up a study guide that would help her prepare for a test next week.

Now she was ready for Professor Lipton's writing assignment. According to Patricia, for this assignment Lipton had asked the class to write about someone going through a difficult time in their life.

The irony of that wasn't lost on her. If there was any subject that she could write about from first-hand experience, it was this.

She turned in her chair to look out through the large window. A few moon-silvered clouds appeared phosphorescent against the velvety blackness of the night sky. Moonlight dappled the placid surface of the pond and outlined the shadowy shapes of the encroaching trees.

As she looked out on this beautiful scene, she began thinking about the past several months, the past several years... her life. She thought of the people she loved so much — Robert and Cheryl, and all the beautiful people whose paths in life had crossed her own. For some crazy, unknown reason, she even thought about Donald Lipton.

She opened her eyes and looked out the window at the moonlight glittering on the surface of the pond. Looking up, she saw at least a thousand stars. *Oh, how beautiful it all is.*

Her thoughts switched from life and love and laughter, to more real thoughts of her illness, death, and sorrow. Why did it have to be this way? She had a million unfulfilled dreams, a million kisses, and so many hugs left to give. Would there be hugs in Heaven?

Still deep in those thoughts, almost unconsciously, Julie turned back to her computer and began to punch the keys. Somehow, every emotion she had been suppressing for months found their way from the deepest part of her heart to the tips of her fingers — a visceral connection with the keyboard. She wrote about her own life, about love and joy and pain and sorrow, about how grateful she was for the years she'd had, and how much it hurt to think about losing it, to think of loved ones continuing their lives without her, of Matthew who wouldn't even know his grandmother except by what others told him.

They were painful thoughts, but this time they brought no tears. Instead, they brought words. For hours, she typed, and thought, and wrote as a real writer does, with her heart.

Chapter Fifteen

Wednesday, April 30

As I held little Matthew close to my breast, my heart just didn't seem able to contain all the love I was feeling. Time seemed to stop. So much love, so much perfection still unmarred by life's dilemmas.

But there was an ache in my heart too, knowing most likely I would never see my little grandson take his first steps, speak his first words. God, I begged, let me live long enough to let even the smallest fragment of my love live on inside this tiny heart.

The radio was playing softly in the background, oh... how timely even life's music is... Whitney Houston's beautiful voice went straight to my heart as she sang "And I will always love you...."

Julie cradled the sleeping baby in her arms and smiled down at him. *Matthew*, she thought. *A beautiful name for a beautiful boy.*

The room was silent and shadowed. Cheryl lay sleeping in the bed, still exhausted from the difficult delivery of the night before. Robert and Tom had gone to the hospital's cafeteria downstairs for coffee. Julie was glad to have some peace and quiet, as she relished holding this new life in her arms.

Tom had called just after dinner the night before. Robert and Julie had barely made it to the hospital in time, and were in the waiting room when Cheryl's husband came out with a big grin and the news that they had a new grandchild — a six-pound grandson.

With the sleeping child in her arms, Julie found herself thinking about Donald Lipton's next writing assignment: a conversation between a little boy and his grandmother. Suddenly it seemed easy for her to project herself into the role of the grandmother, and to project Matthew into the role of an eight-year-old facing a dilemma of heartbreaking intensity to him. She would have to write it that afternoon, since it was due the following day.

She'd gone back to class on Monday and turned in the paper about the dying woman who was thinking about all that she would be missing in life. She silently dared Professor Lipton to challenge her presence in the classroom, but he'd only given her a twisted grin.

It was the same grin that had infuriated her so many times — but this time it didn't. Now that she knew the horror he'd been through, she was seeing Donald Lipton in a different light.

She'd fielded questions from Patricia and Rick and others in the class, telling them that her allergies had gone crazy and left her with a killer sinus infection. She was pretty sure that Patricia didn't buy it, but she had the grace not to pry.

Now Julie looked into Matthew's sparkling eyes and beautiful face, and began thinking about Cheryl when she was little. To Julie, her daughter was the most important thing in her life. She had devoted twenty-four hours a day to her family, and she knew that Cheryl would do the same.

Tears brimmed in Julie's eyes and spilled over as she thought about the future. More than anything else, she wanted to be a grandma to Matthew, to see him grow up. But she knew that wouldn't happen, and the bitterness weighed heavily in her heart.

She wiped away the tears, angry with herself. This was a joyous occasion, and she'd managed to turn it into a pity party for herself. Yes, life would go on after she was gone. She should've been able to accept that by now.

She looked down at Matthew again and gently caressed his cheek. He stirred slightly in her arms, but did not awaken. *Sleep, my precious little boy,* she told him. *May God be with you now and forever.*

~

By the following Friday, Julie was feeling miserable again. She had attended all of her classes that week, and spent some more time in the library doing research for her term paper in psychology. Only three weeks of school remained, and she didn't want to end up in a panic situation with any of her final class assignments.

As she sat in Donald Lipton's class on Friday morning, she closed her eyes, wishing she had stayed home. She'd had chest pains all night, and hadn't slept more than twenty minutes at a time. Her chest was still hurting, and she felt so emotionally flayed that she was sure she would burst into tears at the slightest provocation. Don Lipton was certainly capable of provoking tears. He could've probably wrung them out of Hulk Hogan.

On the previous Wednesday, he had given her a *C+* for the piece she'd written about the dying woman. There were no comments on the paper. For some reason, she couldn't work up the energy to be angry about the grade.

When he entered the room, Lipton seemed more quiet than usual, as if he were preoccupied by some deep thoughts. Even before taking attendance, he pulled out three assignments to read to the class. Julie hoped he wouldn't read hers.

She wasn't in the mood to hear his reaction to her latest assignment about the grandmother. She'd had a rough night with very little sleep.

She was dismayed when Lipton picked up one of the papers and began reading, and she realized it was hers. She had put her entire self into this, and that self wasn't up to being torn apart and humiliated today.

He read quietly through to the final sentence: *"Her love for this child would live on in the world long after she was gone."*

As he finished reading, she looked down at her clasped hands, determined not to let his critical remarks upset her. But for a long moment, Lipton said nothing. When she looked up at last, she saw that he was still staring down at the paper he held.

Lipton looked up at last, and when he asked the class for reactions, his voice cracked a little. Looking around, Julie realized for the first time that others in the class were sniffling and wiping their eyes. Several of them made various comments about how touching it was, and Lipton agreed.

"Julie, this is very good," he said, looking directly at her for the first time. "You've finally done it. For the first time, you have touched the depths of human emotion. It's *very* well done." Turning his head to take in the entire class, he added, "This time, Julie didn't succumb to her tendency to overwrite drama, but instead brought the scene vividly to us, the readers, through realistic dialogue and characterization." Don closed his eyes for a moment of silence before he finished: "The unconditional love of a woman for a little child — the essence of eternal love which displays the deepest of human emotions."

Julie sat rigidly in her seat, blushing furiously. She felt the eyes of all her classmates on her. This was almost as bad as the ridicule she'd become accustomed to.

"It takes courage for a writer to delve that deep, to look

into that mirror of emotions," Lipton continued, his eyes returning to Julie. "That, people, is how a writer can touch the hearts of others. And *that* is what writing is all about. It's about touching people in ways they've never been touched. It's about teaching them to look at familiar things in new ways. You have touched mine, Julie," he added, "and believe me, that's an accomplishment."

~

Patricia and Rick and several others came up to her after class to tell her how good the story had been. Don Lipton remained seated at his desk. After the other students had gone, Julie walked up to him.

"Thank you," she said, fighting back tears.

"Thank *you*," Don said. "I knew you could do it. Writing is hard work, Julie, but you have the ability to write anything you can feel with your heart. As a matter of fact...." He paused, looked down at the desk for a moment, then lifted his eyes back to hers. "I think you should write a book."

"A book?" She wouldn't have been more surprised if he'd suddenly sprouted antennae from his forehead. "A book about what? Do you know how long it would take to write a book, Dr. Lipton?"

"Please," he said, "call me Don. And yes, I have some idea of the effort that goes into writing a book."

"But I wouldn't even know where to begin," she protested. "It's... well, it's an overwhelming idea."

"Start with a journal," he suggested.

She frowned. "Like a diary? I already do that."

"Well... a diary is more of a chronicle of what's happening in your life. In your journal, you should take a few minutes every day and jot down something that you feel in your heart. Eventually, the thoughts will begin to come together. I believe in you, Julie. I know you have a lot to share with others."

"And you don't?" Julie surprised herself with the question.

"I don't write," he said quietly. "I teach writing. Remember?"

"But you used to write," she said, knowing she was venturing into territory she should stay out of. But she was unable to stop. "I came across some of your poetry and short stories while I was doing some research in the library. They were beautiful, Don. When are you going to write again? What are you waiting for?"

For a moment he looked so forlorn she wanted to reach out and hold him in her arms. But Don merely looked into the distance, and then back at her. "I don't know the answer to that. I just don't know. My past has too many weeds."

"Weeds?"

He got to his feet and walked around the desk. "Are you ready to go?"

Julie could tell she had gotten too close to Don Lipton's inner feelings. How she wanted to reach out and tell him that she cared, that she ached in her own heart for his past loss.

But all she said was, "Yes, I'm ready."

She left the classroom ahead of him, and turned toward the parking lot while he went in the opposite direction toward his office.

In an odd sort of way, she felt that she had crossed the barrier that for so many years had separated Don Lipton from the rest of the world. For the first time in months, she felt hopeful and satisfied that maybe she had made a difference in someone's life.

She kept thinking about that look on his face when she'd asked about his own writing. It was as if his face had turned into a deep well of sadness there for a moment, and she knew he hadn't meant to let down his defenses in that way. He'd revealed the depth of his soul to her for just an instant. He'd given her a glimpse of himself.

That was something no man had ever done. Certainly not

Robert, not in all the years they'd been together....

Thinking about that made her realize how much different the two men were. While Robert was usually quiet, reserved, and respectful, Don — at least in the classroom setting — was loud and brash, and certainly didn't consider the student's feelings. She would never forget how he had gone to great lengths to humiliate her in the past. In fact, until a few minutes ago, she had doubted if he even knew the meaning of the word "respect."

Thinking now of the sadness she had seen on his face, she realized that the tough-guy exterior was most likely a cover to hide the hellish pain he harbored in his heart.

Lost in her thoughts, Julie got into her car. She sat there for a moment without starting the engine, still thinking it through.

Was it the nature of men to work so hard to hide their feelings? Did it mean they weren't sensitive? Or was it something else — a fear of displaying a weakness. She thought that was probably the case with Robert. He had even frequently made the comment that women were such babies.

Come to think of it, she had never seen Robert cry. Even years ago when Julie had miscarried and their second child, a little boy, was stillborn, Robert just said, "Don't get so torn up, Julie. Some things are meant to be. If there was something wrong with the baby, we're lucky it happened now."

By no stretch of her imagination had Julie ever been able to think of that loss as "lucky." She had wept for weeks over the loss.

If emotions were just for women, what about Don Lipton? What made him so different? She'd seen depth of emotion in his poetry. Maybe it wasn't fear at all that made him appear so dispassionate, but rather guilt over what had happened so many years ago. How could anyone lose two loved ones and not feel torn apart?

All these questions and more kept invading Julie's mind, and she wondered why she felt so drawn to him. Was that what Cheryl had sensed so many weeks ago? Cheryl had suggested that there was more behind Julie's feelings toward Donald Lipton than frustration over the grade she was receiving in his class. Julie had shied away from that question... but now she wondered.

And the wonder turned to certainty. She was, she had to admit, drawn to him. But why?

As she sat there thinking, going over the past few months, she realized that even when Don Lipton was giving her a hard time, he was still taking her seriously. That was something Robert had never done. Sometimes she almost felt that Robert would be happier with a robot that would carry out his programmed orders without fussing about it.

She laughed to herself as she tried to visualize a mechanical lady programmed to have dinner on the table at 5:46 p.m. — no earlier, no later. Or maybe by pushing another button, it would iron Robert's shirts — making sure, of course, that there was no starch in the collars. She giggled aloud when she wondered what buttons he would need to push to get a goodnight kiss. Or maybe he wouldn't even need one. Lately, that didn't seem to be very important to him.

Her thoughts shifted back to Don Lipton. Deep within her heart, she knew that Donald Lipton would never have been satisfied with a robot. He would want the flesh and blood and mind and soul of a woman. He wouldn't want a woman who would have dinner on the table at the precise same time each evening. He wouldn't want anyone to choreograph his life. He would want someone who would surprise him, someone with the independence to have her own thoughts and dreams... someone who wouldn't be afraid to share those dreams with him.

She drew in a deep breath and let it out slowly. *Julie Hunter, how your mind can wander!* she admonished herself.

Still, though, she sat there a moment longer, thinking. Then, with another sigh, she reached forward and turned the key to start the engine.

~

On the way home, Julie stopped at a store and bought an extra-large composition notebook, and later labeled the cover, *To Touch a Heart*. Before going to bed, she opened it to the first page, wrote the date at the top and made her first journal entry. It was about Cheryl and Matthew, and generations of love.

Julie sat there at her desk for a long moment. Again, she felt the urge to talk to Cheryl about her feelings. But this time she didn't draw back. She reached for the telephone and dialed Cheryl's number.

"He wants you to what!" Cheryl exclaimed when Julie told her about Don Lipton's suggestion.

"He thinks I should write a book," Julie repeated. "He said... well, he liked my last writing assignment. Said he thought I could write a novel."

After a brief pause: "Mom, are you sure he was serious? I mean... you can't stand this guy, right?"

"Well... maybe I judged him too quickly—"

"Honestly, Mom." Cheryl seemed a little confused. " I don't understand. The last time we talked about him, you were counting the minutes until the semester ended. You couldn't wait to be rid of that... I believe you called him a jerk. Now you almost seem to be fond of him. What happened?"

Julie found herself smiling, and wasn't even sure why. "I... don't really know. It's just... well, sometimes I think I see a gentle side of him... a side that he covers up for some reason." Julie remembered the scene she had witnessed with Don Lipton and the little boy in the courtyard. "I watched him once when he was helping a little boy at the college. The boy had fallen down and hurt his hand, and Don couldn't do enough to comfort the little guy. And he was sincere, too. I wouldn't have believed it if I hadn't seen it with my own eyes."

"Are you kidding me? You never mentioned that before."

"I know. It just seemed so out of character. And as I recall, by my next class he was right back to being Mr. Tough Guy again. But now I know there's another side to him."

"Leave it to you, Mom! You always did know how to bring out the best in people. I think you're getting soft on this guy."

Julie felt herself becoming somewhat defensive. "All right, young lady. See if I share anything with you again." She had considered telling Cheryl about the automobile accident that had resulted in the deaths of Lipton's wife and daughter, but remembered the promise she had made to Rick. "I really think I should say goodbye. I can tell you're tired of talking to me anyway."

"I'm sorry, Mom. I didn't mean to offend you. It's just that this entire college and writing and the other stuff is new to me. Don't forget, you've always been my stay-at-home mother. I need time to adjust."

"I hear you! Right now you remind me so much of your father. Neither one of you believes I can do anything more creative than baking apple pies and mending socks. Why don't you just call me Cinderella?"

Cheryl sighed. "I think I hit a nerve. I apologize. Really, Mom, I think you should write a book. I remember all those stories you made up and told me when I was growing up." She laughed. "Especially the ghost stories. They were great! I'm going to tell my own children those stories. I always thought you should put some of them down on paper."

Julie smiled. She was pretty sure Don Lipton had something more serious in mind than ghost stories for children. "Thanks, Cheryl. I don't know for sure what I'm going to do. But I just wanted to see what you thought. How's Tom doing?"

They chatted for a few more minutes, then said their goodbyes. For a long moment after hanging up the phone, Julie sat at her desk looking out at the pond.

~

Cheryl slowly returned the telephone to its cradle and leaned back in her chair, still thinking about the conversation she'd had with her mother. It was peculiar, to say the least. All along, her mother had been saying how awful this Professor Lipton was. Now, suddenly, it seemed that everything had changed.

Cheryl knew it was more than just the fact that Professor Lipton had given her mother some compliments on her writing. It was deeper than that, and for some reason, Cheryl found that it was troubling her more than a little.

She picked up the evening newspaper and tried to bury herself in the front page stories, but she couldn't concentrate.

That does it, she thought, tossing the newspaper aside. *I've got to see this man for myself.*

She didn't know for sure why it was so important to her. It was just that after hearing so many varied reports about Professor Donald Lipton over the last few months, her curiosity was getting the best of her. She wanted to get a close-up look at this man. Maybe she would see a hint of what it was that was driving her mother crazy. It shouldn't be difficult to find him. After all, she knew where he was every day.

But when would be the right time to do it? She would have to plan this, to do it at a time when she knew she wouldn't run into her mother at the campus. *That* would take some explaining, all right.

Wednesday was Tom's day off. She could leave Matthew with him and go secretly looking for this Don Lipton. Then she remembered that Matthew had a well-baby checkup scheduled for this coming Wednesday, and she didn't want to miss that. There were only a little over two weeks left in the semester, so she couldn't wait too long. Perhaps the following Wednesday —

For a moment Cheryl began to feel foolish. After all, her mother was forty-five years old. She had always been quite capable of taking care of herself, and she would doubtless feel insulted if she knew her daughter was sneaking around behind her back.

Then Cheryl remembered the time years ago when she had first started dating, and Julie had followed Cheryl and her date to the movies. Her mother had questioned the boy's character, but Cheryl had begged and pleaded until her parents had finally allowed her to go with him.

Julie, with her motherly instincts, had sensed that the lad had more on his mind than seeing the movie, and she was right. She was sitting behind them in the last row balcony seat when she realized that Cheryl was trying to fight off a pair of wandering hands. Unable to control herself, Julie forced herself through the barrier of knees and pulled her daughter to her feet. Cheryl had been surprised, but very relieved to see her mother.

"Are you ready to go, babe?" Julie had said, keeping her composure. "It's getting late, and you have to get up early tomorrow."

Without saying goodbye to the boy, mother and daughter exited the theater. Julie had never mentioned the incident. Never once had she reminded Cheryl that she had warned her about the boy. Cheryl knew that her mother figured she had learned a lesson, and indeed she had.

Cheryl had never held it against Julie for sneaking around and checking up on her and her date. On the contrary, she felt indebted to her mother for saving her from what might have been a horrible experience.

With these thoughts in mind, she finally gave up arguing with herself and just decided to do it. She could go down to the college next week. She knew that Tom wouldn't under-stand at all, so she just wouldn't tell him what she was going to do. Of course, she didn't want to lie to him. She would just tell him she was going to the grocery store — and that's what she would do. Then she would make a little side trip to the college that she wouldn't mention to him.

Grinning to herself, she pushed herself out of the chair and headed into the nursery room to check on Matthew. She knew she was being foolish. What could she possibly gain by just seeing Professor Don Lipton?

She had no idea, but she was still going to do it. After hearing so much about this guy, she just had to see him for herself.

Chapter Sixteen

Friday, May 23

For better or worse, I made it through the semester. I've done well — with one notable exception, of course. But I don't want to think about Professor Donald Lipton now. I realize that he has been the subject of far too many of these diary entries. I passed his class, at least, so I won't have to ever see his smug face in front of a classroom again.

Patricia and I had lunch together, and I was distressed to learn that she'll be moving to Boston soon. I'll miss Patricia. She was always there for me when I was feeling down....

By the following Monday morning, Don Lipton's attitude and demeanor had once again reverted to that of a rude, ego-tistical know-it-all. Julie wasn't sure what she'd expected — but not this. If anything, he was worse than before, as if he was disturbed because he'd been coerced into revealing a small bit of humanity to the class... and to her.

And that, she decided, was most likely the problem. He'd gotten too close, and now something inside him was pulling back. Alienating himself from others was his security blanket, and she had no idea what she could do about it.

As the days continued toward the end of the semester, Julie completed her term paper for her psychology class and maintained her straight-*A* average in all the classes except Donald Lipton's. The pain in her chest worsened, though, and this time it didn't ease up after a few days. Dr. Cole insisted that she go into the hospital for further tests, and she kept putting him off.

"Just another couple of weeks," she promised. "Then the semester will be over, and I'll be all yours."

Robert — at least when she saw him — seemed to be pleased with the way the plant modernization was proceeding. The work was on schedule, and he was feeling optimistic that everything would work out after all. But he was still fully immersed in it, fretting over every detail and having daily meetings with the engineers and project foreman. Julie didn't even try to talk to him about her own problems. It would've been a waste of breath.

Actually, she was glad that he had his own work to occupy his time and his mind. Since he still wouldn't admit to himself that she was seriously ill, it was much easier for her to be spared the hassle of trying to explain her pain, her constant exhaustion, and most recently, her lack of appetite. Over the past two weeks, she had started losing even more weight.

One bright spot in Julie's life was little Matthew, who was doing great. Cheryl had gone home the day after he was born, and Julie stopped by their house almost every day on the way home from school. She desperately felt the need to cherish Matthew for as long as she was able. Matthew was sheer glory and innocence.

She reluctantly accepted the fact that she would probably be getting a *C* in Lipton's class, despite her one *A+* and a few *B's* afterwards. Lipton had told the class that half of their final grade would be based on the final assignment, which was to be a short story of 3,000 to 5,000 words due on the final day of class. He told his students that they could leave a stamped envelope with him if they wished their story to be returned to them.

~

Julie leaned back from the computer and stretched, wincing as a spike of pain ripped through her chest. After it had passed, she slumped down in her chair, wondering how she could keep going.

For hours, she had been trying to put together an idea for her final writing assignment. Robert had come home late from the office, and after a quick dinner had immediately gone out to the shop to work on his beloved Thunderbird. A new dashboard had been delivered by UPS that afternoon, and he was eager to work on the car's interior. Julie knew that working on the car relieved the stresses of the plant.

The day before, Julie had registered for the fall semester, even though Dr. Cole had all but said she would never be able to finish it. Her blood tests had shown that her disease was getting the upper hand, and the daily fatigue and pain told her that her body was giving up.

Mentally, though, she wasn't ready to submit. She had to have something to look forward to, and she believed that enrolling for the next semester would give her that. She wanted ed to fight this disease to the end. She had decided not to take summer classes, so her body could have three months of rest.

At the moment, though, she faced a more immediate problem. She had been struggling for some time with the final story for Don Lipton's class. She had already written a twenty-page story which Cheryl and Patricia said was very good, but she kept tinkering with it, knowing in her heart that it wouldn't impress Don Lipton.

She kept thinking about his comments in class, about how her other story touched the readers with emotion, and about how simple that story had been to write. He'd said that for the first time, she simply showed everything to the reader and allowed the reader to experience and feel it for himself, and had resisted the urge to overwrite.

She turned to look out through the window at the pond. The setting sun had cast a golden glow over the water. Shadows were gathering in the far corners of the property, and although she couldn't hear them, she knew the crickets and cicadas had begun their nightly racket.

Her mind remained on Don Lipton's words. Maybe that was what she had been doing wrong. She had been trying too hard and had been getting tangled up in the little details without keeping her eye on the real issues.

The door opened behind her, and she turned as Robert came into the room. She was surprised to see that he'd already showered and put on his pajamas. "Oh... I thought you were still working in the shop."

"It's after ten, Ju," he said, sounding annoyed. "I'm going to bed. Which is what you should be doing. Dr. Cole—"

"I know," she interrupted. "Dr. Cole wants me to get more rest. This is the last time I'll be up late, Robert. After this, I'm done for the semester."

He grumbled something she didn't hear, gave her a kiss on the cheek, and left. A moment later his footsteps were shuffling down the hallway toward their bedroom, and Julie's mind was back on what Don Lipton had said about her writing.

Real issues.

Thinking about that, she got her laptop computer and went out to sit on the redwood deck at one edge of the pond. It was a pleasant night, and it was very quiet and peaceful out there with only the insects in the surrounding trees to keep her company. She inhaled the night air.

With the lighted screen of her laptop computer, the moonlight would be more than enough to work by. But the peaceful atmosphere didn't seem to be giving her the inspiration she'd hoped for.

She stared at the blank screen for a long moment, then leaned back in the padded lawn chair and closed her eyes. Her final assignment for Lipton's class was due at eight o'clock the next morning, and she still hadn't even started it. Unless she wanted to use the short story she'd already written... but she knew it wouldn't be good enough for Don Lipton.

Don Lipton....

With her eyes closed, she again saw those photographs in the newspaper from so many years ago... the charred wreckage of the car, the door gaping open, a blackened blur of the interior....

She shuddered, and knew she couldn't hope to imagine what it must have been like for Don Lipton when he saw that car and imagined the horrible final moments of his wife and daughter.

Julie wondered how she would have reacted if something like that happened to her. Would she have shrunk back into a shell as Lipton had done? Would she be bitter, unwilling to allow herself to become close to others for fear of losing them? Would she feel guilt because she'd lived and others had died?

An evening breeze touched her face, cooling the tears that began to flow. Her heart seemed to knot in her chest, and a story of death and guilt and unending sorrow began to form in her mind, fragmented at first like the rippled image of the sunset she'd seen in the pond, then gradually merging into a vision.

She opened her eyes, shifted the small computer on her lap, and began to type.

As she wrote, the newspaper articles about Don Lipton and his family kept flashing through her mind. She tried to understand how hopeless a man would feel after losing the two people he most loved in the world. To blame himself for their deaths had to be a hell of its own.

By the time she finished the story, dawn was painting the eastern sky a delicate rose color. She knew Dr. Cole would be upset with her for neglecting her much-needed rest. But she also knew that the rest would come later. Too soon, it would come, and the rest would be much too long.

As if to punish her for staying up through the night, a sudden flare of pain lanced through her chest. She sat perfectly still, her breath coming in gasps as the pain needled into her with quick, hard bursts. Never before had it been this bad.

After a few minutes, it eased up — enough, at least, that she thought she could make it into the house and swallow two of the pain pills.

She slipped the diskette out of the computer and clutched it in her hand. For better or worse, it was done.

A shooting star scratched its fire across the lightening sky, and like a child, she wished on it. Birds in the trees surrounding the pond had come to life and were calling out in their various warbles and cheeps and twitterings. She wanted to lean back in the chair and close her eyes, but she knew that if she did, she would fall asleep instantly.

Of course, she couldn't do that. In a little over two hours, she had to turn this story in to Don Lipton. And for once, she didn't care whether or not he liked it. She didn't care what grade he gave her for the class.

~

"Well, folks," Don Lipton said, staring out at the students from his usual perch on the edge of the desk, "looks like this is the last day you'll have a chance to see my smiling face up here." He paused, but if he was expecting polite laughter, he must have been disappointed by the dead silence. He cleared his throat. "I guess those of you who bothered to show up must have brought your final assignment."

Julie took slow, calming breaths in an effort to ease the pounding of her heart. Her final assignment lay on the desk in front of her, eighteen pages of neatly printed prose. She felt as if it had been wrung out of her by a giant fist, and she had no idea how Donald Lipton would react to it.

Last night, sitting out there at the pond, writing this story had seemed the most natural thing in the world. But now, as she looked at Donald Lipton, she cringed inwardly thinking about how he might react when he read it. *It was a dumb thing to do,* she told herself for at least the hundredth time. It would certainly hit too close to the truth for Lipton. What could she have been thinking?

At least I won't have to see him again, she thought. She knew she couldn't have faced coming back into this class again after he had read her story.

"Well," Lipton said after he'd collected all the assignments, "I wish I could say it's been fun." He offered the smirk that was supposed to be a grin. "It's been real, though. I'll say that." Without another word, he tucked the assignments under his arm and strode from the room.

Patricia glanced over at Julie and issued a sigh of relief. "It's been real all right. Ready to go celebrate?"

Julie's eyes were still on the door Donald Lipton had gone through, and she had to resist an almost overwhelming urge to run through it, chase him down, and wrestle her assignment from him before he could read it.

"Julie?"

She looked over at Patricia and forced a smile. "Celebrate? You bet!"

They decided on lunch at one of the most expensive restaurants in Freeborn.

Julie had a final exam in business math, and completed it in less than half the time that was allowed. Then she met

Patricia at the restaurant... and that was when Patricia gave her the news.

"Boston!" Julie exclaimed, staring across the table at her friend. "But... *why?"*

"Allen got a big promotion," Patricia said in a tone that was almost apologetic. "We just found out about it a few days ago. His company wants to put him in charge of their plant in Boston. It's a great opportunity for him."

Julie put down her fork, forgetting all about the grilled chicken caesar salad in front of her. "What about *you,* Patricia? Do you like the idea?"

"Sure!" Patricia exclaimed. "I've lived in California all my life. It'll be nice to have a change. Allen says they have some great colleges and universities in Boston, and with the raise he'll be getting, I won't have to work anymore."

"But don't all of your children live in this area?"

Patricia's face lost some of its exuberance. "Yes... and that's the only thing I don't like about it. My family, and of course, friends like you. I'll miss everybody. But our kids are grown now. It might even be better for them to get us out of their hair and let them live their own lives. I made Allen promise to let me come out once or twice a year for a visit."

Julie forced a smile. "Well, then, congratulations! It sounds wonderful." She felt a terrible sense of loss, even though she had known Patricia for only a few months. Patricia had been the only real friend she'd made in school, and she felt that she was losing something important. "You'll call when you get there, won't you? I want to have your address and telephone number."

"Of course I will," Patricia promised. "Julie, you'll be the first one I'll call. I'll really miss you."

Julie picked up her fork and went back to work on the salad, looking down at it so Patricia wouldn't see the tears brimming in her eyes.

Chapter Seventeen

Cheryl's plans to go to the college for a first-hand look at Professor Donald Lipton had seemed destined for failure. On the day she'd expected to carry out her little self-imposed espionage assignment, Tom had been called in to work unexpectedly because of a problem at one of the stores in the district. He hadn't gotten home until late.

With the end of the semester approaching, Cheryl knew she would have to act fast, but she didn't know what to do with Matthew. She didn't want to entrust him to a babysitter at this young age, and she could hardly take him with her to the college. Tom hadn't had any more days off during the week, when Cheryl knew she could find Professor Lipton at the college. She didn't want to ask her mother to watch Matthew; Julie was already under too much stress because of the approaching final exams and papers that were due.

Then, on what she knew was her mother's last day of school, good fortune smiled on her at last. Tom had brought home a briefcase full of paperwork the night before, and he said he was resolved to stay at home and work through it instead of going into the office where he was constantly bombarded with telephone calls. They were nearing the end of their financial reporting period, and he told Cheryl that he absolutely had to get this work done by the following day. His boss had agreed that he should do it at home without all the office distractions.

When Cheryl mentioned that she had some errands to run, Tom immediately offered to watch Matthew for her. He would be taking his afternoon nap, anyway, but even if he awakened, Tom said he wouldn't mind spending a little time with him. It would be a nice break from the drudgery of the paperwork.

Julie called a little before noon to say that she was done with classes, and that she and her friend Patricia were meeting for lunch to celebrate getting through their first semester.

"Mostly to celebrate being finished with Professor Donald Lipton," Julie had said with audible relief. "Cheryl, I'm so glad to be free of that man!"

Once again, Cheryl marveled at the mixed signals she received from her mother regarding Professor Lipton. That added even more fuel to her determination to see this man for herself.

So she kissed Tom goodbye, admonished him to keep an ear tuned to any sounds from the nursery, and was out the door.

~

The doubts started to harden inside her as she started her car and headed across town toward the college. During the entire trip, she argued with herself, telling herself that she was being silly to go through all this.

When she pulled into a space in the parking lot and turned off the engine, she sat there for a long time looking toward the campus. She could almost imagine the headlines in tomorrow morning's newspaper: *Woman Arrested for Impersonating a Student.*

She smiled at that, and finally grabbed the textbooks she had brought as props and got out of the car.

Entering the double glass doors of the creative arts building, Cheryl immediately saw an elevator. She knew from Julie's description of climbing three flights of stairs that Lipton's office was located on the third floor.

She couldn't understand why her mother refused to take the elevator... but then, there were a lot of things about her that Cheryl couldn't understand lately. Maybe part of it was her own fault. Perhaps she was so wrapped up in the excitement of becoming a mother herself, that she hadn't taken time to listen properly.

Well, she would try harder from now on. Right now, though, she intended to go up to the floor where Lipton's office was and — hopefully, at least — walk past and maybe see him inside. That was all she wanted. Just a glimpse. She wasn't going to push her luck by trying for more.

The elevator stopped at the third floor and Cheryl, still feeling guilty, stepped into the hall. To her left was a large office marked *General Admissions*, but to her right was a long row of offices belonging to the instructors.

Great, she thought, *so far, so good.*

But when she found the door with the sign identifying Lipton's office, the door was tightly closed. She could see that a fluorescent ceiling light was turned on, but there was no sound or sign of activity. That made her wonder if he were there.

For almost half an hour, Cheryl paced back and forth, holding the books awkwardly in arms that were growing tired, keeping the office door in sight.

Finally, her resolve began to weaken. Several people who looked like teachers, and several others who were obviously students, had already noticed that she was hanging around, and had asked if they could help her. She'd managed to come up with some vague statement about meeting someone here, but she earned more than one suspicious glance. She was sure her nervousness was showing.

And what, she wondered, would she offer as an excuse if someone decided to have campus security come and question her?

That thought sent a chill down her spine, and was enough to convince her that it was time to give up her mission. It had been a dumb thing to do, anyway.

Not wanting to draw any more attention to herself, she headed toward the elevator. When the door opened, she hurried inside and bumped into a man trying to get out.

"Oh!" Cheryl dropped her books, and one of them landed on the man's foot. "Gosh, I'm sorry!" Then she looked up at him, and her breath caught in her throat.

The man was Professor Donald Lipton.

Even though Cheryl had never met him, she knew it was him. Her mother's description had been very specific about his salt-and-pepper beard, graying hair, and that haughty smirk on his face.

"Professor Lipton!" she stammered before she could stop herself. "I'm sorry!"

"You already said that." Lipton reached down to help pick up the books, but not without his usual sarcastic comments. "If you were trying to throw these at me, I would suggest you practice first... your aim is terrible." He gave her the books, which she nearly dropped again as she jammed them under her arm. Then he looked at her more closely. "Do I have you in a class?"

"Uh... no, sir." Then she realized she'd called him by name, and he was probably wondering about that. "I just... well, I've heard about you, sir."

He issued a short bark of laughter. "No doubt. Good thing for you that you aren't in one of my classes." Lipton rubbed his foot. "This feels like at least a low *D*. You know... *D* for 'dropped' or *D* for 'dumb.' What's the big hurry, anyway? Why don't you kids watch where you're going?"

Still muttering, Lipton walked off the elevator and strode on down the hall, and Cheryl pushed the button to the first floor. She wondered how her mother could possibly feel any attraction at all for this jerk. He was even worse than she'd said.

But still... Cheryl had always thought her mother was a good judge of character. Could first impressions of Professor Donald Lipton be so far removed from the actual man?

There had to be more to him than met the eye. Cheryl was determined to find out just what it was about him that seemed to intrigue her mother so much.

But she was sure of one thing: She wasn't going to let herself morph back into Cheryl Merrow, Private Investigator, to find out. She just wasn't good enough at that game.

Chapter Eighteen

Monday, May 26

Even before I turned in my final assignment, I began to feel concerned about how Don Lipton would react to it. I had no doubt that he would be upset by the story... and probably furious at me for daring to write about something that was so personal to him.

Today I finally got his reaction. I couldn't have been more surprised....

Over the next few days, Julie got caught up on neglected housework and began getting a little more rest, as she'd promised Dr. Cole.

On Monday morning, she went out to do some grocery shopping. She was tired when she pushed open the door leading from the garage and eased through it with two bags of groceries in her arms. Then she heard the ringing of the telephone.

"Darn!" she muttered, kicking the door closed with the heel of her shoe. She hurried over to the kitchen counter and set down both sacks. One promptly fell over, spilling canned goods across the counter, chased by a head of lettuce. She caught the lettuce, but several cans rolled off the counter and escaped across the floor to the other side of the kitchen.

Exasperated, she spun around and snatched the phone off its wall receptacle. "Yes?" she snapped, sure that it was Robert calling to remind her to run some meaningless errand.

There was a moment's hesitation before a man's voice came through. "Is this the Hunter residence?"

"Yes. This is Julie."

"Oh, well... Julie, this is Don Lipton. Did I catch you at a bad time?"

Her breath caught in her throat. Don Lipton was the last person in the world she'd expected to hear from.

But it didn't take a mind reader to figure out why he was calling. He'd read her final writing assignment, and now he was calling to tell her what a thoughtless, insensitive person she was.

"Julie, are you there?"

She realized at last that his voice didn't sound angry. More... tentative. A little nervous, even.

"Hello?"

She cleared her throat at last. "Yes, Professor Lipton. What can I do for you?"

"Well... for starters, you can call me Don. Haven't I said that before?"

She frowned. Was he actually trying to sound friendly? "Okay, Don."

After an awkward pause, he said. "Julie, I was wondering if we could get together to talk for a little while. Could you come down to my office?"

"Talk?" she asked doubtfully. "About what?"

"I've read your final paper, Julie. I just want to talk to you about it."

She felt her shoulders tighten, and she slumped down into a kitchen chair. "Dr. Lipton... Don, I did turn in a stamped, self-addressed envelope for the return of the story as you suggested. Can't you just mail it to me?"

"Of course I could do that. But this is... well, I'd really like to talk to you about the story. Could you come to my office?"

Finally, too tired to argue, she reluctantly agreed. "I suppose I can come. Can you give me half an hour?"

"Sure." He sounded relieved. "See you then." The telephone went dead.

Julie slowly replaced the receiver and sat staring at it, as if it had asked her a question that had no answer. In her mind, she went back through the story she had written for her final assignment, and shuddered as she considered the possible reactions she might expect from Don Lipton.

He had to know that the story was really about him, even though the main character was named Paul Keller. That was the story that had come to her as she sat out by the pond, and it was Paul Keller that she'd written about through that night with the crickets chirping all around her and the moonlight gleaming off the water.

The Paul Keller of Julie's story was a gifted pianist who lost his family in a house fire. He'd been out of town on a concert tour when the furnace malfunctioned, causing the fire that killed his wife and young son. He'd blamed himself for not being there when they needed him, and for not spending more time with them when they were alive.

He gave up his promising career and sank into oblivion, refusing to allow himself to get close to someone again, turning away from others who might have brought him joy.

She'd brought all this into one scene as Paul Keller stood at the edge of a lake, staring out at the sun reflected off the water, thinking about his loss and his life. All the anguish she'd felt had come from thoughts about Don Lipton and his own loss — and she'd done the best job she could to bring out that emotion in her story.

It had all seemed so clear to her at the time. But now she wondered exactly what she'd hoped to accomplish by writing the story. Donald Lipton was sure to see that the pianist was really another version of himself, and that the house fire represented the accident that had killed his wife and daughter.

He probably felt — and with good reason — that Julie had invaded his private territory with this story. Despite the tone of his voice on the telephone, he was surely furious with her. No doubt he was going to rake her over the coals.

She wasn't sure she would blame him. She hadn't meant to rub his nose in his past. She hadn't really thought in terms of trying to accomplish anything at all with the story. It was just something that had come together in her mind, and she'd felt compelled to share it.

She pushed herself wearily to her feet, then noticed the groceries still lying scattered on the floor. She started to reach for them, then changed her mind. They could wait. She had to get this meeting with Don Lipton over with. Otherwise, her nerves might just jump right out of her body.

Grabbing her car keys, she headed for the door.

~

Don Lipton was waiting in his office when she arrived just after three o'clock. She almost hoped he would've given up on her and left, or that he would change his mind and just mail her manuscript back to her, after all. But no, he was right there, sitting at his desk, frowning as he read through assignments.

Great, she thought. *He hasn't even seen me yet, and he's already in a bad mood.*

When Don looked up and saw her, he merely waved to the chair across from him, then pushed the stack of papers into an open drawer.

"Some kids never learn to follow the damned instructions," he said.

She sat down without asking him which kids he was referring to. She didn't want to get into that kind of discussion. On the desk in front of him lay her own manuscript. Her gaze fixed on it as if held there by super-glue.

Don picked it up and held it in his hands for a long moment. When her eyes finally lifted to his, she found him watching her.

"This," he said quietly, "is the best piece of writing I've ever seen from a student. Best, by far. I not only gave you an *A+* for the paper, but an *A* for the class."

Julie realized that her mouth was gaping open. She closed it, swallowed, and said weakly, "You did?"

He nodded. "I know I've often said in class that grades aren't important, but I can see that for whatever reason, they are important to you. There's no way I could give you a *C* or even a *B* after reading this story."

"Well... thank you." She didn't know what else to say. This certainly wasn't what she'd expected to hear from him.

"I really believe that you have the ability to put that kind of depth and feeling into all your stories," he continued. "All you have to do is have the courage to reach down into yourself for it. Of course, writing doesn't have the security of mathematics. But if you're brave enough, you can reach out into that unknown territory every time you sit down to write."

"Well...." She was still struggling to understand his reaction to her story. Was it possible he had missed the connection between himself and the character of Paul Keller in her story? She decided to be more direct. "Why, exactly, did you like this story so much more than the others?"

He looked down at the manuscript on the desk in front of him. "For one thing, you've really brought out this character Paul Keller. You set the tone and the mood so perfectly with the description of the sunset across the lake... and you brought that to the reader *through* Paul Keller. The reader gets to know Keller as he sees that scene through Keller."

Julie's eyes moved again to the story, and she thought about that scene she'd written. Paul Keller had taken a walk to a large lake near his rural house, and as he stood at the water's edge, he noticed all the beautiful things around him. That's where the entire scene unfolded, and the reader's understanding of the pain and guilt that Paul Keller faced every day of his life.

Don picked up her manuscript, flipped to the second page, and started reading. "'Paul watched as the sun touched the lake's edge and flowed into it, spreading out like golden fire across the rippling water. He could almost imagine that it was reaching out to embrace him in its warmth. From all around him came the singing of birds, the whisper of wind through high branches, and to his ears it became the most beautiful music....'" Don broke off suddenly and looked up at her. "Do you see what I mean, Julie? You're giving all this to the reader through Paul Keller's emotions. That's why it's so special. You're doing more than just describing this place. You're taking the reader into Keller's innermost feelings as he *experiences* it."

Julie realized now that she hadn't even thought about the technique she was using as a writer. It had seemed natural to describe this sunset through Paul Keller's interpretation of it. As she had sat there at her own pond with the computer in her lap, it was as if she had *become* Paul Keller.

At this point in the story, she had not revealed to the reader any of Keller's past or his crushing feelings of guilt. But as he stood there by the lake, it became obvious to the reader that Paul Keller was haunted by memories of something terrible that had happened many years ago. All the details of his surroundings — the rippling water, wildflowers, birds, fresh scents — came together in a way that brightened his heart. He felt that nature was beginning to heal him. His thoughts went to his wife, Michele.

Don continued reading from the story. "'He felt the warmth of the golden glow, and for a moment it was Michele's arms holding him again, Michele whispering his name. He stood motionless, wanting only to hold onto this moment as long as he could.'"

Julie knew what came next. As the sun moved lower and its golden light reflected across the lake, all the peace and serenity came crashing down around Paul Keller in a sudden reawakening of all the terrors. The sun turned the water of the lake to fire, and in that instant the fire from the past roared back, consuming the joy and wonder he'd felt. The lake vanished, and Paul's mind conjured up the image of their house, fire raging through it, flames licking from windows already blown out by heat, racing along the eaves to begin eating away at the roof.

And in his mind he could hear the screams from inside....

Sickened, he turned away from the view of the lake and the golden sunset.

"'The unwelcome scene Paul Keller's mind produced was one his eyes had never seen,'" Don read aloud. "'But his imagination had constructed it thousands of times over the years. What he had actually seen so many years ago was the burned-out husk of his house after he returned the next morning from a concert stop in Chicago. And he had never heard the screams because he wasn't there to hear them when his wife and son burned to death, clutching each other in that upstairs bedroom.'"

Don stopped reading for a moment and cleared his throat. He didn't lift his eyes to Julie, but she could see that they glistened with tears.

Paul Keller had felt the weight of guilt over the years because he was convinced that if he'd been at home, he would have saved them. Keller had given up his career and his music, and hid himself from the world, taking a job as a music teacher in a small-town high school and doing his best to alienate everyone around him.

"Well," Don said at last, placing the story almost reverently on the desk in front of him, "as I said, that's the best piece of writing I've ever seen from a student. You begin by bringing beauty and peace and nature to the reader through Paul Keller, then you demonstrate how it all became a horror to him because of the guilt that has infected his soul. The guilt won't let him live and enjoy the beauty of life. That's very effective use of contrast. The characterization is solid, and you've used great physical details of setting to help bring it all out."

She stared at him. Of course she liked the positive comments about her writing. But was that all he was going to say? He was telling her all these things that she had done right from a mechanical standpoint — but didn't he realize that the story was really about him? Was it possible he'd completely missed that? Could he be so blind to himself?

"As I said before," he continued, "all you have to do is have the courage to dig that deep inside yourself every time you sit down to write. If you can do that, you'll be able to turn out pieces like this every time."

"Well...." She bit her lip. "Thank you. I'm glad you liked the story."

He gave her the lopsided grin she'd seen so many times in class. "Is that all you have to say? Does that mean you're not ready to commit yourself to digging for that emotion every time? Does it mean you aren't ready to be courageous in your writing?"

His voice had once again taken on that superior tone, and she felt herself flare. "I have courage, Dr. Lipton. If you knew me better, you'd know that—"

"I'm glad to hear it, because I haven't been seeing much of it in your writing. What I've been seeing is someone who's afraid to face the tough things in life." He tapped his finger against her manuscript which still lay in front of him. "Maybe this is just a fluke, after all."

She felt heat rush into her face. "You have no right to talk to me about courage. You can't face the truth when it's staring you right in the face." She reached forward to snatch her manuscript off his desk, and waved it in front of him. "You've just touched the surface of what I wrote in this story. *You're* the one who won't delve into the real emotion. That's what you always accused me of doing, but it's *you* who are afraid to face the past."

He stared at her, his eyes narrowing. Then he pushed back his chair and stood. "Well, I can see it was a mistake to try giving you some positive feedback about your writing. You even want to argue about *that.*"

"That isn't the issue, and you know it," she shot back, getting to her feet. "You've been hiding and withdrawn completely because of an accident that happened twenty years ago. You, sir, have been putting up shields to keep people from getting too close to your own emotions. My God, can't you see that? Can't you see that *you're* Paul Keller?"

She knew she had stepped way over the bounds into territory she'd promised herself never to go, but she couldn't help herself.

"Like Paul Keller, you blame yourself for an accident that killed your family. I'm truly sorry about your loss, and the blame you assumed. But that is a part of a past that can't be changed. Damn it, you've given up your own successful writing career to teach creative writing at a community college. You could have reached into your own emotions and touched others with your writing. How can you talk to me about lack of courage? How can you dare to judge me?"

Lipton stood frozen in place, staring across the desk at her. After a moment, he spoke in a voice that was dead calm:

"Are you finished?"

"Not quite," she snapped. Her chest was twisting in agony, and she knew that allowing herself to get so upset wasn't helping. But this had been building for a long time, and she was powerless to stop it from pouring out of her. "You were a brilliant writer, and you gave it up because of your own fears. Who are you to tell me about lack of courage? *You're* the one who has stuck his head in the sand."

Then her voice broke and she knew she could say no more. Turning abruptly, she left the office. She kept her head down, not looking back as she headed toward the flight of stairs that led to the first floor. As she reached the top of the stairs, she heard a loud voice behind her.

"Ms. Hunter!"

Shakily, she turned around, expecting the worst.

Don Lipton pointed toward the elevator. "You may not be aware that we have one of those things. You know, the thing that you get into and it goes up and down both ways so you don't wear yourself out on the steps."

Julie stared at him, and finally noticed the slightest smile on his lips.

"Come on, doll," he said. "I'll ride down with you."

Caught off guard, and slightly touched by his concern for her taking the stairs, she walked with him to the elevator. In silence, they waited for the door to open. Two students exited as they stepped inside.

Don pushed the down button... then he turned suddenly and put his arms around her. Her first impulse was to step back from this contact, but then her emotions took over and she found herself returning the hug.

"I was wrong about you," he murmured. "You certainly do have courage."

She couldn't speak. His arms felt both strong and gentle at the same time. His face was buried in her hair.

Then the elevator eased to a stop and opened with a quiet swoosh on the bottom floor.

Don stepped back and looked down at her. "Are you okay?"

Julie wasn't sure, but she knew for certain that things would never be the same. "I'm fine," she answered shakily.

"Good." He smiled. "I'll be teaching the summer. If you like, we can get together sometime... to talk about your writing. I still think you should write a book."

Julie felt as if she'd just stepped into a whirlwind. Things were happening too fast. Her eyes met his. "Are you sure you'll have the time?"

"I'll make the time," Don promised.

Chapter Nineteen

Wednesday, May 28

Six months. That's how long Dr. Cole says I might live. If I take care of myself and do everything he tells me to do. And if I'm lucky. Six months.

Don Lipton took me to his gazebo today. It's in a wooded area near his home. It's really beautiful there, with wildflowers of every imaginable color. He talked about Emily and Abby, and we talked about my illness. He keeps telling me I should write a book.

A book? When I only have six months?

The tea in her cup had gone cold, but Julie sipped it anyway. She had been sitting there at the kitchen table for an hour, since returning from Dr. Cole's office, but she was not aware of the passing time.

Never before had she felt so depressed. A sense of loss greater than anything she'd ever known had settled deep inside her.

Maybe six months, Dr. Cole had said. *Less, if you don't get the rest you need.*

Now there was little doubt. The tests Dr. Cole had conducted over the past few months combined to paint a grim picture. During today's visit, she had sensed that he was holding back, not wanting to give her the bad news. Robert was gone on business for the day, and Dr. Cole kept suggesting that they come back tomorrow, when they could both be present.

Julie wouldn't let him off the hook, though, and finally he'd come out with it. *"Six months,"* he'd said. "I'm afraid you can't count on more than that." He had insisted that she go into the hospital for a few days so they could try to strengthen her weakening body.

"Why bother?" she'd asked.

He held her eyes as he replied, "Because it could be much less than six months, Julie. We're going to have to work to get that much."

Six months. If she were lucky. That would put it right around Thanksgiving. Reaching Christmas would be a miracle.

That meant, she realized, that she wouldn't even live long enough to complete the next semester for which she'd already registered. She wouldn't see Matthew reach his first birthday. Wouldn't see him walk.

She unconsciously picked up the cup and sipped the cold tea. She felt drained, as if all her tears and emotions had been wrung out of her. She had nothing left to give.

The telephone rang. She pushed back her chair and reached across the counter to pick it up. "Yes?"

"Julie, this is Don."

She sighed silently. "Yes, Don."

After a pause. "Is everything all right?"

How could she possibly tell him just how *wrong* everything was? "Everything's fine. What can I do for you?"

"I was wondering if we could get together for a little while and talk. Could you come over?"

She wished she hadn't answered the telephone. "I don't think—"

"Not to my house. I have a... well, it's a special place I'd like you to see. Please, Julie, I'd really like to talk to you. I'll even come over and pick you up if you don't feel like driving. But please do come. Please."

Please? Donald Lipton was begging her to come talk to him? He was actually asking rather than demanding, and he wasn't speaking with the brash, intimidating voice she had come to hate.

She had to admit that she was curious. Besides, it would be nice to get out of the house for a while and enjoy some of nature's beauty.

"Okay, Don. I'll come over for just a little while. If you'll give me directions, I can drive over by myself."

She wrote down the directions on the note pad next to the telephone.

"Julie, I... well, thanks for agreeing to come," he said at last. "I didn't know if you would."

Again, she was struck by the conciliatory tone. "I'll see you in about an hour, then."

~

Following his directions, she skirted Freeborn on a narrow county road, then took a series of lesser unpaved roads, each narrower and more rugged than the one before, traveling from gravel to dirt surfaces until she came to a lonely dead-end at a green wall of immense trees and lush vegetation.

He was standing right there at a row of tired-looking mailboxes, just as he'd promised, wearing faded jeans and a checked shirt and brown boots with the stitching beginning to bulge up the sides. When she pulled to the side of the road, he came over to open the door.

"Hello," he said, somewhat awkwardly. "Thanks for coming." He took her hand to help her out of the car.

The gesture unsettled her for some reason. She nodded and looked around at the lush vegetation and the array of wildflowers that adorned the shoulders of the road. She saw no buildings of any kind. "You said there was a place where we could sit and talk?"

"It's back in the woods a little ways." He gestured behind him, and she saw a narrow footpath leading into the trees. "The path is a little overgrown, I'm afraid. I spent the morning clearing it as much as I could. We used to walk along this path almost every day, but I haven't gone down it now for ages."

She looked at him. "We?"

He nodded. "My wife and daughter and I."

Julie didn't respond. She knew that his heart must be heavy carrying all that grief inside for so long.

Blades of sunlight lanced through the trees as they walked slowly along the grassy lane. The wind rustled from time to time. A bird flew over, racing hard, banking into the woods.

At one point, when she stumbled on a root, Don reached over and took her hand in his own. "Do you mind, Julie?"

Instead of giving a verbal answer, Julie squeezed his hand. Together in silence, they continued down the path. They crossed a little stream over a wooden footbridge that looked weathered but stable. Julie was overwhelmed as she looked around.

"This is a beautiful place, Don."

"Yes." He smiled at her. "For some reason, today it seems even more beautiful than ever. Look at all the violets over there along the woods." Don stopped and gathered up a bouquet and handed them to Julie. "Here you are, madam."

Julie was elated. What a beautiful gesture. "Thank you. They're beautiful."

A few minutes later, passing between a pair of large California sycamores that bent together to form an archway, they came to a place where sunlight poured into a break in the forest. At the far side of the clearing, the trail led into another section of woods in which spruces, laurels, and sycamores grew closer together than elsewhere.

In the middle of the clearing, a wooden gazebo sat amid a sea of brilliant wildflowers. There were too many varieties for Julie to name, but they created a collage of colors that moved gently with the breeze, contrasting beautifully against the deep green foliage.

The gazebo itself had seen better days. It was hexagonal in shape, with wooden rails and a sharply peaked roof. Three steps led up to the door. The rails and steps were badly weathered, and some of the shingles had been blown off the roof.

"I haven't been out here in a long time," Don said. "But we used to have some very special times here." He released Julie's hand and walked ahead, up the wooden steps to open the door of the gazebo. He turned around and offered Julie his hand again and helped her step inside. The wooden benches were covered with dust and cobwebs.

Don took a handkerchief out of his pocket and used it to brush away the worst of the cobwebs, then lifted the top of one of the benches and took out two cushions. They were dusty, but otherwise in good shape. He went to the opening and slapped them together to get rid of the dust, then lay them on one of the benches.

"I should've cleaned this place up," he apologized. "I'll do that before we come back out here."

She sat down beside him on the bench and looked out over the railing at the wildflowers. She could almost imagine that she and Don were in a boat that was floating in a fantasy lake of colors. "This is absolutely beautiful, Don." She turned to look at him. "Did you build this gazebo?"

He nodded. "When Abby was little. It was a place for us to come for picnics and just to get away for some peace and quiet." He pointed toward the pathway that led further into the woods. "That loops around to the back of our house, about a half mile away. Many, many times, we walked down that path with a picnic basket. Emily and I would sit here and talk about our plans for the future, and my writing projects. Together, we would watch Abby explore the beauties and mysteries of life for the first time."

She kept silent, allowing him to relive the memories and share them with her at his own pace. The expression on his face was not bitter or sad or angry. It had the peace of remembrance.

He pointed out something else to her. "See that chain hanging from the oak tree over there? That was part of a swing I put up for Abby. She loved that swing. I can still see her pumping those chubby little legs to make herself go back and forth. And sing... she did sing! She was so tiny, and she had the voice of a cherub. She knew the words to so many children's songs, and sang one after the other as loud as she could. After each one, she would turn around to see if we had heard her, and then she would begin the next one. As long as we kept clapping, she kept singing." He released a heavy sigh. "God, how I miss my little girl."

He fell silent for a moment. She reached over and took his hand without speaking. He squeezed hers gratefully.

"I think about them every day, Julie. Every day, I think about how old Abby would be now, and I try to imagine what she would be like. In my mind, she has grown up through all these years. Her first day of school, her first boyfriend, high school graduation... I've imagined all those first things for Abby, knowing she would never experience them. Many of the girls in my classes would be her age now. I try to imagine what she would look like...."

His voice broke, and this time she was the one who lifted her arms and hugged him. He leaned against her, his shoulders shaking with silent sobs. A sudden gust rustled the canopy of leaves above them, and she thought about how complex this man was — this man who seemed to have as many hues as the wildflowers around them.

Don pulled back at last, brushing a hand across his face and clearing his throat. "You were right about everything, Julie. I blamed myself for what happened to Emily and Abby. I still do. I was the one who lost control of the car. If I had been more careful, it wouldn't have happened. Emily tried to tell me I was driving too fast for the rainy conditions, but I wouldn't listen.

"Then it happened, and I was the only one who was saved." His hand moved up to touch the scar above his eyebrow. "This is all I got — a little memento. It seemed so unfair. *I* should have died in that crash. Emily and Abby should have been pulled out, not me."

He had to stop for a minute, and she held him, moving her hand up to press it against the back of his neck.

"I couldn't write anymore after that. I just couldn't. It was as if I had died inside... just like Paul Keller in your story." He issued a bitter, humorless laugh. "You won't believe how hard I tried to convince myself that your story really wasn't about me. I actually succeeded, for a while. I couldn't believe that you had been able to see me so clearly."

"I was afraid I had hurt you," she said softly.

After a moment, he replied: "Seeing the truth can hurt. And you were right — I didn't want to see that truth. You brought it out all too clearly in your writing. Now I know why I was so hard on you about your class assignments. It wasn't because there was something wrong with them. It's because you were demonstrating the same kind of passion in your writing that I once had, and had given up. Something inside me kept wanting to get closer to you, but then the pain and guilt would make me pull back. Again, I was just like Paul

Keller in your story. I know I must've come across as hot and cold to you. It must have been terribly confusing. I'm so sorry. I hope you can forgive me."

"You're forgiven," she whispered, too unsure of her own voice to attempt saying the words aloud.

Don straightened on the bench and again brushed a hand across his eyes. He looked around. "After Emily and Abby were killed, I never came back to this place. As you can see, the place has been deteriorating... pretty much in synch with my life."

"You've never... well...."

"Let myself get close to another woman?" He shook his head. "No way."

"But Don—"

He stopped her by lifting his hand, and gently placed it on her cheek. "What about you, doll? You already know my life story. Don't you think I should know a little more about yours?"

She shrugged. "There isn't much to tell, I'm afraid. I got married really young — right out of high school, in fact. Within two years, we had a daughter and my husband was running a business. Things have... well, they've gone pretty well for us. We were having some problems with the business, but it looks like Robert is taking care of them. My daughter, Cheryl, just had her first baby. A little boy."

"Ah... so you're a grandma!"

She smiled. "Yes, and I love it."

He laughed. "Sounds like you've had a marriage made in Heaven."

"Well... I wouldn't say that, necessarily." She looked away, feeling uncomfortable with the direction the conversation had taken. "Robert is a good man. He has always provided well for me."

She felt his eyes on her, but he didn't pursue that subject.

"What about other family? Your parents? Brothers and sisters?"

"I was an only child," she told him. "My father was a wonderful man. I loved him dearly, and he always treated me like a princess. He died from a brain hemorrhage when I was twelve. My mother remarried a few years later, and now they live in Florida. I don't see much of her."

"Why not?"

Julie sighed. "She never liked Robert very much, and they don't get along. She used to come out to see us every few years, but that eventually dwindled. Her health isn't good now, either."

"That's too bad," he said. "My parents are old, but still as feisty as ever. They live up in Colorado."

"Do you see them often?"

He shook his head. "Not as often as I should." He paused, thinking. "I should make it a point to visit them more often. They may not be around too many more years."

They sat in companionable silence for several minutes while the birds chirped and twittered and sang, and the breeze rustled the wildflowers and tall grass around the gazebo. Finally, Don cleared his throat.

"I have a confession to make."

She looked over at him. "Yes?"

"I know about your illness."

It took a moment to sink in. Then her eyes widened in surprise.

"I suspected something right away," he went on. "In class, you often didn't look as if you were feeling well. Then I found your pill bottle in my office. Apparently, you dropped it there when you came to talk to me that first time."

She remembered dropping the keys in his office, and later she hadn't been able to find the pill bottle. When she hadn't found it in her car, she decided to forget about it. The bottle was almost empty, anyway.

"A friend of mine works in a pharmacy, so I asked him what the medicine was for." Don took her hand and held it between both of his. "God, Julie, I'm sorry. Sorry for not telling you about the pills earlier, and sorry for what you're going through."

He sounded like he cared, and sudden tears rolled down Julie's cheeks. "What gave you the right to snoop into my medical problems, anyhow?"

"The same thing that allowed you to snoop into my past, I suppose. In an odd sort of way, doll, I think we both cared enough to find out what was making the other one hurt. I don't know why I was so hard on you after that. I suppose I was angry, too. I've already lost the two people in the world I cared most about. Now I would be losing someone else who was already starting to mean something to me."

"Mean something to you?" She stared at him incredulously. "You treated me like dirt through the entire semester."

He turned to face her more directly, his eyes on hers. "I've made a lot of mistakes in my life, Julie. I'm just now beginning to recognize some of them. Tell me... how bad is it? Your illness, I mean."

She couldn't hold his gaze. Instead, she looked out at the meadow with its ocean of flowers. "Dr. Cole says I probably won't live past Thanksgiving, if that long. I'm so scared. I'll be going into the hospital for a few days next week, but I don't think Dr. Cole believes it will do any good. The disease has caused too much damage." She started crying harder. "God, Don, I so love being a mother to my daughter, but for years I've been planning on pursuing my own dream. I didn't realize I would run out of time. I always had it figured out, everything lined up in an orderly fashion just like a mathematics formula. My life was perfect, then this damned lupus came along and screwed up everything."

Don extended his arms and held her close. "I'm sorry, doll. It's just so incredibly unfair. You can't imagine how sorry I am."

Another long silence drew out while he held her in his big arms with her head pressed against his chest.

"Julie," he said at last, "do you realize how much you've touched me with your writing? How much you've changed me? That piece about the pianist... well, believe me, it had the impact you were hoping for. You've made me see everything in a new light."

She didn't trust herself to respond, so she just held him tightly and remained silent.

"Can you understand why it has been so hard for me to talk about this... not only with you, but with anyone?"

"I think so, Don. I doubt if anyone can know what you have been going through."

"*You* know, Julie. You brought it all out in Paul Keller." His questioning eyes met Julie's. "Why did you try to understand me, love?"

Julie thought for a moment. "I guess because the Don Lipton I saw in the classroom and the one I saw a few times when he didn't know I was watching were so different. I saw you one day in the courtyard with a little boy who had fallen down. Don, you were so gentle with him."

"You saw that?" Don was surprised.

"Yes, and somehow I knew that no one could fake such compassion."

He pulled her close, and for a long time they sat there on the dusty bench without speaking. Julie knew that communication didn't always require words. Sometimes, just being together was enough. After all these years, he was ready to accept the fact that another person could care for him. He needed her, and somehow being there for him seemed so right.

"Oh, my love, my very special love," he said at last, "I apologize for getting so angry with you that last time in my office. When I called you that day and asked you to come see me, I really thought talking to you might help me explore my inner feelings. But... but I still wasn't ready to admit what my gut feelings were telling me. Suddenly, there you were telling me how Paul Keller was so much like me, and I felt threatened and began lashing out at you. Can you ever forgive me, Julie?"

"There is nothing to forgive, Don. You were reacting the only way you knew how."

Another silence drew out. Don broke it at last.

"Julie, I have to ask you something. I have to know. What finally happens to your guy, Paul Keller? In the short piece you wrote for my class, the guilt and inner conflict remain unresolved. Tell me, please, does Keller ever become whole again?"

"Wow... what a complicated question." She thought for a moment. "Oh, Don, I'm not trying to avoid answering you. I really don't know how to answer that. I do know that the scars run deep, and I just don't know if Keller will be able to heal them." A pensive look covered her face. "Don, I don't even know if he *wants* to be healed, since he feels that he deserves all the pain."

Don took his hands and lifted Julie's chin toward his face. He spoke softly, as if afraid to hear her response. "Tell me, doll, do you think your Paul Keller could be healed if he really wanted to be... I mean if he was willing to work at it?"

Julie considered this. "Yes, Don, I think Paul would be strong enough to do that, but only if he sincerely wanted to purge the poison of guilt and regret from his soul."

He nodded slowly. "I understand what you're trying to say. And Julie, I think you ended your story too soon. I honestly think you have something very important to tell other people. With your writing, you can touch ever so many hearts, just as you've touched mine. I think you owe it to yourself, and to others, to expand your story into a novel. You have the feelings, the skill to reveal all this to readers, and to let them see how a man like Paul Keller can be healed."

Julie thought about that for a moment, and then put the question back to him. "Tell me, please, what do *you* think would heal the soul of a man like Paul Keller?"

Without hesitation, Don answered. "Well, babe, I think the love of a woman could do it. Keller would have to allow himself to fall in love again. Not to let another woman take Michele's place, but to give himself the gift Michele would want him to have."

"Do you really think he could fall in love again?" she asked quietly.

He nodded. "I think he could." His voice was choked. "Maybe he already has."

They sat for a long time, hugging each other warmly. It had seemed natural to come into his arms. It seemed even more natural to linger there a little while, past the point of a casual hug between two new friends.

Chapter Twenty

Friday, May 30

Robert stayed home today to spend some "quality time" with me, but that didn't work out very well. He just can't accept that I'm seriously ill, and that's always coming between us.

Lunch with Don was very nice, though. I can't believe I'm falling in love with this man....

Her entire body twisted with pain the next morning as Julie forced her head up to see the clock. 8:15. She moaned aloud. She felt exhausted, and she had a queasy, thumping headache. She'd tossed and turned most of the night, unable to get Don Lipton out of her mind.

Robert was already gone, of course, no doubt having launched himself into his carefully planned day with his usual mixture of wholesome cereals and skim milk.

This morning, at least, she had something to look forward to. Don had asked her to come have lunch with him in his office. He promised to bring everything they needed, and said the privacy would give them a chance to talk some more. She only hoped she could work up the energy to get there.

During the long night, she had wrestled with a fair amount of guilt over her feelings for Don Lipton, and for the way she'd felt the day before when he held her. But she knew that the comfort she got from being with the burly college professor might be all that would keep her from totally giving up on life. Cheryl was busy with Matthew, and Julie didn't want to interfere in their lives. Robert still found it impossible to even acknowledge that she was seriously ill, and seemed eager for every opportunity to distance himself from her.

The business worries, at least, seemed to be behind them. The work on the plant was continuing to proceed on schedule and within budget, and Robert was pleased that he was able to maintain a high level of production even during the modernization. All of his major customers had signed long-term sales contracts.

Until the work was finished, though, Julie knew that the plant would be occupying most of Robert's thoughts and time. He was leaving the next morning for a two-day trip to Los Angeles to negotiate a new contract with the company that supplied most of the raw paper for the plant.

Julie knew that if Robert hadn't been fully absorbed in the plant, he would've found something else to devote his time to. Anything that would take his mind off Julie and her illness. Julie didn't press the issue. Although she found it increasingly more difficult to understand how he could simply ignore her fears, she knew that Robert just couldn't face the fact that he was losing her. She tried to protect him from any expendable pain, and was usually able to maintain a fake cheerfulness around him. Most nights, though, after he fell asleep, she flooded her pillow with tears.

"Are you awake, Ju?"

She jumped and jerked her head around to the door, a movement which escalated the thumping headache to an excruciating jab of pain up her neck and into the back of her head. She winced.

"Are you all right?" Robert came over to the bed and sat down beside her. He was dressed in tan casual slacks and a beige pullover sweater. "Got a headache?"

She nodded, running a hand over the back of her neck. "I'll take a pain pill. How come you're still here?"

He grinned. "I just decided to take the day off. Called Dick and told him that since I was going to be gone for the next couple of days, I wanted to spend some quality time with my wife." Dick Leach was the plant manager. "There isn't much happening with the modernization today, anyhow. Just clean-up. I thought we could do something together. How's that sound to you?"

She groaned inwardly, thinking of her planned lunch with Don. Of all days....

"That sounds great, Robert," she said, trying to force some enthusiasm into her voice. "What did you have in mind?"

"I don't know. Something active. All you need is a little exercise. That'll perk you up."

Julie rolled over to face her husband. "Robert, do you know what I would like to do? I know it's crazy, but do you think maybe we could dance? A nice, slow dance. Maybe it would loosen me up and make me feel better."

His eyes widened. "Dance? It isn't even eight o'clock. Besides, you know that I never like to dance without a few drinks under my belt."

She issued a silent sigh. So much for doing something spontaneous. "Let me grab a quick shower, and maybe we could have some breakfast and then go somewhere for a walk."

"Sounds pretty good," he said, already turning away from the doorway. "I'll go take a look at the newspaper."

Thirty minutes later she came into the kitchen, showered and dressed. Her headache had eased, but the pain in her chest told her she wouldn't be doing any vigorous walking today.

Robert was sitting at the table, reading the newspaper. He looked up when she came in. "Would you like a cup of coffee this morning? Or tea? I'll make it for you."

"Tea would be fine. Thanks."

Robert was in an unusually talkative mood over breakfast, but Julie was lost in her own private thoughts about Don Lipton and the time they had shared the previous day. She hated the thought of missing their lunch together, but she supposed she would have to call and cancel.

"So what would you like to do today?" Robert asked. "I mean besides dance."

"I'm not sure," she mumbled.

"Surely you have something you've been dying to do with your one and only."

"Whatever."

He frowned at her. "Julie, is something wrong with you today? You act as if you're in another world. First you complain because I don't spend time talking with you. Now that I am, you don't even seem interested."

"Sorry," she said, but she was unable to come up with anything else to say.

"Have you talked to Cheryl lately? Have you seen little Matthew?"

"Yeah, they were here yesterday afternoon for a short time. The baby is getting big." Julie stood up and carried her cup and breakfast dishes to the sink. Again, she had another chest pain. Dr. Cole had told her to call at once if these pains worsened, but she knew Robert would get terribly upset if she ruined his day off. She wasn't up to his misunderstanding and verbal abuse. She decided to try to cover up the pain the best she could.

"Would you like to take a walk down the lane with me?"

Robert asked.

"I'm not sure I feel up to a walk right now," she said. "Why don't you go ahead?"

"Well...." He hesitated. "Since you aren't feeling well anyway, maybe I ought to go on into the office and get ready for the trip tomorrow. I should review our old contract and jot down notes about what I want to change. I'm hoping we can get some price cuts, since we'll be buying more paper. Would you mind?"

Would she mind? What if she did? But in truth, she didn't at all mind. "No, Robert. I'll just take it easy today."

"Good girl." At the door, Robert turned around. "Are you sure you're okay?"

"I'll be fine," she said, wishing he would go.

"Why don't you take a few of those antacid pills? Mom used to have indigestion all the time, too. She swore by those tablets. Want me to get some for you?"

Her temper flared. "No, damn it! Don't keep telling me what I should do." The pain in her chest suddenly spiked, making her gasp. She waved weakly at Robert. "You go ahead. I'll be fine."

He nodded stiffly. "All right. I'll be home for dinner." He opened the door and left. A minute later, Julie heard his truck pull out of the driveway.

She sighed with relief. She still had plenty of time to get to Don's office for the lunch he'd promised.

~

It was just past eleven when she got off the elevator at the third floor of the college's main building. She felt a mixture of sadness and elation at being back here. The classes she'd taken had meant so much to her. All she wanted was a college degree, but now it was clear that she wouldn't be reaching that goal. Again, she wondered what she had done to deserve this death sentence.

She turned down the hallway that led to the specialized educators' offices. Don Lipton's door was closed, but she could see the light through the glass panes. She raised her hand to knock, but changed her mind and twisted the knob, then stepped into the office, closing the door behind her.

Don looked up from his desk, and instantly smiled. "Hello, doll." Then the look on her face registered, and he got up to come around the desk to give her a hug. "What's wrong?"

"Everything!" She held onto him for a long time, sobbing. "I've had it, Don. I can't take it anymore! I'm tired of being sick, and I'm really tired of hurting so much. I hope I die! I just can't wait to die. Oh, God, I'm so scared. Hold me, please, just hold me."

Don pulled her closer. "How's this? Is this what you want? It's okay, doll."

It felt good to be in his strong arms. "But you don't understand—"

"I know I don't, love. Nobody can understand what you're going through. But I can be here for you, and be your friend, and love you."

"But I'm so scared...."

"What are you afraid of, Julie? Are you afraid of dying?"

She looked up at him. "Wouldn't you be?"

"You're damn right I would be. Anybody would be scared if they were in your shoes."

Julie leaned against him with the full force of her body, put her head on his shoulder, and cried. She knew that he didn't mind. Never before had she known such unselfish love.

Don finally backed her up to a chair. "Sit here, and I'll get a tissue." Opening the drawer at the front of his desk, he jerked several tissues out of the box. "They're free today, you know."

Julie couldn't help but smile. What a crazy man. Even in the midst of her greatest sorrow, he found a way to make her smile. She took the tissues and wiped her eyes.

"Are you feeling better now?"

She shook her head. "I'll never feel better. But at least I have you to share all of this with me. Thank you, Don. What would I ever do without you?"

"Let's see... I can't think of a thing. How about lunch?"

She didn't feel much like eating, but she knew she would have to do her best. He had gone out of his way to make ham sandwiches, and had picked up some potato salad at the deli. He'd packed it all into a wicker picnic basket, along with a large, sealed pitcher of iced tea.

"This looks great, Don," she said as he spread a checkered tablecloth on his desk and began laying out the food, along with heavy plastic plates and forks.

"Have you been writing in your journal?" he asked after they had started on the food.

She nodded. "I wrote quite a bit last night. I was writing about little Matthew and how much I'm going to be cheated by not watching him grow up. It stinks, Don. It is so unfair."

"I agree. Life often isn't fair." He paused a moment and drank some tea from his glass, then said, "What about Paul Keller? Have you been thinking any more about him?"

She nodded. "A lot. And I've been sketching out some thoughts about his feelings, and how his story can be expanded into a book. But I still don't feel as if I really know the man." She thought for a moment, then added, "I was hoping you could help me with that."

He grinned. "I'll be glad to, if I can. I suppose I should know him as well as anyone can."

From the look on his face, Julie knew she'd said exactly the right thing. That was the reaction she'd been hoping for. She did want his help in understanding fully how Paul Keller felt about the deaths of his wife and son.

But she had another reason for asking Don for help. She hoped that by examining Paul Keller's heavy burden of guilt and grief, Don might be able to come to grips with his own.

For a few moments, they concentrated on eating their lunch. After the sandwiches and potato salad were gone, they settled back with glasses of iced tea, he in his swivel desk chair and she in the visitor's chair she'd pulled up close to the other side.

"Don," she said, "I know that Paul Keller feels guilt over the deaths of his wife and son. He feels that he should have spent more time at home where he could've protected them. But I'm wondering... do you think Paul would really feel so sure that he could've saved them even if he'd been home when the fire broke out? The fire started in the basement furnace, and Michele and Brian were trapped in an upstairs bedroom. Doesn't it seem more likely that all of them would have been killed even if Paul had been at home?"

He sipped iced tea while he considered her question. "I think he would've felt that he was completely to blame, whether it was rational or not. When something like that happens, Julie, a person loses all sense of reasoning."

"But... when he had time to think about it, wouldn't he realize that he would've probably died, too? And that he would've been powerless to prevent what happened?"

He offered a slight, uneasy shrug. "How can any of us know all the *could have's* and *would have's* in life? Look at all the strange happenings in life. There is no set of rules when it comes to life and death." He paused, and his eyes softened. "You, love, should know that far better than I."

Julie knew Don was right. Even people who appeared to be making all the right choices and decisions sometimes lost in the end. She was losing right now, and there wasn't a thing she could do about it. She knew that instead of frantically exhausting all means to find a way to beat her illness, she had to look instead for ways to make the most of every second of her remaining life. She had found many of those ways, day by day, with Don Lipton.

"What are you thinking about, Julie? You seem lost in your thoughts."

"I'm sorry, Don. I was just thinking about my own life and how happy I am that we have had even this limited time together. Isn't it crazy, love? We both needed this time. I needed it so desperately so you could help me die... and Don, you needed it so I could help you live again."

He looked down at his hands, which were clasped together before him on the desk.

"I have another question," she said softly. "It may be that Paul Keller can't help blaming himself for what happened. But let's look at that from another angle. If he seriously thought about it, do you think Paul would believe that Michele and Brian would blame him for what happened? Would he believe that they would want him to blame himself and cause himself such misery?"

Don shook his head. "No, Julie. If he thought about it, he would know better than that. But all that guilt inside him probably won't even let him see it that way." He looked down at this clasped hands again, then cleared his throat. "And if you're asking me if I think Emily and Abby would blame me for the accident... hell no." His eyes lifted to hers. "Our love was splendid, Julie. Any blame I had was self-imposed. Emily knew I never would have harmed her or our daughter for anything in the world. True love doesn't know blame." He lowered his head and momentarily covered his eyes with his hands. Then, looking again at Julie, he added, "And no, honey, Emily would not have wanted me to be miserable for a moment. She was a lot like you. She treasured each moment of life to the fullest and did all in her power to see to it that others in her life did the same. Emily wanted the entire world to know peace and happiness."

Julie was pleased that Don could finally be open and honest with her, but she could see that the conversation was causing him tension. She knew somehow that she had helped this man she cared so much about, and he in turn had helped her understand Paul Keller better. They had really helped each other. Don was helping her to write a book, and she was helping him heal his soul.

For a brief time, the conversation switched to less painful things. Julie smiled when Don told her how for the first time in years he had "tinkered with a few words" the previous night. He said he was trying to write a poem for a friend, but wouldn't tell her anything else about it.

All too quickly, it was time for him to go teach his last class, and for Julie to leave. She hated these goodbyes.

"Tomorrow's Saturday," he said as he put the checkered tablecloth and remnants of lunch back into the picnic basket. "Do you think you'd feel up to taking a drive?"

"A drive?" she asked. "Where to?"

He smiled. "That's a secret. Just a place I want to show you. I'm not sure about Robert, though. Will he be spending the day at the plant?"

She shook her head. "He's going to be in Los Angeles tomorrow and Sunday." She thought for a moment. "A drive sounds like fun."

"Great! I'll pick you up at three, then." He hesitated. "Promise you won't laugh at my car, though. She's old, and she gets her feelings hurt easily."

She smiled. "I promise."

"Now, I think you need an extra-long hug." He came around the desk. She stood, and he put his arms around her. "There, how's that? Is that good enough?"

"No!" Julie knew nothing would be good enough. Don pulled her close again. Looking down, he put his lips on hers and they kissed.

"Are you ready to go, doll?" he murmured.

"No, please... hold me for just one more minute."

Don pulled away and teased, "Okay, I'm counting. One, two, three...."

Julie pretended to get angry and headed for the door. Don pulled her back and hugged her again. "Now, let's get out of here. I'll ride down with you."

Together, they walked down the hallway to the elevator. When the door closed behind them, Don grabbed Julie and kissed her while gently patting her on the bottom.

Startled, she pulled back and looked up at him. He was grinning broadly. "You'd better watch out, buster," she warned. "I might lose control of myself. I won't be responsible for what happens to you then."

The grin turned into a satisfied smirk. "I'll take my chances, doll."

Before she could reply to that, the door opened to let several other people inside, and she and Don stepped out into the lobby. Giving the appearance of casual friends, Don squeezed her hand. Then, not looking back, he hurried down the hall to his class.

Julie turned the opposite way, which led to the exit near her parked car. She began at once to count the hours, the minutes, until she would see him again.

Chapter Twenty-One

Saturday, May 31

    Don asked me to go with him to see a lighthouse. Although he never said so, I wonder if he used to go there with Emily and little Abby. He keeps telling me how special this place is to him.

    For some reason, it seems so right. A lighthouse — a bright light to guide lost ships, sometimes the only hope in total darkness. Don has to know, to feel in his heart, that he has been a beacon to me....

    A summer storm had been moving in, and it was raining by the time Don reached her home the following afternoon. He had been wanting to take Julie to the lighthouse — but now, for some reason, he was feeling nervous about the idea. He hadn't gone out there since Emily and Abby died. He'd never expected to see it again.

    She smiled and returned his hug as he helped her into the old Plymouth. A few minutes later, with the windshield wipers swooshing rhythmically, they were driving west along a highway that wound through a pretty country of overhanging elms. The underbrush on either side was thick — bright sumac, blue-gray juniper, lots of bushes he couldn't name. On the left, an ancient rock wall meandered in and out of the brush, and on the right a small brook gurgled cheerily east. Scattered ranch homes dotted the landscape along strings of wood and wire fences.

He felt his hands trembling on the steering wheel, and forced them to be still. Emily had always loved this stretch of highway.

"I like your car," Julie said. "She has character."

He smiled. The car was a 1976 Plymouth Fury, a big four- door sedan which had once been gold in color, but was now faded to a sickly beige with spots of rust showing through here and there. The upholstery was still in pretty good shape, but the dashboard had several huge cracks through which yellow padding was visible.

"This is the car I bought after... after the accident," he explained. "Never saw any reason to buy another one since. She's old and tired, but she gets me around."

"At least she has a personality. All the cars today look alike."

"Well, I doubt that anybody would mistake her for a Toyota or Honda."

She laughed. "So when are you going to tell me where we're going?"

"You'll know when we get there, doll."

The trip to the lake took only about fifteen minutes. They talked a little about her book, but for the most part just enjoyed the scenery outside the rain-streaked windows.

Finally, he spotted the sign, and turned onto the little gravel road, rolling slowly down it toward the lake shore. When he turned off the engine, he could hear the rain pelting against the roof.

"It's a lighthouse!" Julie exclaimed, staring out at it.

He reached over and took her hand without speaking.

They sat there for a moment looking through the blurred windshield at the ancient stone structure, dark gray against the lighter gray of the sky. He'd always liked this place, liked the solid, cool feel of the stones when he leaned against them on summer mornings and looked out at the lake. It seemed so long ago.

Don became aware that Julie was looking at him. She squeezed his hand.

"This is the special place you were telling me about?"

He nodded. "I used to come here when I was a kid. Back then, the lighthouse was still in use. There's a waterway that connects this lake to the Pacific, and merchant ships used to come up this way all the time. They still do, now and then, but now they've got sophisticated navigation gear and they don't need the lighthouse anymore. I liked to watch that big light turning, turning, like a big eye looking around at everything. It seemed spooky to me back then, especially when the night was dark and rainy. Later, though, I fell in love with the place."

Gazing out at the lighthouse, she slowly nodded. "I can understand why. And later, you brought Emily here?"

"Yes." After a long pause: "This is where I proposed to her." He looked over at Julie. "Isn't this a silly place to propose to the woman you love?"

She shook her head. "Not at all. It's a place of substance, Don. I can't think of a better place to promise your love to someone else."

He felt an almost overwhelming sense of relief that she'd understood.

"Let's walk," Julie said suddenly.

He looked over at her, surprised. "In the rain?"

"Sure!" She'd already pushed open the passenger door. The chilly, sharp, finely-divided rain hit him in the face as he opened his own door and got out. He felt it trickling inside the collar of his shirt.

"Julie!" he cried. "You'll catch your—" He stopped suddenly.

"My death?" she asked. She laughed and stuck out her tongue to catch the drops.

Don opened the back door of the car and pulled out an old yellow slicker for her, and a blue jacket for himself. He grabbed her as she turned around and around, laughing and playing in the rain. His arms around her stopped the turning, but not the laughing. Even Don began to laugh as they got into the slicker and jacket.

"You look like a little kid," he told her.

"I'm a bird!" she said, lifting her arms. The slicker billowed out behind her like wings. "I'm free, and I want to fly!"

Don held her tightly in his arms, her cheek pressed against the soft wetness of his jacket. With her arms around his waist, she hugged him back. It all seemed unreal to him. He could never remember having been this happy in his entire life. He almost wept for fear it would end when he opened his eyes.

They picked their way carefully across the broken ground and mud puddles. Close to the lighthouse, the ground was smoother, finely pebbled. They held hands, staying close together as they walked. There, under a small wooden shelter, was the granite bench where he and Emily had sat on the afternoon he proposed to her. He'd done it right, with his knees on the ground. They had also sat on this bench the night before that fatal accident.

They stopped under the shallow overhang at the old wooden door to shake some of the water from their clothes. Don could feel it trickling off his sleeves onto his hands. Julie took off the slicker and draped it over the bench. Holding both of his hands and turning him, she moved very close and raised her face up within inches of his. Tiny droplets covered her hair.

Her eyes connected with his, holding him, looking all the way into him. Then she released his hands, reached up, unzipped his jacket and reached her arms around inside of the warm space between the jacket and his back. She pulled herself against his body, laying her head against him.

The smell of her moistened hair, the warmth of her body, the rhythmic rise and fall of her breathing against him, overpowered his hesitancy. Don completed the embrace, spreading his hands across the back of her wet sweater and pulling her in. The sensation of her flourished to a bright sun and overrode all else.

Don breathed deep. He had to say something. His consciousness demanded it — about loving, wanting, needing... but something held him back.

Julie, not moving, began to speak in a quiet whisper. He moved the side of his face down so their moist cheeks touched, and his ear touched the softness of lips. "What?"

She spoke again, the words barely audible against the pattering rain. "I've never known anyone like you. I don't know why you love me... but... God, I'm glad you do."

Don did not respond. He didn't know how to.

With the same hushed, breathless voice, she said, "I can't believe we've met... now..." She brought her head up until their lips touched. The kiss did not have a forcing push, rather a soft blending as each of them wanted to yield to and receive the other's giving.

He did not want the feel of her body to leave. The press of her breasts and abdomen gave him a new perception, a limitless wholeness; her physical joining concentrated all of his conscious awareness toward her.

"Julie... I want to...." His words trailed off.

"Yes?" she prompted softly.

At last, with his heart thumping, he pulled away from her and, still holding her hands, lowered himself onto one knee.

"Julie," he said softly, "I want to propose to you."

She looked down at him, her eyes widening. "Don, how—"

"I want you to be my forever friend, Julie," he said solemnly. "Please say yes. You'll make me the happiest man in the world."

Now tears were streaming down her face as she pulled him up and threw her arms around him. "Yes, Don... yes... forever." Julie drew close and kissed him softly.

Don returned the kiss as he felt his own eyes burning with tears. He could not have believed it would be possible for him to love anyone like this again.

They kissed again, and he held her close to him. Despite the combined warmth of their bodies, the deepening cold eventually made its way through. A deep shiver ran through Julie, shaking her entire body.

Don broke the embrace and found her hand. "We'd better get you home so you can get dried out."

"But I don't want to go yet. Robert's in Los Angeles, so I don't have to rush back and fix dinner. Maybe we could get back in the car and sit for a while. I'll be fine."

"I don't know if that's a good idea. You don't want to catch a cold, doll."

"You'll keep me warm."

She reached for the yellow slicker and draped it over her shoulders, then they walked quickly through the rain, hand in hand, back to the car. As Don was opening her door, Julie turned again to look at the lighthouse.

"How powerful it seems. That so reminds me of you, Don... how you have been the light in my darkest times."

Don could say nothing. He walked around and got into the seat beside Julie. He put his key in the ignition, but Julie reached up and placed her hand on top of his.

"Not yet, Don, please. Can't we sit here for just a few minutes?"

When he saw that she was still shaking from the cold, Don pulled himself away from the seat and slipped his arms out of his jacket. "Okay, have it your way... always your way," he said, giving her a wink. Knowing her life's time was passing too quickly, he wondered if it wasn't the right thing to do, letting her fill her final hours in the way she chose. "But here, put my jacket on. That slicker isn't heavy enough to keep you warm."

With his help, Julie got out of the slicker, and he tossed it into the back seat. Then she stuck her arms into the sleeves of his jacket and immediately felt the warmth of the wool lining along with Don's own body heat, and her chills went away. Don reached his arm around Julie's shoulder and pulled her close to his side.

"There, how's that? Hmm? Is that better now?"

"I'm fine," Julie whispered.

They sat together peacefully for about forty-five minutes, Don giving occasional squeezes and Julie rubbing her hand across the top of his leg in a steady rhythm.

"You're gonna rub a hole in my pants," he protested.

Julie giggled. "You wish!"

Turning toward each other, they kissed repeatedly. Don realized that if they stayed much longer, the kiss wouldn't be enough.

"It's time to go, doll."

She groaned. "Please, Don, just two more minutes."

"You've had your two minutes." But as he pretended to discipline her, he grabbed her again and gave her the biggest kiss ever. "There, how's that?"

She sighed. "I was just thinking about how happy we could have been if we had met years ago."

Don was silent for a moment. Then he said, "We don't know that. I believe that life is all planned out for us, and everything happens in its own time. This is just the way for us... the only way it can be, love, the only way."

"I love you, Don. I'm glad to be your forever friend."

"I love you too, Julie."

Finally, he started the car and returned down the gravel lane to the highway. Julie lay her head against Don's shoulder, and they continued the ride in silence. Both were deep in their own thoughts — thoughts of life and death, and now and forever. Now the lighthouse, like so many things, had become a memory.

"Can we go back there again someday when it isn't raining?" she asked.

"Sure, love, I don't know why we can't."

But both of them knew most likely that *someday* would never come.

~

Since Robert would not be home for dinner, Don suggested that they stop at a coffee shop on the way to her house. Julie was extremely tired, but readily agreed. At least it would give her a little more time with Don before going home to the empty house.

She ate little, though, and it was obvious to Don that she was exhausted.

"This has been a long day for you," he said as they pulled into her driveway. He got out of the car and came around to open the door, helping her out. "Get some rest, doll. I'll give you a call tomorrow sometime, okay?"

She nodded. "Thanks for taking me out there, Don. I can see why it's such a special place for you."

He hugged and kissed her. "Doubly so now, Julie." He gave her a gentle swat on the bottom. "Now get inside and get to bed, okay? I don't want to tire you out."

She smiled and stood on her toes to kiss him again. "I'm glad we don't have any neighbors close by to see all this. Talk to you tomorrow."

"You bet, doll."

Chapter Twenty-Two

Sunday, June 1

Except for the day Cheryl was born, I think today has been the most beautiful day of my life. Thinking about what happened makes me feel like laughing and crying at the same time. Laughing because it was so ridiculous... so incredibly absurd. A grown woman and a grown man, acting like crazy children! But I feel like crying when I realize that these precious moments with Don will end all too soon.

I want to hold onto the happy times, not dwell on the sadness. I know that until that final moment comes for me, every time I look out at the pond, my heart will lighten and sing with happiness....

Julie slept fitfully, and every time she awoke in the darkness, her thoughts were on Don Lipton.

The first day of June arrived bright and sunny. The storm had moved away during the night, and by ten o'clock Julie knew it was going to be a warm, humid day. Early summer was often fickle in this part of California: cool enough for a jacket one day, and uncomfortably warm the next.

Julie went to her study and worked on the book for several hours, then went back again after lunch. Don called a little after three o'clock and said he'd expected to take her out for dinner, but then remembered that he had a business meeting at his church and probably wouldn't get out of that until late.

"I'm pretty tired anyway," she told him. "I'll probably just relax this evening."

She had a soup and salad for dinner, enjoying the luxury of not having to prepare the usual big dinner for Robert, then decided to go out to sit by the pond and watch the sunset.

She was still there an hour later when the moon, a thin sliver of pale light, arose. Little pinpoints of stars glittered like jewels on the water's flat surface.

It's so peaceful out here, she thought.

From all around her came the drone of cicadas and the bleat of crickets. She could hear the occasional muted purr of a car passing by on the roadway in front of the house, and from far away came the persistent barking of a dog.

She felt she should be doing something productive. There was laundry to do, and Robert's shirts needed to be ironed. The dishes from dinner were still stacked in the sink.

But she didn't feel like doing any of those things. For some reason, she didn't even feel like writing. She just wanted to stay here on the chaise lounge and enjoy this peaceful evening. Later, she could do all those other things. For now she was going to allow herself to waste her time — at least, a few minutes of it.

She was so glad that she and Robert had decided to have a pond instead of a swimming pool. Surrounded by grass and the maple trees which would one day provide shade for its entire surface, the pond looked like a miniature version of the small lake that Julie loved to visit when she was a teenager. She had often gone swimming in a secluded corner of the lake, where she was hidden from the other side by heavy vegetation.

She smiled as she remembered the first time she'd gone skinny dipping in that lake. It had been an afternoon in late August, the second day of blistering temperatures in the mid-nineties. The stored heat of the long summer day had radiated off the pavement and buildings in town, and even trees seemed to droop wearily. The air was motionless. On the streets, the sound of traffic was muffled, as if the thick air filtered the roar of engines and blaring of horns.

After a full day of work behind the counter at Mr. Webster's drug store, Julie had stopped by the lake on her way home. She didn't have her bathing suit, but she figured she could dip her toes in the water and perhaps absorb some of its coolness.

As she sat there on the bank, though, she'd been overcome by a sudden urge to jump in. She knew that the lake was deserted, and even if someone happened to drive down the little road, she would hear them coming long before they reached the lake. With the vegetation surrounding her private little cove, she doubted that anyone would even notice her here anyway.

Laughing at the craziness of it, she'd stripped down and leaped into the water, splashing around like a little girl and loving every moment of it. She liked the feeling of freedom, without the confines of clothing. It was as if all her worries had been stripped from her.

She knew it was also partly the sense of adventure — of daring. Even though she felt sure that she would have heard anyone approaching the lake long before they got close enough to see her, there was a sense of risk. She liked that.

Julie had never told her parents about her little adventure. But from that moment on, she stopped by the lake every chance she got and went swimming. Never again had she worn a swimsuit in that lake.

When she'd tried to get Robert to go skinny dipping after they were married, he looked at her with an almost comical expression of shock that she would even think of doing such a thing. She'd never brought it up again, and gradually, under the weight of his disapproval, she stopped doing it herself.

Now, gazing out at the still waters of the pond, the urge came back. It had been an unseasonably warm day, and she smiled, thinking about what it would feel like to slip naked into those cool, dark waters....

Surprised with herself, she realized that she was actually thinking seriously about it. Why shouldn't she do it? She was alone, and there were no nearby neighbors to peak at her through the shrubbery.

Once the notion had taken hold, there was no denying it. She pulled herself onto her feet and, laughing aloud, undressed and draped her clothing over the back of the chaise. The warm night air caressed her, and for a long moment she stood there marveling at how wonderful it felt.

Carefully, she stepped down the grassy bank, shivering slightly as the water level passed her thighs, her waist, and finally her shoulders.

It felt... *terrific!*

She yelled with the sheer joy of it, shouting out to the night sky and the stars. She ducked her head under and swam across one end of the pond, then kicked against the soft earth of the far shore and swam back. She splashed like a kid, throwing up sprays of water that glistened like jewels in the pale moonlight before pattering back onto the pond's surface.

God, it felt great to be alive!

"Julie?"

She froze, her eyes darting in the direction of the male voice. Had Robert returned early from his trip? *My God, what will he think of me?*

Then she spotted the figure coming toward her from the darkened back corner of the house, and realized immediately that the man, whoever he was, was taller than Robert. She couldn't see his face yet, but—

"Are you all right, doll?" he asked, coming closer.

She stared. Could it be...?

Moments later, the figure stepped out of the shadows, and there was no doubt. She sank a little lower into the water. "Don! How did... when did...." She stopped, got a grip on her thrashing thoughts, and said, "What are you doing here?"

"I called earlier and didn't get an answer." Now he was only a few feet away. She knew that in the darkness there was no way he could see her nakedness under the water, but still she drifted back away a few feet farther from the shore. "I knew Robert was gone, so I came by to make sure you were all right. I didn't get an answer at the door. While I was trying to decide what to do, I heard a yell from back here. Sounded like somebody was in trouble, so I came on around. Are you sure you're all right?"

"Yes, yes... I was just...." How could she possibly explain that she'd been yelling out of sheer joy of being naked in this cool water? "I decided to go for a swim. The water was a little colder than I expected."

"Ah...." He nodded. "Gosh, I wish I could join you, but I don't have a—" His words broke off suddenly as he glanced around for a place to sit, and spotted her clothing draped across the back of the chaise lounge. His eyes moved back to her. "No towel?"

She felt hot blood rush to her face, and was grateful for the darkness. "It was... well, sort of an impulse. I didn't really come out here to swim."

He looked at the discarded clothing again. Then his face broadened in a wide grin and he came to squat next to the water line. "So can I assume you're *au naturel?*"

Her face was burning. "No, of course not! What do you take me for?"

Still grinning, he patted the grass beside him. "Well, then, why don't you come up here and join me?"

Her eyes darted to her clothing, then returned to his face. "Don, I... well...."

He threw back his head and laughed.

"What's so funny?" she snapped. "I don't think—"

"You're okay, doll," he said, still chuckling. "There's nothing wrong with skinny dipping. Emily and I used to do it all the time. We loved it! And don't worry. I can't see a thing out there. Your integrity and modesty are well preserved."

She found herself smiling then, and after a moment she moved a little closer. "Robert would go ballistic if he knew I was out here like this... especially with another man present."

"Robert's in Los Angeles, right? What he doesn't know won't hurt him." Then his grin softened into a gentle smile. "Besides, I have no intention of doing anything that might cause hurt to others... or to our own relationship."

She tilted her head and looked at him for a moment, then suddenly slapped her hand into the water, sending a fine spray at him.

"Hey!" He scrambled backwards, shaking water off his hands and arms, then wiping a hand across his face.

Julie laughed. "Take that, Professor Lipton! That's for all the grief you gave me in class."

"You'd better watch out," he said, faking a serious, threatening tone. "I'll come right in there and give you a spanking, if you don't behave yourself."

"Ooh!" she squealed. "Sounds kinky!" She started laughing again. "I dare you!"

"You should know something about me, love," he said, beginning to unbutton his shirt. "I don't back down from dares."

Her eyes widened when he pulled off the shirt and tossed it onto the grass, then bent to untie his shoes. In a moment, his shoes and socks were beside the shirt, and his hands went to his belt.

"Uh... Don...." Her words dried up as he unhooked the belt and unbuttoned his slacks. "Wait!" She turned quickly away, splashing water up around her with her frantically paddling arms. Then she felt her toe touch the pond's muddy bottom, and realized she'd moved close enough to shore to stand. Behind her, she heard the sound of a zipper, then heard another garment hit the ground.

"Don't forget," he said. "You dared me."

"Yes, but—"

That was as far as she got before she heard him enter the water behind her, and gentle waves nudged at her. She turned then and found him three feet away. All she could see was his head — and the wide smile.

"You didn't really...." Her words caught in her throat, and she had to draw in another breath to try again. "You didn't take off... *everything,* did you?"

"Every stitch," he said. "You wouldn't want me to get my clothes all wet, would you? I might catch cold." He moved closer. "Isn't this what you wanted, doll? Isn't this what you meant when you dared me to come in?"

She couldn't speak. He'd moved up until he was directly in front of her. Then he lifted both hands and placed them on her bare shoulders, just under the surface of the water.

"Do you want me to go, Julie?" he asked, his voice soft now. "If you do, just say the word."

She knew the answer immediately. She didn't want him to go. She wanted him to hold her, to press himself against her. And she wanted so much more....

"No," she whispered. "I don't want you to go."

He moved his hands down along her arms, lifting her

hands out of the water. He brought one hand to his lips and gazed into her eyes as he slowly kissed each finger. Heat coursed through her body despite the cool water surrounding her. Then he lowered that hand and repeated the process with the other.

Finally he released her hands and placed his own hands on each side of her waist, drawing her closer. Just before she was sure their bodies would touch, he stopped pulling. He placed his hand under her chin and turned her face to his. She felt his soft lips move over hers with a feather light touch, which became more demanding. She slipped one arm around his neck as his warm, moist lips rocked against hers. His tongue slid across her lips, and she opened hers willingly for him. She was swept with the hollow ache and dizziness of desire, and it took every ounce of willpower to keep herself from melting her body against his.

At last he broke off the kiss and lowered his head to put his cheek against hers. "Oh, my love," he said hoarsely in her ear. "You are so beautiful."

Her body hungered for more. She felt his leg touch hers under the water, but it was a bare whisper, there and gone so quickly she wondered if she'd just imagined it. His hands ran slowly up and down along the small of her back. But even then he kept his body away from hers, although she felt sure that only millimeters of water separated them.

"Don...." she murmured.

Her pulse quickened as he made a necklace of small biting kisses about the base of her neck. With a swiftness that made her heart leap, he trapped her earlobe between his teeth and gave it a delicate nip.

"I feel as if I've known you forever," he murmured, stroking her back with a tenderness that made her shiver.

"Oh, Don...." All she could do was speak his name. She was powerless to say more.

"I'm hungry for you," he said, his mouth moving slowly against hers, more deeply and hungrily by the second, until the erotic pleasure of it, added to the sweet words, brought her arms up around his neck.

Then, with a groan, he drew away and pulled back.

Shocked, she looked up at him. "Don, what's wrong?"

"This isn't a good idea," he said, his voice husky. "In fact, it's the dumbest thing I've done in a long time." He came close and kissed her again, but this time his lips did not linger. "Turn around, doll. I'm getting out."

"No!" She startled herself with the vehemence in her voice. Then she reached out to touch his arm, and smiled. "Don, can't we just enjoy the pond for a little while? You're right. Going too far would... well, it's not a good idea. But the night is warm, the water is cool, and the stars are out. Can't we just swim for a little while and enjoy this beautiful evening together?"

He looked uncertainly at her for a moment, then smiled and nodded. "I can't think of anything I'd enjoy more than a swim under the stars with the woman I love."

For the next hour, they were like two happy children, splashing each other, swimming, and diving to the bottom of the pond. Neither of them gave another thought to the other's nakedness. It seemed perfectly natural to be together in this way, unashamed of their bodies. This was not, Julie realized, a sexual experience. It was something much deeper... It was a loving experience, and for certain it was something she would treasure for as many days as she had left.

For a while, even the pain in her chest seemed to ease, as if to give her a break so she could enjoy the evening.

Eventually Julie began to tire, though, and Don was the one who saw it in her face and suggested that it was time to stop. He turned his back while she got out of the pond and went into the house for towels.

Wrapped in terry-cloth robes, they pulled two chaise lounges up side by side at the water's edge and sat there for another hour, talking and holding hands while the night air turned cooler. It was past midnight when they picked up their clothing at last and took it into the house to dress — in separate rooms.

"This has been the most wonderful evening of my life," Don said as they stood together at the front door. He framed her face in his hands and kissed her tenderly, then brushed a lock of damp hair out of her eyes. "I didn't wear you out, did I? Are you feeling all right?"

"I've never felt better." She leaned forward and rested her head on his shoulder.

He held her tight, his hand stroking her hair, her back. Then he kissed her again. "I love you, Julie."

"I love you, too." She returned his kiss, this time feeling not the hot passion of earlier, but the gentle love from the heart that runs much deeper than physical lovemaking.

A moment later, he opened the door and was gone.

Chapter Twenty-Three

Monday, June 2

I had a long talk today with Cheryl, and I tried to make her see what a special friend Don Lipton has become. I think she understands. At least, she's supportive. I love her so much... more than I can ever express in words.

Robert returned from his trip today and had a big surprise for me. A few years ago — or even a few months ago — I would have been delighted with it. But now it's too late. I know he has trouble accepting that. I also know he didn't like the surprise I had for him: Tomorrow I'll be going into the hospital....

If the pain in her body had eased for the evening in the pond, by morning it had redoubled its efforts to make her life miserable. Her joints ached, and her chest felt as if it was filling with liquid fire with each breath.

She knew that she hadn't been getting enough rest. She probably hadn't helped anything with the trip to the lighthouse and the impulsive swim of the night before, but she would not have given up those few precious hours with Don Lipton for anything. Whatever it had cost her was more than worth it.

Besides, these symptoms had been worsening over the past several days. She felt sure that the pain she was experiencing now would have come regardless of what she had done over the weekend.

She stayed in bed until past ten, then decided she'd better get up and at least be dressed before Robert got home. She thought he'd said he would be home before noon.

She wouldn't have believed that the pain in her chest could get worse, but it did. She was slumped at the kitchen table with a cup of tea when Cheryl called at a little after eleven to see how she was doing, and Julie forced herself to carry on a pleasant conversation despite the spikes of pain.

"How's Matthew?" she asked, wanting to steer the conversation away from herself.

"A little fussy, but otherwise fine," Cheryl said. "I have an appointment with Dr. Wagner for a regular check-up tomorrow."

"Good. Let me know how it comes out."

They talked for a few more minutes, then Julie said she had to go and get some housework done before Robert got home from his trip.

After hanging up, though, she immediately called Dr. Cole's office. He was busy with a patient, but his receptionist assured her that he would call back as soon as possible. Only minutes later, the phone rang.

"Julie, this is David Cole. What's up?"

"You told me to call if the pain got worse. I feel awful today. I can hardly breathe."

"Is anything else bothering you?"

"No... well, yes. My ankles are swollen, and my hands are so puffy I can hardly bend my fingers."

"Did you check your temperature?"

"No, but I don't feel like I have a fever."

"All right. I think you should do as I've been suggesting. I think you should check into the hospital for a few days. Do it right now, Julie. I'll call and set it up. I want to run some tests and see if we can't help you."

"Robert's away on a trip today—"

"Can't someone else bring you?"

"Well...." This was all happening too quickly. Julie didn't want to call Cheryl and tell her that she had to go to the hospital on such short notice. Cheryl would know that Julie's illness was more serious than she had been letting on. And she didn't even want to think about how Robert would react if he got home and found that she'd been admitted to the hospital. She needed a little time to prepare them for this.

"Dr. Cole, it would be a lot easier for me to come in tomorrow. Wouldn't that be just as well?"

"We aren't talking about buying a car, Julie. We're talking about your life. I think you should come to the hospital today—"

"But—"

"And for sure, if you aren't at Tyler General by eight o'clock tomorrow morning, I'm going to come looking for you."

"Okay, Dr. Cole. I'll be there in the morning. I promise."

"Take it easy today. And if the pain worsens, you go right over. Promise?"

"I promise. Thank you, David."

"Okay, Julie. I'll see you in the morning."

Just as she was hanging up the telephone, Robert opened the front door and came in with his small suitcase.

"Hi, honey." He put down the suitcase and came to kiss her on the cheek. "Who were you talking to?"

Julie hated to tell him, but she knew nothing would be gained by putting it off. "Dr. Cole wants me to go into the hospital for a few days. I told him I'd come in tomorrow morning."

Robert scowled. "Is that really necessary? What's wrong? Doesn't Cole have enough sick patients that he has to keep running these tests on you?"

She stared at him. "Don't be silly, Robert. He wouldn't put me through all of this just to keep busy."

"Maybe he wants to remodel his office and needs the money," Robert said. "Listen, Julie, the new corrugating machine is being installed in the plant tomorrow. I'll have to be there all day. I can't take a chance of something going wrong. Do you think you can get Cheryl to take you to the hospital?"

She couldn't believe what she'd heard. He really wouldn't even take her to the hospital? "I suppose I can try...." Then she remembered that Cheryl had an appointment to take Matthew to the pediatrician. "But—"

"Good girl." He was already turning away. "I've got to grab some lunch and get down to the plant. I got some price breaks in Los Angeles. Can't wait to tell Dick about them. Fix me a quick sandwich while I wash up, okay?"

Julie stared after him as he hurried down the hall. Then, wincing, she got to her feet and went to the refrigerator.

～

Julie was lying down that afternoon when Don called.

"Hi!" he said brightly. "How's my little mermaid doing today?"

That made her smile. "This little mermaid will be staying on dry land for a while, I think."

He laughed. "That's probably a good idea. I was wondering if you'd want to have lunch with me tomorrow. We can have an office picnic again and talk about the book. Do you like egg salad?"

She opened her mouth instantly to say yes, that she would love to come and have lunch with him. Then she remembered her conversation with Dr. Cole. "No...."

"Well, then, how about pastrami? The deli near my house has the best pastrami you'll ever taste."

"It isn't that, Don. I just can't come tomorrow." She realized that she would have to tell him that she would be going to the hospital. Dr. Cole had said she would probably be there for several days. There was no way she'd be able to hide that from Don.

"For tests?" he repeated after she'd told him.

"Mostly. Dr. Cole is hoping they can...." Her voice faltered. "Well, that they can find a way to buy me a little more time."

"Then you have to do it," he said. "You have to grab any chance at all. What time will you be going in? Can I come up and see you?"

"Sure," she said, marveling at how his simple question made her feel so much better. "I'm not sure what time I'll be getting there, though. Dr. Cole wants me to check in by eight o'clock, but Robert has something important going on at the plant."

This brought a short pause. "He can't even find the time to take you to the hospital?"

"He has to be there," she said. "And I don't want to ask Cheryl. She's taking Matthew to the doctor tomorrow. But I can find somebody—"

"You just did," he told her. "I'll pick you up a little after seven."

"Don't you have a class in the morning?"

"I'll have somebody else take it. That's no problem. You just be ready to go, okay?"

"Well... okay, if you're sure it's no trouble."

"I'm glad to do it, love. I'll see you then."

She had just hung up from talking to Don when the phone rang again. Sighing, she picked it up. "Hello?"

"Mom?" It was Cheryl's voice. "Is something wrong? You sound awful."

"Just tired."

After a brief pause: "I talked to Dad a little while ago. He says you're going to have to go into the hospital for some tests tomorrow."

Julie closed her eyes and lay back on the bed. She hadn't even thought about the possibility that Robert might tell Cheryl about it. He hardly seemed concerned about it himself. Julie had been hoping to play it down as much as possible. The last thing she wanted to do was cause Cheryl and Tom to worry about her.

"Mom? Are you still there?"

"Yes, Cheryl—"

"Why didn't you tell me you were going into the hospital?"

"I didn't want you to worry, honey. I still don't. There's nothing you can do besides pray for me, and I know you already do that. I can't believe your father got you so upset. He knows I didn't want to cause you distress."

Cheryl responded as if she hadn't heard a word Julie had said. "Mom, I can't believe you. You know that I want to be there for you. It's much more stressful when you hide all these things from me. Now listen to me. Dad said he has to work all day tomorrow. I have an early appointment for Matthew, but I'll be done in plenty of time to take you to the hospital by ten. I won't take no for an answer."

Julie hesitated momentarily. "Dr. Cole wants me there at eight—"

"Then I'll just call and change Matthew's appointment. He's getting better, anyway—"

"I don't want you to do that, Cheryl. I knew your father had to work, so I already asked a friend to take me."

This brought a momentary pause. Then: "A friend? Who is your friend?"

"I've asked Don Lipton to take me tomorrow, honey. He

only has two classes over the summer session, and he wanted to do it. He knows how concerned I am about Matthew, and he was trying to help both of us. Please try to understand."

"Don Lipton is...." Cheryl's words trailed off, and another pause drew out. "He's a *friend* now? Mom, you're finished with his class. I don't understand why you've even kept in touch with him. You always said he was a total jerk. I can't believe you would rather have a jerk take you to the hospital than your own daughter."

Julie issued a brief prayer for Divine help in explaining all this to her daughter. "I'm sorry, Cheryl. I know this is hard for you to understand." She glanced downward for a moment, then refocused on her daughter. "When Don read my final assignment, he thought... well, he gave me an *A* in the class—"

"An *A!*" Cheryl repeated incredulously. "Mom, I thought you said you were getting a solid *C.*"

"I was," Julie replied. "But he really liked that final paper. In fact, Don is helping me develop a novel, Cheryl. And yes, I see him now and then. The 'jerk' has become a very good friend."

"Well...." Cheryl seemed to be at a loss for words.

"I know that Don and I have had our ups and downs," Julie said. Suddenly it became important to her to make Cheryl see Don in this different light. "Cheryl, I learned something about Don Lipton that changed the way I saw him. It was a terrible thing that happened twenty years ago."

She went on to tell Cheryl about her conversation in the cafeteria with Rick Marston, and her subsequent research in the library that uncovered the newspaper articles about the accident.

"It was awful, Cheryl. Seeing that car, and knowing what Don must have felt like when he woke up in the hospital and learned that he was the only one who had survived. It had a dramatic impact on him. He gave up writing, even though it was clear he was a gifted writer. I think it tore him all up inside."

"Well... that sounds pretty bad, all right," Cheryl agreed. "Since he was driving the car, it must be especially horrible."

"I already told you about the time I saw Don with the little boy at the college," Julie said. "That made me realize that the real Don Lipton is still inside there. It was the caring, loving man who must've existed before that terrible accident. Now I know that Don maintained this rough exterior in order to keep people from getting too close to him. His heart was shattered by the accident. He knew the only way he could protect himself from losing such love again was to never feel it again, so he made certain by being the tough guy that he wouldn't get involved."

Cheryl took a moment to absorb that. "I can understand how that could happen. But... well, Mom, then how do *you* fit into the picture?"

Julie sighed. "Oh, honey, that is so hard to explain. When I thought about what Don went through after the accident, and how it changed his life—" Suddenly Julie found herself crying. "I hurt so much for him. Really, Cheryl, he is such a beautiful person. I am so lucky to have him in my life. I don't ask you to understand me... but babe, as my daughter, I am asking you to trust me."

"Mom...." Cheryl's voice faltered. When she spoke again, her words were filled with compassion. "Mom, I trust you, and I trust your judgment about people. You were right about Tom, weren't you? If you hadn't told me what a great guy he was, I might never have gone on a second date with him. I know Professor Lipton must be special for you to care this much for him."

"He is, Cheryl," Julie said. "Believe me, he is."

"What was that final assignment you were talking about? You said he wants you to turn it into a book?"

Julie told Cheryl about the story she'd written about the pianist Paul Keller, and how Don had reacted to it.

"Wow!" Cheryl exclaimed. "That took a lot of guts, Mom. There's no way you could've known how he would react. Weren't you afraid he would get mad?"

"I was terrified," Julie said. "But that only sank in after it was too late, after I'd already turned in the assignment. When he called and said he wanted to talk to me about it, I was sure he was furious. At first he had a hard time fully accepting that the story was really about him. But now we've been able to talk openly about it, and he's letting his true feelings show for the first time in twenty years."

"That must make you feel pretty special yourself."

There was no way, Julie knew, that she could ever express just how special it made her feel. "I think Don knew that I needed to empty my heart out to someone, too. Now I'm letting it all come out in my writing." She paused to draw a steadying breath. "I have so much to say to the people I love. My book will let me do that."

"Wow...." By now, Cheryl was also choking back tears. After a few moments of silence, she continued. "All right, Mom. I'll come down to see you tomorrow, if you're sure you don't want me to take you—"

"There's no need, really. Take care of Matthew, and I'll see you later in the day. Goodbye, honey."

After returning the telephone to its cradle, Julie sank back onto the bed.

∼

"You look much better," Robert said that evening when he got home and came into the kitchen. Despite the terrible pain, Julie was preparing dinner. "Did you take those pills like I said?"

She shook her head without looking up from the stove. The tuna casserole — one of Robert's favorite dishes — was out of the oven, and she was ready to put everything on the table. "I don't need antacid pills, Robert." She almost added, *That's for heartburn, not for heartache*, but decided she didn't want to go into those waters.

Robert looked as though he was going to say something, then changed his mind. Instead, he sniffed appreciatively. "Dinner smells great, Ju. Thanks for going to so much work." He kissed her on the cheek, then unfolded the newspaper and wandered into the dining room.

Ten minutes later, they were seated across from each other at the table.

"Delicious!" Robert said after tasting the casserole. He sounded as if he meant it. "You're the best cook ever, Ju."

"Thank you, Robert," she said quietly. She really didn't feel like talking, but she felt obligated to ask how his day had gone, even if he seldom asked about hers. "Does everything look good for the installation of the new machine tomorrow?"

"Sure does," he said brightly. "I can't believe how well it's all turning out. We're actually a little below budget. Can you believe it? The engineers were able to use the existing housing for the corrugator, so that saved having to build a new one. It'll mean that everything will be finished a couple of weeks ahead of schedule, too."

"That's nice, Robert," Julie said, trying to work up a little enthusiasm. All she could think about was that she would be admitted to the hospital in the morning, and the more she thought about that, the more scared she became of those tests Dr. Cole would be running.

"You bet it's nice," Robert said.

When he didn't say anything else, Julie looked up and found him grinning at her. He looked like the proverbial cat that had swallowed the canary.

"What is it?" she asked. "What's wrong?"

"Do I look like something's wrong?" he asked, still grinning.

She knew he was up to something, and she didn't have the patience to dig it out of him. Robert was like a little boy when he had a secret to share. "Come on, Robert. I'm too tired to play guessing games."

His grin didn't falter even the slightest. "Ju, I've got a surprise for you."

She waited, beginning to feel a little uneasy. This had to be something big for Robert to be playing it up so much.

"I've been thinking about something special we should do together," he went on. "The plant has been taking up all my time lately, and I know you haven't been feeling very well. What we really need is a vacation. We need to get away from everything and get ourselves recharged. What do you think?"

She stared at him. She hadn't been able to get Robert to take a real vacation in years. "Where would we go?"

Now the grin widened even more. "Oh... I was thinking about Rome."

Her eyes widened. Surely she'd heard him wrong. "Rome?"

"You bet! In September the plant will be up and running again. I told Dick that I was going to take my wife on a dream vacation, and he'd just have to hold down the fort for a week." He reached across the table and took her hand. "Ju, you'll love it over there, and it'll be beautiful in September. I've already talked to a travel agent. She's getting it all together. Think of it, Ju. A week in Rome!"

He leaned closer, watching her expectantly, the grin fixed in place. She knew he was waiting for her to fall all over herself thanking him for his thoughtfulness and gushing about how much she was looking forward to the trip.

But at the moment she just couldn't work up that kind of reaction. She was worried sick about what Dr. Cole's tests would turn up, and her chest was aching terribly.

"Robert, I...."

"I know it'll be expensive," he said, his face almost glowing with pride. "But heck, if I can't spend it on you, what can I spend it on? And I know Dick can handle the plant. Besides, I'll be just a phone call away, if a problem comes up."

How could she tell him that there was no way she would be able to go to Rome with him in September? She didn't even know for sure that she would still be alive then. If she was, she was sure she would be feeling even worse than she was now. Why had he waited until now, when she was too sick to enjoy such a trip?

Besides, a week in Rome would mean a week away from Don Lipton. She couldn't even bear to think about that. Every moment she could spend with him was precious to her now.

As she was thinking about this, Robert picked up his fork again and attacked his food, eating rapidly and talking about everything they would see in Rome. He'd gotten some brochures from the travel agent, and she was going to book some tours for them in advance so they wouldn't miss anything.

"She says September is really the best month to be there," he said. "The weather is still nice, and we won't have the heavy crowd of summer tourists. I know it'll make you feel better, Ju. All you need is a change of scenery and a little relaxation—"

"This morning you said that all I needed was some antacid pills," she reminded him.

He looked a little irritated. "I was just telling you what my mother always used to do for those stomach pains. If you want to have some expensive tests in the hospital, then I guess that's what you'll do."

She put down her fork and stared at him. "Robert, do you think I *want* to go into the hospital tomorrow?"

He shook his head. "No. But I do think you're putting way too much stock in what that doctor has been telling you. If you'd just get some rest and take it easy, you'll feel better. In fact, just thinking about this trip in September will probably be enough to boost your spirits. Why don't you call Dr. Cole back and cancel those tests for tomorrow?"

"I'm not going to cancel anything. But you don't have to worry about taking me. A friend from the college said he'd do it."

"Some friends you have," Robert snapped. "What kind of friend takes you to the hospital when you aren't even sick? Wake up, Julie. The entire bunch of medical processionals are using you for a guinea pig. Can't you see that?"

Julie could no longer hold her anger back. "Damn it, Robert, who do you think you are? Why don't you grow up and get real? I'm so damned sick, but as always, you walk around ignoring it all. This time it isn't going to help you. Can't you even pretend to care what's happening to me? And you can forget about that trip to Rome. If I'm still alive by then, there's no way I'll be able to go."

Julie ran into the bedroom and threw herself onto the bed. She needed to cry, but she knew that Robert wouldn't care if she did. She felt so terribly alone.

A short time later, Robert opened the door and said, "I'm going over to the shop for a while."

Julie didn't respond. She didn't care where he went, or for that matter, if he ever came back. She pulled the blankets up over her eyes and tried to shut out the world.

Chapter Twenty-Four

Tuesday, June 3

Well, Dr. Cole, you win. I have finally agreed to go to the hospital for a short time for more extensive testing and treatment. I don't want to go, and I don't want to know whatever it is the tests will prove. My entire body is aching; my heart as well. It aches from the pain of my illness, and more so from the pain of finding love too late in life. I'm not sure which of the pains is worse. Both will be gone soon, and so shall I....

The hospital was set against the backdrop of the distant mountains that were part of the Sierra Nevada. It was an L-shaped, two-story structure, very modern in design, a striking mix of flat planes and graceful curves faced in dark green and gray stone. It was surrounded by a parking lot and by immense expanses of well-maintained grass, shaded by a few trees.

After parking and going in through the main lobby, they were directed around from here to there, and eventually found themselves seated at one of those little cubicles across from a middle-aged, bespectacled woman who asked Julie about insurance, medical history, religious affiliation, and who to contact in case of emergency. She seemed suspicious about the fact that the man who had brought Julie to the hospital was not her husband. Not once did she make full eye contact with Julie, and she made not the slightest effort to seem friendly. Clearly, Julie was just part of her work day. Her job was to make sure no blanks were left on the forms, and she approached it with cool precision.

After blood was drawn and an electrocardiogram was administered, Julie was wheeled up to the second floor. The nursing station was positioned at the center of the rooms like an island in order to give the nursing staff quick access to the patients. Julie and Don saw several of these patients shuffling down the halls in their wrinkled hospital gowns, connected by various tubes to wheeled IV stands which they pushed along beside them.

Don waited outside her small private room while Julie got undressed and slipped into the shapeless hospital gown. It immediately made her feel even more vulnerable. Her room, with its sterile, light-blue walls and tile floor, was typical of other hospital rooms Julie had seen. Various pieces of medical equipment clung to the wall behind the bed or stood beside it, ready to be attached to her in order to monitor her body or administer medicines to it.

"Looks like you're all set," Don said after he had come in and sat in the chair beside her bed. She noticed the gleam of sweat on his brow, even though the room was uncomfortably cool to her.

"Are you okay?" she asked.

He nodded and forced a grin. "I didn't realize it was so obvious. I hate hospitals."

She was going to ask why, then realized it would have been a dumb question. He had regained consciousness in a hospital room twenty years ago, only to learn that his wife and daughter were dead. He had probably lain in a hospital bed for several days, grieving for his loss. It was no wonder that he didn't like hospitals.

She took his hand and squeezed it. "You don't have to stay."

"No, I'll be all right." He looked at the clock on the wall. "I'll have to leave in time for my afternoon class, though. I figured you'd be tired of me by then, anyway. So what kinds of tests will they be doing?"

"More blood tests," Julie said. "Sometimes I wonder if they haven't already gotten it all. Dr. Cole says he wants to do some kind of kidney test, too."

"Not too painful, I hope."

"He said they would be using a local anesthetic for it. Anyway, they won't be doing that until tomorrow. I can spend the whole day thinking about it."

"Well... you could," he said. "Or you could spend the day working on your book. You brought your notebook with you, I assume?"

Julie nodded toward the bag leaning against the wall. "Yes, sergeant, I brought it. Can I rest a while before working on it, sir?"

He laughed and leaned over to kiss her on the forehead. "You can work on it after I'm gone. I expect to see lots of progress when I come back tomorrow."

She attempted a half-salute. "Yes, sir!"

~

Don left a little before noon, and Julie did manage to get some writing done before Cheryl came by to visit her. Because of Matthew's age, they wouldn't allow him on the floor, but Julie felt uplifted with Cheryl and her usual cheerful disposition.

"I'm glad you're here, Mom," she said, sitting in the same chair Don had been in a few hours earlier. "I'm hoping Dr.

Cole will find something that will help."

Julie didn't tell Cheryl that all Dr. Cole was hoping for was to find a way to extend her life for another few months. "What did the doctor say about Matthew?" she asked, wanting to deflect the conversation away from her own health.

"He didn't find anything specific, but he wants to see Matthew again next week. He said he thinks Matthew might have colic. I hope he's wrong. Kendra's daughter had colic for two months after she was born. Kendra said it was a nightmare."

Kendra Kessler — now Kendra Landrum, Julie reminded herself — had been Cheryl's best friend since they were freshmen in high school. "There are worse things to have than colic. It wouldn't be the end of the world." When she saw Cheryl smile, she said, "What's so funny?"

"How many times you have said those words! 'It's not the end of the world.' Mom, I remember as a little girl, falling down on the pavement in front of the house and scraping my knee. Although it was a minor hurt, at such a young age it seemed major to me. I began to cry, and when I was sure that I had your complete attention, I cried even harder. I'll never forget how much better it felt when you washed my knee and applied medication and a bandage. You kissed my cheek, held me close, and whispered, 'Honey, I know how much it hurts, but believe me, it's not the end of the world.' Do you remember that?"

"Of course I do, Cheryl. And that was a pretty deep gash. But I couldn't let you know that I was worried, or you would have been hysterical."

"Now the truth comes out. You said it again when I was engaged to Michael. Remember how you tried to encourage me to take time and be sure I had found the right person for a lifetime partner? I was 'head over heels in love' with that jerk. I couldn't imagine why you didn't want me to marry him. After all, what could a mother know about such things?"

Julie smiled as she recognized signs of her daughter's maturity. "Now don't be so hard on yourself, honey. We all needed time to grow up. Some people never do."

"Gosh, Mom, I'll never forget how crushed my heart was when I realized what a rat Michael was. I didn't think I could possibly go on living."

"Oh, I do remember. You were so unhappy, and I felt so helpless. Unfortunately, someday you'll learn for yourself that one of the most difficult parts of being a mother is to watch your child suffer over something which is beyond your control. You can love her and tell her you care, but it doesn't take the pain away. You pray and hope that she learns something from the experience that will bring her happiness in the future."

"Mom, did I ever tell you how much I appreciated it when you didn't tell me I told you so, even though you did a hundred times. I knew from the beginning that you didn't approve of the relationship. But instead of shoving my mistake in my face, you just held me close and let me cry. Then, sharing my sadness as only a mother could, you told me, 'I truly know how much you are hurting. But believe it or not, this isn't the end of the world.'

"You were so right. Only a year later, I met my Tom, and you know the rest. Oh, Mom, I love him so much! And now we have little Matthew... I have never before felt so loved or so happy. Life seems almost too perfect."

Cheryl was beaming as she talked of her life, and Julie felt satisfaction in knowing her daughter would be able to know the love she had known... the love of a man... the love for a child....

Suddenly her mother's silence triggered a painful reality for Cheryl. Scooting over closer to Julie, she threw her arms around her and hugged her with all her might. "Oh, I love you so much, Mom. Why do you have to be sick? It is so unfair...."

Cheryl began to cry.

For a brief moment, Julie remained quiet, lost in a world of her own, seemingly so far away. Then suddenly her eyes met her daughter's. Even in the midst of her own private hell, she put her "little girl's" feelings first.

"Now what are *you* crying for?" she asked gently. "I'm the one who's sick. You've got to be brave enough for both of us. Oh, God, Cherrie, I know how much this hurts you. But regardless of what happens to me, you've got to be strong. You have your Tom and beautiful little son, and your father to take care of. No matter what you think right now, I promise you, honey, this isn't the end of the world." She gave Cheryl another squeeze, then drew back. "Now you get back home to your little boy. If he isn't feeling well, he needs his mama."

Cheryl drew back and wiped the tears from her eyes. "He's got his papa right now. Tom came home for lunch. He brought some work with him and told me to stay as long as I needed. I think Matthew is in pretty good hands." She pulled a tissue from her purse and blew her nose. "Dad says you don't want to go to Rome with him."

Julie sighed. She realized that she shouldn't have been surprised to learn that Robert had been blabbing about her again. "There's no way I'll be able to go, Cheryl. This disease... well, I won't be getting better. I'll be feeling even worse in September. I only wish your father had asked me a couple of years ago."

Cheryl wiped at her eyes again. Julie saw that she would need some repair to her mascara. "So do I, Mom. It's too bad that Dad has always been so tied up with the plant. But I think he really wanted to go this time."

Julie thought about that. "It's probably another example of denial for Robert. He doesn't want me to be this sick, so he just plans a trip to Rome assuming I'll go and that everything will be fine."

"He's having a hard time with it," Cheryl said, still sniffling. She blew her nose again, then put away the tissue. "Have you been working on that book Professor Lipton talked to you about?"

Julie nodded, and felt a surge of renewed strength just thinking about the book and about Don. "So far it's going really well. I don't know...." She'd been about to say that she didn't know if she would have time to finish it, but decided she didn't want to hurt Cheryl even more. "I'm hoping it'll turn out to be a good book."

"I'm sure it will, Mom." Cheryl leaned over the bed and kissed Julie on the cheek. "I love you, Mom." Then she got to her feet. "Guess I'd better go home and relieve Tom. If I know Tom, he's probably ordered a pizza from Gambino's and can't figure out why Matthew doesn't like the anchovies."

Julie laughed. "Thanks for coming by, Cherrie. I'll see you tomorrow?"

"Wild horses couldn't keep me away," Cheryl promised.

~

That afternoon, the nursing staff and lab workers kept Julie busy, taking her seemingly all over the hospital for various blood tests, x-rays, and other procedures she barely understood. Dr. Cole had said he was going to put a rush on the results so they could know as soon as possible what they were up against.

Julie was exhausted when Robert came by after dinner. He had stopped at the gift shop to buy a Hershey bar for her and the evening newspaper for himself. He gave her a hasty peck on the cheek and handed her the candy, which she placed inside the bedside table in case she wanted it later.

"Sorry I'm late," he said, reaching for the television remote control, which hung by a strap from the bed rail. He clicked on CNN. "It took a little longer than I'd expected to get the new corrugator installed. It looks great, though. It'll run nearly twice as fast as the old one, with only a fraction of wasted linerboard." He sat in the chair beside her bed, kicked off his shoes, and placed his feet on the blankets beside her. Light brown socks, of course. "How are you feeling, Ju?"

She started telling him about all the tests she'd been subjected to that afternoon, and about how tired she was — but it was clear that his attention was already focused on the news broadcast. She gave up and remained silent while he made his usual comments about politics and crime and education, and anything else that happened to come up on the screen. What Robert lacked in attention to her, he more than made up for with opinions about everything else.

She lay there quietly, struggling with an impulse to scream and throw something at the television... or at Robert.

He turned the television off only when Dr. Cole came in an hour later for his evening rounds, and Robert actually seemed to go out of his way to be polite. Dr. Cole said he expected to have at least some of the test results back by the next morning, and he instructed Julie to rest and to eat as much as she could while she was in the hospital.

Eat more and get more rest. His usual refrain. Julie nodded and promised to try.

Robert didn't stay long after the doctor had gone, and Julie didn't mind. Robert seemed even more uncomfortable in the hospital than Don Lipton.

Later, Julie tried without success to fall asleep, and she wondered how any of the patients were expected to get the rest they needed. There was constant noise from outside her open door: the beeping of monitors, the clatter of passing carts, the moans and coughs of other patients, the ringing of telephones at the nursing station.

If she could somehow manage to ignore the noise, there was the bed to deal with. The mattress was hard, and every time she moved, the plastic mattress cover under the sheets crackled like a thin layer of breaking ice.

Eventually, she managed to fall into a restless sleep, and awakened exhausted to the whispering, early-morning hush of the hospital and the scent of disinfectants.

Chapter Twenty-Five

Cheryl made it a point to visit her mother just before noon the next day. Again, Tom was able to come home for lunch, and said he actually preferred having the chance to get away from the telephone at the office and take care of some paperwork. He also enjoyed having some time to spend with Matthew, and said he would be glad to feed him lunch.

Matthew wasn't as fussy as he'd been the day before, and Cheryl was hoping that it would turn out just to have been a mild case of indigestion rather than colic. As her mother had said, it wouldn't be the end of the world — but Cheryl would be just as happy to get through this period of Matthew's life without having to deal with colic. Besides causing a fussy baby, she would hate to see her son going through the pain of cramps.

At the hospital, she found her mother lying in bed, looking almost as pale as the bed sheets. Smiling, she leaned over to kiss Julie on the cheek. "How are you doing, Mom?"

"I'm fine," Julie answered, although Cheryl felt sure that she was working hard to put some strength and conviction into her voice. "These doctors just want to prod and poke on me a little more before they let me go home."

She didn't *look* fine, and Cheryl was even more worried than before. Julie's face was drawn; her eyes looked like dark smudges of weariness. But Cheryl decided not to comment on that. Her mother didn't need to have someone telling her how bad she looked.

"I brought some magazines," Cheryl said, placing the stack on the bedside table. "I just gathered up several that I know you like."

Before Julie could respond, the door behind Cheryl opened. She turned, expecting to see a doctor or nurse entering the room — and froze. It was Professor Donald Lipton.

"Hi, Don," Julie said, instantly perking up. "Come on in. I was just talking to my daughter, Cheryl. Cheryl, this is Don Lipton, my former writing teacher... and my friend. And look at the beautiful flowers!"

Lipton was clutching a bouquet of multicolored flowers in his left hand. But for a moment, Cheryl couldn't even breathe, much less acknowledge the introduction. She could only imagine how embarrassing it would be if he recognized her. When she had visited the college that day to check up on him, she had tried to make herself look like a student. But that had consisted only of carrying a few books and wearing the jeans and pullover that was the most common attire of college-age girls. She hadn't done anything to conceal her actual appearance.

She could only hope that in this different setting, Lipton wouldn't recognize her as the student who'd dropped her book on his foot.

"Gl... glad to meet you, Dr. Lipton," she said, finding her voice at last. "It is 'Doctor' isn't it? I believe that's what my mother used to call you."

Lipton gave Cheryl an odd look — a slight tilting of the head and narrowing of the eyes. "Yep, I do have a 'doctor' before my name at college, but 'Don' will be just fine." He paused, studying her face. "You look a little familiar, young lady. Have we met before?"

Cheryl felt the blood rush to her face under his scrutiny. "No, I don't think we've been introduced before." Well, that was a sort of truth, she thought miserably to herself. She just wanted to get out of there. "Well...." she said, edging toward the door, "it looks like you have enough company without me right now, Mom. I'm sure you have a lot to talk about. I'll see you again soon, Mom. Probably tomorrow." She forced her eyes back to Don Lipton's. "It was nice to meet you, Professor Lipton."

"Oh, the pleasure was all mine," Lipton said with that half-smirk she'd seen there at the college elevator. And there was that look in his eyes again — that amused, knowing look. Was she just imagining it, or was he laughing at her?

She offered another shaky smile at her mother, then turned quickly and fled from the room.

~

After the door closed behind her, Julie turned a quizzical look at Don. "What was that all about?"

Smiling, Don sat down in the chair beside the bed. "What do you mean?"

"Cheryl... well, she was acting peculiar, to say the least."

"Ah, well." He reached over and patted her hand. "Young ladies often find themselves at a loss for words when they're in my presence." He held out the bouquet. "These are for you, doll."

"They're beautiful!" she exclaimed. The stems of the flowers were wrapped in a dampened paper towel, and as she looked more closely, she realized it was an unlikely combination of roses, carnations, marigolds, and violets. "Did you get these in the gift shop downstairs?"

He had a smirk on his face. "In a way." He got up and filled one of the hospital's plastic water containers from the sink, then put the flowers in it and set it on the windowsill.

"In a way?" she repeated, puzzled. From the look on his face, she knew he was up to something.

"Well... I happened to be coming in just as one of the hospital workers was loading up his cart to deliver all the phoned-in orders to the rooms. Like the gentleman I am, I offered to carry some of them for him, since his cart was already full. I made all the deliveries on this floor for him."

Her mouth dropped open as she realized what he was saying. "You *stole* those flowers?"

"Naw... well, just one flower from each of the arrangements. They'll never be missed, but they sure made up a nice bouquet, don't you agree?"

Julie had to laugh. "You're incorrigible, Donald Lipton."

"That's me, doll." He came to sit on the side of the bed next to her. "Are you doing okay? Were the tests rough today?"

"Yes, to each," she answered, unable to stop herself from thinking about the contrast between Robert's visit and Don's. Robert's main interest was the newspaper and the television. Don's concern was clearly for her. "The tests were awful, but I got through it okay. I'm feeling pretty good."

"That's great, doll." He glanced at the door, then leaned over quickly and kissed her gently on the lips. "I want you to get out of here as quickly as you can."

For the next hour, they talked about Paul Keller and the novel Julie was writing about him. And for that hour, her mind was taken away from her own problems. She felt that she was getting to know Paul Keller better every time she and Don talked about him. And through Paul Keller, she was also getting to know Donald Lipton.

~

The rest of the day passed slowly, with another visit from Robert in the evening, and a long night.

It was only a little after six o'clock the next morning when Julie gave up trying to go back to sleep. She'd awakened before dawn, her body aching and her mind on Don Lipton.

She showered, brushed her hair, and slipped into a clean gown before breakfast came. This was a hearty meal with a cheese omelette, toast, potatoes, and fruit — Dr. Cole's orders, no doubt — but she could only eat a few bites of toast and finish the glass of orange juice.

Cheryl called at a little after eight o'clock to see how Julie was doing, and even put Matthew up to the telephone so Julie could hear the little sounds he made.

She was surprised when Don Lipton showed up before nine.

"Hi!" she said the moment he appeared in the door. "I thought you'd be teaching class this morning."

"Not until ten," he said, coming across to the bed and giving her a quick kiss on the lips. She savored those kisses, and wished only that they could last longer.

"I'm glad you came," she said softly.

They spent a half hour talking about his classes and her writing, and about what they would do after she got out of the hospital.

"I'm fixing up the gazebo," he said. "I forgot to tell you about that last night. New paint, new cushions for the seats, and a new roof. I'm also clearing away the weeds from around it. That'll take a little while, but I want to make it look brand new again."

She smiled. "That's great, Don. I'm looking forward to seeing it again."

"You will," he promised. "I have another place I want to show you, too."

"Oh?"

"Yeah, but I want it to be a surprise. You just have to get out of here so we can do it."

She knew he was trying to cheer her up, and she was grateful for that. But when he spoke of all the things they would do together, she felt the tears welling in her eyes. Even after she got out of the hospital, they would have precious little time to spend together.

Don reached to the bedside table for a tissue. "Only a quarter today, doll," he said softly, holding her while she cried.

~

Fifteen minutes after Don had to leave for his class, Dr. Cole arrived on his morning rounds.

"Good morning, Julie. Do you feel better today? Did you sleep well?"

"Which one do you want me to answer? Both answers are the same, *no and no*. Of course, if you have some good news about the tests, I'm sure those answers will change."

Instead of replying to that, Dr. Cole went around to the bottom of Julie's bed and pulled the blankets away from her feet. "Are your ankles still so swollen?"

"Oh, they seem much better when I stay off my feet."

He placed the covers back around her feet and gently sat down on the bed beside her, his face grave. He looked down at her tiny hands, and then picked up one of them in his own.

Julie thought she knew what was going through his mind. She had shared with him all of her thoughts and hopes for the future, and despite his training and experience, he wouldn't be able to prolong her life much longer. She felt an unexpected pang of sadness, and this time it was for him, not for herself. It wasn't his fault this was happening to her.

"Julie, if there was anything at all I could do for you, I would do it. You know that, don't you? You and Robert are both very special to me — although at times I would like to kick him right in the... well, right in the bottom."

"Yes, I know that. Robert really does love me, David. He

just doesn't know how to show it in ways in which most people understand. He's trying his damnedest to hide his feelings. He must be so torn up inside."

"I know, Julie. But you need him now, and you don't have time to waste on his moods."

"How bad is it, David? Has the prognosis changed? I mean, how long do I have?"

He drew in a breath and let it out slowly before replying. "Right now, I'm afraid we're going to be fighting just to keep things as stable as possible. With the condition you're in, things could go downhill very quickly. Your last urinalysis contained large amounts of protein and blood, which alerts us to kidney disease. There are a number of studies that can be done to test this in a lupus patient. I strongly suggest that we begin the necessary ones immediately. Time is of major importance."

She felt tears well up and spill down over her cheeks. She had been hoping for a miracle, that the tests would reveal that the lupus had somehow reversed, and that she was getting better. From the way she had been feeling lately, she knew that was a long shot. But she had not given up hoping for that miracle.

Now Dr. Cole was all but telling her that the battle had been lost. All they could do was hope to buy her a little more time before admitting defeat entirely.

"What sort of studies are you talking about?" she asked, her voice breaking. "I'm so tired of all these tests. Please... can't I just go home?"

"We have to find out for sure to what degree your kidneys are involved. Most of the tests are simple and relatively painless. I've ordered a few more blood tests for this morning. The major function of your kidney is to rid the body of waste products and excess fluids. We need to do more blood tests to measure whether the kidney is carrying out this function properly. The tests will also tell us if waste products are being adequately removed by the kidney and not building up in the blood."

She sighed. "Is there anything else?"

"Yes. I also want to run a twenty-four-hour urine collection. Studies done on your urine collected over a twenty-four-hour period are very sensitive in determining kidney function. These studies measure the kidneys' ability to filter waste products, and the exact amount of protein lost in the urine over a twenty-four-hour period."

Julie rolled her eyes. "That sounds like fun."

"I've also already ordered some x-rays for this afternoon. These will show the size and shape of your kidneys, and are commonly done before a kidney biopsy to help guide the physician doing the biopsy. I've scheduled the biopsy, too. That will determine the extent and severity of kidney disease."

Julie was trembling. "David, if I'm going to die soon anyway, why should I go through all this? Why can't I just go home?"

He squeezed her hand. "The best we can hope for is to give you a few more months, Julie. It might at least give you more time to be with Robert and Cheryl. What about that beautiful new little grandson? You might even be able to finish that book you were telling me about. Isn't a few more months worth a couple more days of your time now?"

Julie looked over at the bedside table and saw her manuscript lying there. It had already started growing from a collection of notes into a real book. She thought of Don, and about how much he wanted her to complete the book before she died. She thought to herself that she would do anything to have more time with her very special friend.

"All right," she said, fighting back tears. "How is this biopsy done? Will it require surgery?"

"It's just minor surgery under a local anesthetic," he said. "The doctor will insert a needle through the skin of the back and remove a small piece of the kidney. Then we can examine the specimen under a microscope to determine how much inflammation or permanent damage is present within the kidney. This will help us determine the best form of treatment."

She nodded. "Okay, David. I'll have the biopsy. When will you have the results from it?"

"By late tomorrow or early the next morning." He patted her leg through the blankets and got up from the bed. "I'll be back to see you later tonight, Julie. Hang in there."

As Dr. Cole was leaving the room, a cheerful, middle-aged female lab technician entered with her tray of vials and tubes to draw Julie's blood. Later, she handed Julie a plastic cup to use for the first of twenty-four urine specimens.

"They think you got sugar or something?" she asked. "Diabetes, I mean?"

Julie didn't feel like talking. She shrugged her shoulders. "Who knows," she said as she headed into the bathroom.

～

The rest of the morning passed quickly. Around 10:40, Don called from his office at the college to see how her day was going, and Robert's call came a little later.

After lunch, two very young male orderlies came in with a gurney to take her down for kidney x-rays.

"Hey, guys," she said, "I can walk, you know."

"Sorry, lady, hospital policy," said the red-haired one. "The ride's on us."

"Great," Julie muttered. "If you aren't sick when you get here, they make sure you are before you leave."

The orderlies looked at each other, but didn't respond. She was just another cranky patient to them, she figured. One led the cart while the other pushed Julie on down the hall to the elevator.

"Will you be taking me back up to my room when I'm done with the x-rays?" she asked when they reached the first floor.

"Not right away," answered the red-haired one, obviously the spokesman of the two. "After this, you're going across the hall for a kidney biopsy. I'm not sure how long that'll take."

"Kidney biopsy? Right now? Shouldn't I have my husband or somebody here with me?"

"Is there someone back upstairs we can get for you?"

Julie thought for a moment, then answered, "No, no one is here. I'll be fine."

The x-ray took only a few moments. Then she was taken to another room and helped onto a table. A young intern who introduced himself as Dr. Willard explained that he was going to do the biopsy.

"It should be relatively painless," he said.

Julie was apprehensive, but the procedure went quite well. Before she knew it, she was taken back upstairs to her room. Now began another wait to hear what the tests showed, and what Dr. Cole planned to do next.

Later, Robert stopped in and announced that he could only stay for a little while because of a late meeting back at the plant. He sat in the chair next to her bed, and this time he didn't turn on the television.

"Are you going to be all right tonight, Ju?"

"I'm okay," she said. "I just want to go home."

"It must be rough." He took her hand and didn't say anything else. Julie thought that he seemed a little more concerned than usual. He was letting his defenses down, and for a few moments, she sensed the real depth of his love for her. Her heart ached knowing the sadness her illness was causing him.

Robert left for his meeting after about forty-five minutes. For once, he volunteered to come back in the morning so he would be there while Dr. Cole was making his rounds. Julie began to wonder if Dr. Cole had talked with Robert and suggested that he be there.

~

Around 7:00 that night, Don came into her room. Without saying a word, he walked over to the bed and kissed her. "How are you doing? Been a rough day?"

All the emotions, all the tears Julie had dammed up inside let go. She threw herself into Don's arms. "Thank God you're here. I'm so afraid, Don...." Julie's voice broke and she could talk no longer. All she could do was cry.

Chapter Twenty-Six

Friday, June 6

I'll be having surgery tomorrow. When I came into the hospital, Dr. Cole said he wanted to have further tests and give me a chance to rest and regain some strength. He didn't say anything about surgery, and my stay in the hospital has been anything but restful. He says the surgery will be fairly minor, but it's still upsetting.

One good thing has come out of this, though. Robert has finally been forced to accept the fact that I'm dying....

When Julie awakened the next morning, she was surprised to find Robert already sitting in the chair beside the bed, reading a newspaper. Dr. Cole had given her a sedative the night before, and she was feeling fuzzy as she stretched and yawned.

Robert looked over the paper at her. "Hi, Ju. How are you feeling?"

"Groggy," she replied, reaching to the bedside table for a glass of water. After sipping, she said, "How come you're here so early? I didn't expect you until later this morning."

"Dr. Cole called last night and asked me to be here at seven," Robert replied, folding the newspaper and putting it on the floor beside the chair. "Said he'd meet me here."

Julie frowned. "Did he say why?"

"Just said we had to talk about treatment."

Before Julie could ask any more questions — for which Robert doubtless had no answers anyway — Dr. Cole came in.

"Ah," he said, nodding at Robert. "Glad you could make it."

"Will this take long?" Robert asked. "I have an important meeting this morning."

"Your meeting is of little importance, my friend. This time your wife comes first."

Robert leaned over and kissed Julie on the cheek, then stepped back. "So what's the news?"

Dr. Cole looked down at Julie. "How are you feeling this morning?"

"Hungover," she told him. "I think you tried to kill me with that sleeping pill you ordered."

"You really needed that." Dr. Cole walked around to the side of the bed. "Julie, your tests confirmed what I have suspected for the last few days. Let me try to explain. As I told you yesterday, the primary functions of the kidneys are to maintain the fluid and salt balance in the blood, and to remove waste products. These jobs are quite essential. If the kidneys fail for any reason, wastes start to accumulate and the body becomes overloaded with fluid."

"That's what's happening to me?"

He nodded. "Your kidneys are failing, Julie. In the hardest terms, if something isn't done immediately, you will die."

"What do you mean by *something done?*" Robert asked.

"Julie needs to get on dialysis at once. That's done with an artificial kidney machine."

Robert frowned. "Will she have to come back to the hospital for that?"

"There are two options. Usually, patients undergo a three-hour hemodialysis session at the hospital three times a week. We can do it that way, or we can use another method in which the dialysis fluid is instilled in the abdominal cavity through a permanent percutaneous access device. This allows patients to self-administer their therapy. Used solution is discarded, and fresh solution infused daily."

"We could do that at home?" Julie asked.

Dr. Cole nodded. "In my professional opinion, that's your better choice since it'll allow you to receive your treatments at night while you sleep. Just a little training will be required. You'll still be able to remain somewhat active, and it's the least expensive of the choices."

"Are there any risks?"

"There's risk involved with everything in life," he answered. "I don't have to tell you that. With the implant, there is always a chance of exit-site infections and peritonitis. Risk, sure... but without the dialysis, you have no chance at all."

Robert looked at Julie, and then back at Dr. Cole. "Heavy stuff."

"Damned heavy," Dr. Cole agreed. "There is no right or wrong choice, but the decision has to be made now."

"Is she going to need this forever?" Robert asked.

Dr. Cole glanced at Julie, and she knew what he was thinking. In her case, *forever* wouldn't be long at all. "Sometimes patients only need dialysis until they can find a suitable kidney donor. Often with a transplant, they're able to live a fairly normal life. But—"

"So what's the big deal, Doc? Can't you get her a new kidney? Can she have one of mine?"

"It isn't that easy, Robert. In Julie's situation, the kidney failure is only a small part of the picture. Her most recent x-rays show that the lupus has also affected the outer lining and the valves of her heart."

"Her heart?" Robert repeated. "That sounds serious."

"It *is* serious," Dr. Cole said patiently. "That's what Julie and I have been trying to tell you."

"What about a heart transplant? People have that all the time, don't they?"

Again, Julie saw Dr. Cole glance at her. Robert was holding onto his denial right to the end.

"Julie would never survive either a heart transplant or a kidney transplant," Dr. Cole said to Robert. "She wouldn't even be put on the waiting list for a transplant. Even if we could give her new organs, the lupus would just attack them, too."

"Well... well...." Robert seemed at a loss for words.

"Human bodies aren't like '58 Thunderbirds, Robert," Julie said gently, reaching out to touch his arm. "You can't just keep replacing parts as they break. Sometimes you just run out of things to do. Right, Dr. Cole?"

He nodded solemnly. "With some diseases, that's unfortunately true. The kidney dialysis I'm recommending will buy a little time, but I'm afraid that's all it'll do. A little more time."

Robert's face changed as he gradually absorbed what they were telling him, and was forced against his will to accept the inevitable. "You mean... you're saying... she's really going to die?"

Dr. Cole nodded slowly. "Within just a few months, at best. I've gone over this with Julie. She's been able to accept it, even though I know it has been terribly painful for her. Now *you're* the one who must accept it. She needs you now more than ever."

Robert walked over and took Julie's hand in his own. His voice was low and husky when he said, "Can we have a few moments alone?"

"Of course. I have other patients on the floor. I'll go see them and then come back here. We'll need to know which way to proceed with the dialysis. Take your time and try to decide what will work best for the two of you."

When they were alone, Julie sat up on the edge of the bed, and Robert leaned down to hold her. For the longest time, no words were spoken. It became difficult to tell whose tears were whose. They cried together as they had never cried before. Both of them knew that this was the beginning of the end. Although they often had difficulty in expressing their past feelings, at this moment in their lives, words weren't needed at all. Julie knew no words had ever been thought of to convey the message in her heart.

Later, Dr. Cole returned and the decision was made. Julie would have the tube inserted into her abdominal cavity. Specialists would teach Robert how to hook her up to a machine every night so it would handle the dialysis while she slept. During the day, she would still be free to come and go.

She knew she would never again have a normal life, but *normal* didn't matter anymore. The important word was *life*. More than ever before, Julie wanted to live, to breathe, to feel, to love. She had moments to share, memories to make, a book to finish.

Please let me live long enough to complete this final gift of my love. Oh, God, oh, please.

Dr. Cole scheduled the surgery for the next morning, and told Julie she would have to stay in the hospital an extra day or two to recover and get the necessary training for the dialysis.

Robert stayed for the remainder of the morning, and when he left for work, he promised that he would be back later. Don called to see how she was doing, but she didn't feel like telling him everything over the phone. He said he would come straight to the hospital when his afternoon classes ended. Although he didn't say it, Julie could tell from his voice that he sensed something more than usual was wrong.

When Don arrived, the scene of the morning repeated itself. They were two people in love, trying to sort it all out. Both of them knew that their time together was running out, but neither was able to do a damned thing about it.

"We'll never be able to do all the things that we planned," Julie said.

Don couldn't deny that. Instead, he held her close and tried to calm her with his words. "We will do all the things that we can, and what we aren't able to do physically, love, we will do in our heads."

This only made Julie cry more. How could one feel the breezes blowing off of the lake, know the warmth of a hug, do a million other things... in her head?

"No!" she cried. "I don't want to do things in my head. I want to *really* do all those things!"

Tears began to fill Don's eyes as well. He placed a large hand on both sides of Julie's face and wiped away her tears with gentle motions of his thumbs. "We will do as many things as time allows together. If a time comes when you're too weak to go places, then I'll sit on the bed beside you, and you can shut your eyes, and I'll tell you all about the other places. We can go there together in our heads, Julie... in our heads and in our hearts."

As her eyes met Don's, Julie knew there was nothing left to say. He was there for her, and somehow in her heart she knew that he would never walk away.

She gently removed one of his hands from her face and held it tightly between her own, then leaned her head back against the pillow and closed her eyes. Trying not to think at all, she drifted off to sleep.

~

When she opened her eyes again, Cheryl was sitting quietly in the chair beside the bed.

"Hi," Cheryl said softly, leaning over to kiss Julie on the

cheek. "I decided not to wake you."

"Oh, you should have," Julie said, reaching down to press the control to elevate the head of the bed. She sipped from her water glass and felt a little better. "How long have you been here?"

"Only fifteen or twenty minutes."

Don had apparently gone while she was asleep. "Tom's watching Matthew?"

Cheryl nodded, smiling. "He seems to be doing pretty well with this father-son bonding thing."

Julie returned her smile. It felt good having Cheryl there. "You are so lucky, babe. You have such a nice husband... and now that beautiful little boy. Do you really know how blessed you are?"

Cheryl lowered her eyes. "I know, Mom. I never take either one of my men for granted. I only hope I can be as good of a mother as you were. Mom, do you think I'll have all the right answers for little Matthew when he needs them?"

Julie turned her head, making direct eye contact with her daughter. "None of us have all the answers, honey. But I'm sure you'll do just fine. Many of a child's questions are about things we adults have experienced ourselves, and hopefully have learned from."

A few moments of quiet passed. Suddenly, Julie felt the need to talk to Cheryl about the seriousness of her illness. She, who had repeatedly told her daughter that most of her life's significant problems didn't mean the end of the world, knew those words wouldn't work this time. Indeed, the end of the world as they had shared it was very close.

"Cherrie, give me your hand." She took her daughter's hand and held it between both of hers. "I am very sick, baby, and there is nothing I or anyone else can do to make it better. Honey, I've been trying to protect you from the pain, always hoping for a miracle. But I know now that there isn't going to be one this time. Cherrie, baby, it is just about the end of life's road for me. Damn, I don't want to die. I'm sorry... I never wanted to hurt you."

Julie reached up and pulled her daughter close. For the longest time, wrapped in each other's arms, they remained silent. When Cheryl regained her composer, she spoke softly to her mother.

"I've known the truth for a long time, Mom. Dad has been filling me in. He is so scared too. I know he tries to hide it, even from himself at times. But he's hurting big time." She wiped her eyes with a tissue. "Has Don Lipton been visiting you every day?"

Julie nodded. "He's been here several times." Suddenly, for some reason, Julie felt that she had to talk to Cheryl about Don. She wanted her daughter to know there was another kind of love... the love she had found when she needed it most. "Honey, There's something else I would like to talk to you about."

"Sure, Mom, anything."

"It's about... about my friend, Don Lipton. I just wanted to let you know that Don has become a very special person to me... at the very least, a most beautiful friend."

Cheryl nodded slowly. "That wasn't hard to figure out, Mom. The question is, just how special of a friend is he?"

Julie sighed. "Cheryl, in a way that only he could, Don has come into my life ever too late. Yet he has filled many of my final moments with the deepest, purest love." Julie stopped for a moment, and then went on. "Honey, do you remember when you were a little girl and I took you to the parade? You were so afraid of the drums and noise and all. Remember it was cold outside, and although I had dressed you in a heavy coat, you were still cold and shaky. You were crying and wanted to go home.

"Then, suddenly, a big fuzzy teddy bear popped out of the

costumed crowd. He walked over to us and picked you up and gave you the biggest warm hug. You stopped crying almost at once, and in your wee little voice you whispered, 'Now I feel better. He makes me feel good.'"

"Sure I remember... barely. Life was so simple then, Mom. All it took was a hug from a big burley bear to take away my fears and keep me warm. So what's the point?"

Julie smiled. "The point is, Cheryl, that nothing is going to make it all right for me again. But when I hurt, when I am scared to death, when I feel ever so shaky and cold, Don Lipton gives me the biggest teddy bear hugs, and at least for the moment I find the strength to go on. I sometimes live for another one of those hugs. Cherrie, Don has touched the deepest part of my heart with his love."

"But...." Cheryl had a doubtful look on her face. "You still love Dad too, right?"

"Oh, yes! It isn't like they're competing with each other. And Cheryl, the love between Don and me is strictly in our hearts."

Cheryl took a deep breath, then released it in a whoosh of air. "Wow! I suspected there was some kind of deep feelings between the two of you." She paused, then smiled. "In fact, Mom, I have a confession to make too."

Julie lifted an eyebrow at her daughter. "You have another man in your life?"

Cheryl laughed. "Hardly. Believe me, I don't have room for another one."

"Then what is it?"

"Well, a while back, I went to the college one day to get a look at Dr. Lipton—"

"You what?"

"I went to his office to see if I could catch a glimpse of him. I don't know why. I just wanted to see what he looked like. But he wasn't there. After I gave up and was leaving, we literally ran into each other on the elevator. I dropped one of my books on his foot, and he made some sort of crazy remark. I was too frightened to listen to what he was saying."

Julie couldn't help laughing. "You are crazy! Checking up on your mother's friends." A softness covered Julie's face. "I love you so, baby. Thanks for looking out for me."

"God, I love you too, Mom. And this thing with Don is okay. I know you'll do whatever your heart tells you to do, and I know you'll do what you believe is right. No matter what, I'll always be here for you too, and I'll help you through all of this in any way that I can. Thanks for sharing with me, Mom." Cheryl wiped her eyes again with the tissue, then got to her feet. "I'd better be going." She tried to force a faint smile, but was only partly successful. "I'm not sure if I'm ready to trust Tom to put Matthew down for the night. It's a pretty complicated project. I'd better supervise."

Julie reached out a hand, and Cheryl took it, giving her a reassuring squeeze.

"I love you, Mom," Cheryl said, her voice breaking.

"I love you too, baby," Julie whispered.

A moment later, Cheryl was gone and Julie lay there staring up at the ceiling, her eyes blurred by tears.

Chapter Twenty-Seven

Right on schedule at nine o'clock the next morning, the surgical team came in with the gurney to wheel her to the operating room. Julie was nervous, even though Dr. Cole had promised that this would be a minor surgery. As she looked at the faces of nurses, technicians, doctors, and even visitors in the hallways, she felt even more compromised. They all looked at Julie as if they knew how ill she was, then looked away quickly as if they were afraid they might catch what she had.

As she was wheeled into the operating room, she caught a glimpse of the greenish-blue walls and brown-tiled floor. Two huge ceiling lights were positioned on large tracks in the center of the room. The narrow operating table looked like something that might have been used to restrain prisoners in a medieval torture chamber. At least, that was the way it seemed to Julie at the time.

After she had been positioned on the narrow table by the anesthesiologist, Julie glanced up at the nurses setting up the surgical instruments. Then she saw the surgeon standing by the side holding up his hands, with water dripping from them.

She realized that she didn't even know his name. Dr. Cole had surely told her, but with everything else, she had completely forgotten.

"How are you doing, Julie?"

Julie looked up at Dr. Cole. "Okay," she mumbled.

"You'll be asleep soon," he promised.

Finally, she saw the anesthesia mask come up over her face. She closed her eyes, and it was as if a dark curtain were being slowly drawn.

~

When Julie regained consciousness in the recovery room, the catheter was in place and Dr. Cole told her everything had gone perfectly. Over the next few hours, Julie saw several members of a renal team, consisting of a nephrologist, dietitian, nurse, social worker, and mental health professional. Their job was to make sure everything went smoothly with the dialysis therapy at home.

The dietician carefully explained that Julie would have to change her diet, avoiding large amounts of protein and adding ketoacid and amino acid supplements. Dr. Wallace, a family psychologist, explained that Julie's quality of life and social role function would largely depend on her understanding and positive participation in her own care. The renal team also explained that exercise and physical training programs would be important to Julie's physical well-being.

Julie felt that her life was becoming an unfamiliar routine, almost as if she was a stranger trapped inside the body of someone she used to know.

~

Two days after surgery, when the renal team felt confident that Julie could handle her home dialysis, she was released from the hospital. She faithfully followed the exercise program, and most of the time tried to follow the recommended diet.

Over the next week, she recovered from the surgery and eased into her new schedule with the nightly therapy. While some days she rested until late morning, most of the time she was up by nine, dressed and ready to do one more thing... perhaps for the last time.

During Julie's first week at home, Robert was unusually attentive, but before long he had fallen back into his old habits. While the modernization project was going well and nearing completion, it still required that he spend long hours at the plant. Or so he said, anyway. He often came home just in time to help start the dialysis treatment.

Because Julie was hooked up to the machine every night, Robert began sleeping on a fold-down sofa bed he'd brought into the bedroom. On rare occasions, Julie would wake up at night and find him quietly sneaking under the blankets beside her. He would cuddle as near as the tubing allowed, and lay his face against hers. Although he usually remained silent, there was a mutual understanding of hearts.

Once or twice, Julie thought she heard Robert crying, and she knew that his sorrow was tearing him apart. Her heart went out to him, knowing she was the cause of that anguish, and there wasn't a thing in the world she could do to lessen it. Most of the time, she pretended to be asleep so she wouldn't embarrass him, but on one occasion, she felt the need to share.

"Robert, are you okay?" she asked quietly.

He cleared his throat. "Why wouldn't I be?"

"Are you crying?"

Robert's voice broke, and he began to tremble. "Oh God, Julie, I feel so helpless... so hopeless. I... I thought if I kept believing that you would get better, then you would. I've been praying my heart out, Julie. Damn, I just don't know what to do. I'm so scared, Ju... so damned scared."

"Hold me, Robert. Just hold me. I know you love me. There's nothing anyone can do. We have to make each moment count, take one day at a time. Just hearing you say that you love me means so much. I never totally doubt that, but sometimes I need to hear it. I'm scared, too."

Neither of them slept through the rest of that night. They talked and they cried. They sought comfort and gave it in return.

Near morning, Robert went back to the sofa. By breakfast time, Julie discovered that he had reverted back to denial, and no mention was made of his nighttime visit.

"You look much better today, Julie," he said, glancing at her over the newspaper. "I thought that new medicine would work. As soon as you get back in shape, we'll talk about that trip to Rome. Maybe we can do it next spring."

She didn't bother to reply to that. She knew there would never be a trip to Rome — or anywhere else, for that matter."

~

As the days passed, Julie slowly settled into her new routine with the days spent writing and the nights with dialysis treatment. Cheryl and Matthew came to visit often, and it seemed that each time they did, little Matt had some new "first time" accomplishment to show his grandma.

Over the next few weeks, Robert spent as much time as possible at the plant. He had told Julie that this was the only way he could deal with her illness — by keeping busy.

Julie regularly exchanged letters with Patricia Davis, and enjoyed hearing how her friend from college was doing in Boston. Patricia had said that she would be coming back to Freeborn in the spring to visit her children, and was looking forward to seeing Julie again. Julie didn't tell her that she probably wouldn't be alive by then.

Don came nearly every day. On good days, Julie somehow found inner energy, and they took long walks and spent hours sitting side by side in the gazebo, talking about anything and everything.

One day while they were sitting in the gazebo, he asked about Matthew. "How is your little grandson doing? Still keeping his mom up at night?"

She shook her head. "That just lasted a few days. The doctor has given him a clean bill of health."

"Good. Cheryl looked pretty tired when I saw her there at the hospital."

"Well...." Julie thought back to the encounter between Cheryl and Don, and the confession Cheryl had made about her incognito trip to the college. She knew that Cheryl had felt terribly flustered about running into Don unexpectedly there in Julie's room. "She had a lot on her mind at the time."

"Hmm...." Don said noncommittally. "You know, she looked very familiar to me. I'm sure I've run into her somewhere before." He shifted in the seat and drew Julie closer to him. "Of course, Freeborn isn't that large. I've probably seen her at the grocery store." Pause. "Or maybe even at the college. You said she was a student there a few years ago, didn't you?"

"Yes. But... well...." Julie hesitated. It was silly, she decided, to keep this little secret any longer. "Actually, Don, I think you saw her there not long ago."

"Oh?"

The tone of his voice made her turn her head to look up at him, and she found him smiling.

"What's so funny?"

He burst out laughing. When he was finally able to catch his breath, he said, "Julie, I know exactly when I saw Cheryl at the college, and I think I've figured out why she was there — books, ponytail, and all. I almost became a casualty of her little espionage operation." He lifted his foot slightly and waggled it. "Luckily, I didn't end up on crutches."

It was her turn to laugh. "Cheryl told me what happened. I don't know what got into her, Don. She's usually so level-headed."

"No need to apologize, doll. After the stories you must've told about me, she was probably dying to see this ogre you had for creative writing."

"No, Don, that wasn't—"

"Shush!" He put a finger to her lips. "If that's what you told her, you were exactly right. I was an ogre. And I don't blame Cheryl for wanting to get a first-hand look at me." He removed his finger, then lowered his head and kissed her. "But there's no need to embarrass her. We'll just keep this to ourselves, okay? She doesn't have to know that I recognized her."

She smiled. "That's a good idea." She drew in a breath and sighed contentedly. "I'm glad we have some things to laugh about, Don. Sometimes I'm afraid I'll forget how to laugh."

"I hope you don't." He tilted her head up and kissed her again. "And I sure hope you don't forget how to love."

~

One day he took her to his house, which was about a half mile from the gazebo. The house was painted forest green, blending in so well with the wooded area around it as to be nearly invisible. The porch was screened-in, with a wood-frame screen door mounted on squeaking hinges and reined in by a complaining steel spring.

He had obviously made an effort to straighten up the house before she came over. This, she reminded herself, was the house he had shared with Emily and Abby, but over the years, most of the feminine touches had faded. The living room was cluttered, the furniture stodgy and a little seedy-looking. The room's nicest feature was the fireplace, a huge stone job with a hearth wide enough to sit on. There were several chairs that looked comfortable but not expensive, a coffee table that had once been expensive but now had a long chip gone from the side, two bookcases, and a small television.

He waved her to the sofa, then brought iced tea for both of them and sat down beside her.

"How's the writing coming along?" he asked.

They had been talking about her book almost every day, and on more than one occasion Don's input had gotten her over a stumbling block. It seemed to her that over the past few weeks, Don Lipton and Paul Keller had both gone through a transformation. Julie had come to think of it almost as the metamorphosis of a butterfly pulling itself out of its cocoon and spreading its lovely wings. Julie had felt fortunate to be present when it happened — to both Don Lipton and Paul Keller.

"It's going well," she replied. She sipped the tea, then set the glass on the coffee table and turned toward Don. "I've been thinking a little more about Lisa, though." In her book, Lisa was the woman who had fallen in love with Paul Keller. She was the one who, with her love and gentleness, had pulled him out of his cocoon.

"Is something bothering you about her?" Don asked with some concern.

"No, not really. I'm just curious about something. When Lisa met Paul Keller, he was almost completely withdrawn, hiding himself away from others and responding in ways that were sure to drive them away—"

"He was being a jerk," he said in his usual blunt way.

"Exactly. So what I was wondering was this. If Paul Keller was such a jerk, why was Lisa drawn to him? What did she see in him that others couldn't see?"

For a long moment, he sat without replying, staring out across the room as if studying something on the far wall. Finally he took her hand.

"I'm not sure, Julie. Why would someone like Lisa fall in love with Paul Keller? He certainly did nothing to deserve her love."

She started to say something, then saw the thoughtful

expression on his face and decided to give him a little more time with her question. It was clear that he was taking it seriously.

"Lately I've been thinking more and more about the nature of love," he said at last. "Poets have written about it. Singers have sung about it. God knows, thousands of books have been written about it. Lovers have been proclaiming their love for one another from the time speech and language first came about — and they were probably doing things to *show* their love for one another long before that. But what *is* love? Is it something we can really define and understand?"

She squeezed his hand and remained silent, giving him more room to explore his thoughts without intrusion.

"I first learned about real love when I met Emily," he said quietly. "And when Abby was born, I learned that there are at least two kinds of love, each just as deep as the other. My love for Abby was much different from my love for Emily, but it was just as strong." He paused again for a long moment before continuing. "Over the years, I've thought a lot about that. What *is* love, anyway? Biologists who believe that we're all the product of natural selection and evolution would say that it's built into all of us as part of our survival instinct. The strong feeling we have for someone of the opposite sex furthers the human race through procreation. And the love we feel for our offspring leads us to do anything to protect them, thus allowing them to live longer and have offspring of their own—"

His words suddenly choked, and Julie knew that he was thinking of Emily and Abby, and that terrible day they had died. And he was thinking of the lives and love that had been stolen from him.

She held his hand, letting that be the comfort he needed. She didn't want to interrupt him with words of her own.

"Anyway, that's supposed to be the way it works," he went on at last, barely above a whisper. Then he cleared his throat and put more strength into his voice. "A few years ago I read an article by a psychologist who had a different slant on the meaning of love. He said it's all tied up in our own ego. He said that we love someone else if we love the image of *ourselves* that we see reflected back from that person. In other words, if we feel accepted for who we are, we're more likely to love the person who accepts us and reflects that image of acceptance back at us through word and action."

Again, he fell silent, and this time she sensed that he was waiting for a response from her.

"I've thought a lot about love too, Don," she said softly. "And I've reached the conclusion that it's a mistake to analyze it too much. It's a gift, and somehow I think God would be happier with us if we just accepted his gifts without questioning why he gives them to us."

He nodded thoughtfully. "You're probably right. I know one thing. *Thinking* about love all these years didn't help bring it back to me." He pulled her close. "It took another person to make me see it again, and feel it." His voice had grown husky with emotion, and now he cleared his throat before going on. "That's probably the way it is for Lisa in your story. Maybe she doesn't even know what she saw in Paul Keller. I suppose she just had the ability to see things other people couldn't see." He looked down at her then. "Just like you did, Julie. You made me feel love again even though I did everything I could to turn my back on it. You wouldn't let me."

Julie didn't trust herself to speak. They sat there for a long time, finishing the iced tea and enjoying each other's closeness. No more words were needed for the moment. They understood each other perfectly.

~

They came back to his house on one other occasion, but spent most of their time together at the gazebo down the lane. Sometimes she would show Don her most recent writing, and he would make corrections and offer suggestions.

Julie sensed that by helping her write, Don was finding renewed interest in his own. Sometimes she would ask him to help her even when she really didn't need it.

"I'm stuck!" she told him one day over the phone. "You've got to help me, Don. I need a word... I can't think of the right word."

"What kind of word do you need?"

Julie thought for a moment. "Well, I need a word that means all the things that happen between two memorable events in a person's life."

"Hmm... give me an example," Don suggested.

"Okay. Say, like between someone's birth and death... or marriage and divorce. I need a word that covers everything in between. Do you understand what I'm trying to say?"

"Of course. And I know the exact word you need. Intraslop. I-N-T-R-A-S-L-O-P. How's that for a word, Julie?"

Julie giggled. "I never heard of that word before."

"Neither did I. I just made it up." She heard him chuckle.

"Then I'll use it. I like it. Your 'intraslop' will be a part of my book. Now that's real love." She giggled again. "Can you even imagine what a computer grammar checker — or better yet, a creative writing instructor — would do with that word? Thanks, Don."

"No problem, doll. Anytime. Anything you need."

Julie loved the times she spent with Don. They always found something meaningful to do together. Occasionally, Julie would have a day when she was exhausted before she even got up in the morning. Then, as he had once promised, Don would sit on a chair by her side and mentally take her to places. Sometimes it hurt her knowing they would never really go there, but most of the time, his presence near her at that moment in time was enough.

That was indeed all that they could be certain of — that one precious moment in time.

Chapter Twenty-Eight

Wednesday, October 22

There is that song again.... There's a place for us, a time and place for us....

Well, world, my time is now, and the place, well, the place is anywhere that we can be alone together. Don told me about a little cabin in the woods that belonged to his parents. He used to go there with his wife and daughter. He's finally ready to go back again... this time with me, his forever friend. I pray that I can somehow help him to live again... before I die....

The sound of the phone ringing on the bedside table awakened Julie. She had been experiencing an unusual amount of pain the previous night, and she had taken a pill to help her sleep. Now she didn't want to wake up.

"Julie, are you okay? This is Don. You sound groggy, doll. Did I wake you?"

Gathering her senses, Julie answered, "Oh... hi, Don. Yes, I think... I guess I'm awake. I had a rough night, but I think I'm better this morning... not sure."

"I was thinking about stopping by for a few minutes. I'd

like to look at those new pages you said you had added to your journal. Do you think I could come over for a little bit?"

The sound of Don's voice served as an immediate stimulant, and Julie became more responsive. "Sure... yeah, that would be okay. No, I meant to say that would be *great.* I would love to see you this morning. I'll go now and unlock the side door. You don't have to knock. Just come on in when you get here."

"Okay, doll. See you in a few."

Standing up too quickly, Julie was temporarily overcome with dizziness. She wasn't sure if it was caused by the pill or the disease. *Not that it matters much....*

She waited to catch her balance, then leaned over and gathered her white silk slippers from beside the bed. Putting them on, she walked slowly to her bath to freshen up before Don arrived. She thought about getting dressed, but at the last minute decided against it. Instead, she gathered the silk robe that matched her gown.

Putting it on, she walked into the study and pushed the master switch on her computer. While she was waiting for the system to bring up the program manager, she walked over to the large window on the east side of the room. This was always one of her favorite places to be in the early morning. The sun was just rising over the pond, and this morning Julie thought it was breathtaking.

"Oh, God, how perfect," she whispered to herself. "How perfect."

~

Don had arrived and, as instructed, had let himself in. Seeing the light on in the study, he figured that was where he would find Julie. Walking quietly into the room, he found her still staring out the window. Seeing her standing there dressed in that beautiful gown, he thought she looked like an angel.

"Morning, doll. What are you looking at?"

"Oh, hi, Don." She turned and smiled at him, then turned back to the window. "I didn't hear you come in. Look! See the sunrise on the pond? Isn't it beautiful? I was just wondering what could possibly be better than this in the next life. I do love life, Don." Julie's voice broke as she whispered the words.

"Yes, it is beautiful, Julie." He came up to stand beside her, and put his arm around her. "Can you recall when you saw your very first sunrise? Mine had a beauty unsurpassed by any I have seen since. I remember it so well."

Surprised, she looked up at him. "You actually remember your very first one?"

"You bet! I was a small boy, hunting with my father. I was tired and cold, and not even noticing what was going on around me. Suddenly, my father pointed toward the sky, and he told me to look up. He encouraged me to pay close attention, for I was about to see something splendid and beautiful for the first time. He added that it was something I would always remember, that it would forever be etched in my mind. 'Look, son!' Father was excited. 'See that pink, that turning red, that now red ball over those trees. That, my boy, is your very first sunrise. Always remember it that way.'"

"Wow!" Julie smiled. "How special it must have been for you."

"You know, Julie, I have compared each new sunrise and sunset since to that original one. In each, the beauty is still there... but my father isn't here to tell me to pay attention. To be certain, each sign of beauty, the beauty of each light, adds to the total beauty that I've seen. But none will ever be as great as that first sunrise."

"That is so beautiful, Don. Did you ever wonder what the first sunrise — or ever so many other first things — look like to a person who witnessed it through tear-filled eyes brought on by hunger, fear, or sorrow?" Julie turned toward Don and put her arms around his neck. He leaned over and gently kissed her cheek. "I can't remember my first sunrise, my love, but I will never forget seeing this one with you."

Their embrace tightened, and once again, together they turned toward the window. Both knew in their hearts that no other sunrise would be quite so beautiful to them ever again.

"Are you busy today, Julie?" he asked suddenly. "Got time to take a ride with me?"

She didn't even hesitate. Even the suggestion made her feel better. "Oh... I might find the time. But what about your classes?"

"No classes today," he said with a grin. "I already called and told them I couldn't come in. They'll post a note on the classroom door. I'm sure my students won't mind having a day off."

"Probably not," she said with a smile. "Where did you want to go?"

He kissed her. "You'll see."

~

Don parked the car in the rutted driveway, jumped out, and made his way over to the other side to help Julie. She sat on the edge of the seat for a moment trying to catch her breath before getting out.

What a neat place, she thought.

While not very large, the cabin looked comfortable and had obviously been well cared for. The driveway was lined with big-leaf maples and horse chestnut trees. Many of the leaves had turned to shades of red and brown, and a multitude of them had already fallen to the earth to once again become a part of it.

Julie kicked at the leaves with her foot as she walked along the bark pathway toward the door. She noticed the many summer flowers that were now dead and leaning over, as if to bury themselves in the soil. *You are unfair!* her heart said to them. *Spring will be back before you know it, and you will live again.*

"Did you ever see such a beautiful, secluded place, Julie?" Don said. "Emily and I used to love coming here." For the first time, she noticed that his brow didn't furrow in pain when he mentioned Emily's name.

Suddenly Julie reached up. "Look, Don. See what I have?" She stood grasping a tiny blue feather. "I just caught it as it was falling down from the sky. A little bluebird dropped its feather as it was flying over us."

"Yep, I see it, Julie. What does the feather mean to you?"

Julie tried to explain. "Don, don't you see? If that bluebird hadn't dropped this feather, we never would have known it had crossed our path. Even at this, all we know about it is that it was blue. We don't know its size, where it was going, what sort of things it likes to eat. All we will ever remember about it is that it was blue."

"So what are you trying to say, love? Is it so very important for you to know anything else?"

"No, Don, not about the bird." She paused, looking closely at the feather. "This conversation isn't really about the bird. It is about me. This feather has made me wonder what I will leave behind so that those I have loved, those whose paths I have crossed in my life, will remember me. Have I left more than a simple blue feather for Cheryl and little Matthew to remember me by? Have I made any positive changes in their lives?"

He reached out and hugged her. "Wow, doll, this has really got you thinking, hasn't it?"

"Yes... can't you see? Can't you understand that all of a sudden I am forced to become aware of my own mortality? Oh, Don, I don't want to be just a remembered name. I want to do something, anything special to set me apart from the rest."

"And that you are, love. You are writing your book. Your very precious gift of love for all of us will live on in your book.

Julie, as long as a single copy of your book exists, your love will be a real part of the world. Think about that."

She nodded, then lifted the feather and let the breeze catch it. When she released it, it drifted out past the driveway and settled into a clump of vegetation. "And I'll return this to the world, too. It isn't mine to keep. Maybe somebody else will find it someday and feel as special about it as I did."

Don stood there quietly with her for a moment. Then, taking Julie's arm, he led her to the door of the screened-in porch. "After you, madam."

"What's that, Don?" Julie pointed to an antique buggy seat.

"Oh, that was from the buggy my grandfather used when he was courting my grandma."

"Really? That's neat."

He grinned. "Well, maybe I'm just teasing you. I bought that old buckseat at an auction years ago... for only twenty-five dollars. Emily and I used to sit there together and talk about everything under the sun." He paused, and the grin faded. "I even wrote a little poem about the buckseat. Well, about the gazebo, too... and Emily."

She touched his arm. "I'd love to hear it."

For a long moment he was silent, then he gazed off into the trees and began reciting:

"'Tis not the seat that makes the ride,
But the companion on the seat that makes the moment.
'Tis not the sides of the gazebo that make the flowers beautiful,
But the company and the music of the time.
'Tis not the music from a tape that makes the dance,
But the tunes from the heart that make the beat.
'Tis not the place that makes the love,
But the people that are no place that make the moment."

She squeezed his arm after he finished. "It's beautiful, Don."

He cleared his throat. Then the grin was back. "Ready to take a look inside?"

The cabin was toasty warm. Don had been there earlier and started a fire in the cast-iron stove, and the sound and smell of the burning wood filled the tiny room. An old oak ice box sat in the corner, and bookcases made of old wooden crates lined the walls.

"After Abby was born, we sometimes came here on Christmas Eve," Don said, pulling Julie close. "I would get a fire going to warm it up, then we'd open one present each. Abby used to get so excited. She'd want to open everything, of course, but we told her she'd have to wait till Christmas morning for the rest."

Julie hugged him. They stood together for a moment, then Julie moved over to the bookshelves and picked up two books near the top. They were Gene Stratton Porter's *Freckles* and *Girl of the Limberlost*. How she loved those old books.

"Have you read these, Don? My grandmother had the entire collection, and I grew up reading them. They're great!"

He shook his head. "I haven't read them. They belonged to Emily. She thought they were great, too. She wanted to collect all the Porter books so when Abby was old enough to read...." His voice broke. He cleared his throat and continued. "So when Abby was old enough to read, she would have them."

"I'm sorry, Don. I didn't mean to bring up something that hurt you."

His eyes softened as he looked at her. "It still hurts to think about them — but now there's no bitterness, Julie, no guilt. That's the same way Paul Keller feels. I'm closer to him now. It seems that you've helped both of us enjoy life again."

"I hope so, Don. Lisa's love allowed Paul to once again accept the beauty of life. He was able to finally create beauty of his own with the piano."

Don smiled. "Your beautiful love, doll, has helped heal me. Finally, after ever so long, I have this urge to write again. For the first time since that accident, I'm ready and eager to live again."

Julie didn't know what to say. She nodded her head to acknowledge understanding, but remained silent.

Don put his arm around Julie's shoulder and gave her a hug. "You know, doll, you've ruined my reputation on campus. In this last week alone, I received three notes from students thanking me for going out of my way to help them. I think I'm starting to be too easy with these kids. What have you done to me?"

She returned his smile. "I knew you were all heart."

"Yeah, I hear you. But yesterday one of my students turned in a paper that she wrote about her infant son who died from SIDS, and it was so sad, so beautifully written, that I thought about it all evening. Not long ago, this same paper would've had little effect on me. Now, knowing you, my love, death seems so real, so close." He broke off and sat there for a moment breathing deeply. Then he looked at her again. "Are you okay, doll? Are you warm enough?"

"If I tell you I'm cold, will you hold me closer?"

"Probably. Are you cold?"

Julie smiled. "Absolutely freezing!"

Time seemed to stand still as his mouth drew nearer, and slowly her eyelids closed. His mouth moved over hers, as hot and demanding as it had been that night in the pond. Common sense warned her that she ought to tell him to stop. But all rational thought fled as the kiss went on and on. She was conscious only of his nearness, his lips, and the pleasure of being in his arms.

He ran his hand caressingly up and down her back, along her sides and patted her bottom. She could only draw in a quick, unsteady breath, then give herself up to the pleasure that cascaded over her. Tremors shook her body as his lips left hers and seared a path down the length of her slim neck and into the hollow of her throat.

"You taste so good," he whispered raggedly into her throat. "Sweet. Just like honey."

"Don...." She didn't know what to say, what to do. Then she noticed an old radio on the side table. "Does that work?"

He turned to follow her eyes. "No. I think that thing's older than me. Why?"

"I was hoping we could dance."

"Well...." He smiled. "That sounds great to me. Let's do it!"

"But there isn't any music."

"Music, shmoozic! Do we need music to dance? I was under the impression that we could make our own music. There is always a song in my heart when I'm with you, my love. Sometimes it's a happy song, and sometimes a sad one, but always a song... our very own love song."

Julie stood up, and Don took her hand. Looking down into her eyes, he smiled and pulled her close. He was right, they moved together in unison, almost as one, and their hearts were whispering a love song... their very own love song. He moved across the floor with a grace she would not have believed possible.

"How are you feeling?" he asked after a while.

"Tired," she said, then looked up at him. "A back rub sure would feel good." The instant it was out of her mouth, she couldn't believe she'd said it. God, she was a masochist.

"Sure." He laced his fingers with hers and led her over to the sofa. She lay on her stomach, and Don began massaging her neck, kneading the tight muscles. She couldn't stop the sigh that slipped out as his hands moved over the tense muscles of her back. A sense of well-being filled her as she savored the feel of his strong hands through her sweater.

"That feels wonderful," she murmured, a blessed lethargy

seeping into her as the tension disappeared and a warm contentment took its place. Her skin tingled everywhere he touched her. Now his hands were sliding gently up and down her smooth legs.

He leaned over and whispered close to her ear. "Do you like that?"

She didn't trust herself to speak, and instead nodded her head.

He chuckled, and continued running his hands over her back and shoulders.

She felt so good, so relaxed....

Then his hands were under her shoulders, lifting her to face him, drawing her up to him. She kissed him firmly and he kissed back, his strong hands moving restlessly in her hair.

"I love you, my friend," she murmured. Her arms tightened around him. Their bodies, with magnetic force, pulled toward each other. "Hold me, Don, just hold me, please... never let me go."

"I'm holding you, love."

He began to rub the back of Julie's neck with his hand, occasionally allowing his thumbs to brush against the tips of her ears. Once again, she forced her lips to cover his, and kissed him with all the strength she possessed. He didn't resist. Instead, he kissed her back with a strength that overpowered hers. She melted into his arms, closer and still closer. The cabin and the cold seemed to fade away, and there was only the two of them in their own special world.

Julie began to tremble with the intensity of their kiss. The two became fused, closer than they had ever been before, but still not close enough to satisfy either of them. Julie wanted this man, wanted to belong to him completely, to express her love to him with her whole body, not just her lips. The urge was overpowering, even stronger than it had been that night in the pond. She knew that Don felt the same way. He was trembling too, and his kiss was so intense she almost forgot how to breathe.

She pulled back her arms and slipped her hands inside his shirt, and was startled when he suddenly jumped back. In spite of the fact that he had pulled away, his eyes were warm with love, his face glowing with a mixture of happiness and pain.

"Wait a minute, Julie," he said huskily. "Take it easy, now. Give me a second to think."

"No, Don," she murmured. "Don't think about it. This has been building up all along. We both know it—"

"We need to talk about this, doll." Now his voice sounded more controlled. He moved back to the other side of the sofa. "We can't rush into something we might regret later. I know what you want — what we both want — but I'm not sure we'll be happy, even if we go through with it."

Tears began to fill Julie's eyes as she pleaded with him. "I know that with you, I could have no regrets... except that I didn't meet you sooner. I never knew that anyone like you existed, Don. I never dreamed that I could feel this way about anyone before. You've brought so much love, laughter, and comfort into my life. You complete me, Don. I want to be totally yours, in every sense of the word. Please, love, please don't push me away. I know that you want me, too."

"Yep, I know all that, doll. But we need to think before we act. We're not the only ones who'll be affected by anything we do here today. Don't forget about your husband and daughter. You know how much I love you, Julie. I just don't want anything to destroy the beauty of what we've shared together. You are the most important thing on Earth to me, and I want to do what's best for you. If we make love, will we ever be able to really look at each other in the same way? What would it do to our friendship?"

She knew instinctively that he was right. But she didn't want to admit it. "I want you so much that I can't think clearly anymore. I can't bear the thought of dying without ever making love to you. It feels so right just being with you. I need you, Don. I need you so much."

"I know, doll. It's tough. We both want each other. But if we give in to these feelings, I'm afraid we may destroy this precious friendship. Right now, we have a greater happiness than we've ever dreamed of sharing, something most people never know in a lifetime. Do you really want to risk destroying it for a few moments of physical pleasure? I love you so much, Julie. I'm afraid that by indulging ourselves, we'll lose what we have. Do you really want to make love, knowing how we'll feel about it later?"

Yes, Julie's heart whispered. But her mind was stronger now that he had pulled back. She remembered all the good times she and Robert had shared and how much they had gone through together. Robert was a very good man, and it would indeed be heartlessly cruel of her to be unfaithful to him. If he ever found out, it would kill him. She knew without a doubt that he had been faithful to her through all the years of their marriage.

She also thought of her Cheryl, and how much the possible knowledge of an affair would hurt her. *Mom, I trust you, and I trust your judgment about people,* Cheryl had said. Would she believe in "forever with one man" if she found out? Julie knew that things would never be the same. How could she hurt Robert and Cheryl that way after all they had given to her?

But I want him! her heart pleaded.

You already have him, her mind replied. *You have all of them, all of their love and support without having to make a choice between them or hurting anyone. Don is right, and you know it.*

"Oh, Don!" Julie whispered, her eyes filling with tears as they met his. "You're right. I hate this. Why didn't we meet years ago? Of course, you're right. It just hurts so much to admit it. Just hold me. Please hold me."

"I'm holding you, doll. I'll hold you as long as you need me to. Please know how much I love you. I know this sounds terribly crazy, but I love you enough not to go all the way. Do you understand?"

"Yes...." She guessed she really did, although her heart was still reluctant to accept it.

Don turned around and grabbed the quilt off a nearby rack, and laid it on the floor in front of the fire. He reached across Julie and picked up the wool blanket which had been folded on the sofa near her, and spread it on top of the quilt.

"There, madam. Dry those tears."

Don helped Julie down onto the blanket, then joined her. He lay flat on his back, then reached up and pulled her gently down beside him. A lull came over them; there were no words to be said. Their hearts were speaking to each other in the silent language that only they understood. Julie felt warm, safe, secure in the arms of her forever friend. She was safe, and nothing could harm her now.

Julie rolled over onto her side, then leaned up onto her elbow. She rolled her eyes at Don. He tried to smile, and whispered softly, "I do love those antsy eyes, Julie. I will always love your eyes and your beautiful smile."

"Don, when something happens to me, will you know how much I loved you?"

"I'll know, love."

Julie lowered her head and kissed him on the lips. She pulled away for a moment, then leaned forward to kiss him again. She parted his lips with her tongue, and for a moment in time, in the only way allowed, they became one. Oh, how cruel life was to let her taste of such sweetness when it was so nearly over.

For long moments, they lay together. Julie stroked his

beard with her hand. Then she couldn't help herself; she started sobbing.

"What is it, doll?" he whispered. "What are you thinking about?"

She wiped at her eyes. "I was just thinking about you and Emily and Abby here on Christmas Eve. Christmas was always a special time for my family. When I was little, before my father died, we always used to go out on Christmas Eve and sing carols. And our tree... Dad used to go into the forest and find the best one. Sometimes he'd look for hours. Then Mom and I would decorate it with strings of cranberries and popcorn. Mom would fix a special dinner on Christmas Day. Roast duck, with mashed potatoes and gravy. We'd have that wonderful smell in the house while we were opening presents."

He hugged her close. "Sounds like you had a great family."

"I'm afraid I won't ever see another Christmas," she said, sobbing again. "If I had just one wish, that would be it — that I could live long enough to feel the joy of one more Christmas."

"You'll have it," he said, hugging her. "I promise."

Chapter Twenty-Nine

It had been a busy day for Cheryl. It was Tom's day off, so Cheryl had decided to leave Matthew at home with him and take care of some errands she'd been putting off. They had left Matthew with a babysitter a couple of times to go to dinner and a movie, but she didn't want to do that any more than necessary while he was still so young.

She had gone shopping and dropped off some clothes for dry cleaning, and decided to stop by to visit her mother on the way home.

"Mom?" she called out as she came through the front door.

There was no answer.

"Mom?" she called in a louder voice. The house was silent, and sudden panic clutched Cheryl's heart. "Mom! Are you here?"

"Cheryl?" It was her father's voice, coming from the kitchen area.

Almost sagging with relief, she hurried into the kitchen and found him pouring a cup of coffee. "How come you're home?" she asked quickly. "Where's Mom? Is she okay?"

"Sure, she's okay." He stirred in a spoonful of sugar, then looked up at her and grinned. "Should I take those questions in order? Let's see... I'm home because I was working on some damned papers last night for the plant and left 'em here. Had to come back and get them, and decided to have a decent cup of coffee while I was here. I don't know where Julie is. She was gone when I got here, and I figure she's visiting one of the neighbors or running an errand or just taking a walk. She doesn't always check in with me, you know."

Cheryl felt a flash of annoyance at his flippant tone. "Well, she's really sick. I never know when...." She let the words trail off. She'd been about to say *I never know when I'll get the phone call saying she's gone,* but she decided that was better left unsaid.

"I know, babe." He sighed, then took his coffee to the table and sat down.

"Do you really, Dad? Do you know? Do you know how scared I am when I think about losing Mom? Aren't you scared to death yourself?"

"Of course I am. Do you think I'm heartless?"

"No, but sometimes you would like Mom — and me, and the rest of the world, for that matter — to think you are."

He thought about that, then shrugged. "Maybe you're right, Cherrie. I haven't been fair to your mother. Some days if I think about it long enough, I could go crazy. Julie is a fine lady. I rarely show her, but I'm very proud of her and all she has done for both of us."

Cheryl sank down into the chair across from him. "But why haven't you told her that, Dad?"

He sipped coffee, then put the cup on the table and wrapped his hands around it as if to absorb its warmth. "I can't answer that. Maybe it's just the way I was raised myself. I guess I never looked at all the extra special things your mother did as being more than what was expected of her as my wife."

"And now? Have you changed your mind about any of that?"

Robert looked at his daughter and, drawing his lips tightly together, nodded his head. "Oh, baby, I've been such an uncaring fool. It is so much easier for me to keep myself wrapped up in my work than to face reality. I truly believed that if I ignored certain things long enough, they would go away... or at least get better. I've never lost anyone in my life before who wasn't old enough to die. I truly thought at first that your mother was playing this lupus thing up to keep me home with her more. But now, almost too late, I realize that she was only asking for what she should have had all along... my love and support." Robert lowered his chin to his chest.

Cheryl realized how torn up Robert was about Julie. She knew he was feeling guilty that he hadn't given her the support she needed over the years, and that he hadn't before now recognized her worth and value.

Ashamed of showing his weaker side to his daughter, Robert straightened on his chair and almost instantly seemed to revert to his old self. "I don't know where the heck your mother is now. She never stays home anymore. For someone who claims to be deathly sick, she sure has a lot of ambition when it comes to running around."

Cheryl was pretty sure that Julie was with Don Lipton. They had been spending a lot of time together, and she realized that she should feel more troubled by this. Her mother had told her that Don was a very close friend, but Cheryl knew it was actually much more than friendship... at least "friendship" in the usual sense of the word.

In truth, Julie was getting something from Don Lipton that she had never gotten from Robert. Don was taking her seriously and encouraging her to grow in ways that Robert never allowed.

Cheryl had no doubt that her parents loved each other.

But she also knew after the conversation she'd just had with her dad that he would be crushed if he found out that Julie was spending so much time with Don Lipton.

"Did your mother tell you her crazy idea about writing a book?" he asked. "Can you imagine someone of her intelligence cranking out a *Gone With The Wind,* or something like that? Crazy lady!"

"Yeah, Mom did mention the book to me. But I don't think it's a crazy idea. If it makes Mom feel better about herself and helps fill her hours, I think it's great. Even if nothing ever comes from it, it's good therapy for her."

"Well, I think she's spending entirely too much time on this foolishness." Robert refused to see Cheryl's point of view. "She should be resting, or at least be spending more time with her family. She should be doing something that makes her happy."

Knowing how important this book was to Julie, Cheryl jumped at the chance to protect her mother's interests. "I think writing *does* make Mom happy. I think she enjoys writing about people she loves."

"Then why the hell does she cry every time she's working on that book?" he demanded. "That doesn't sound like anything someone who is happy would do. I suppose now you're going to try to convince me that they are tears of joy. You might as well hang it up, Cherrie. This book thing is no good."

Cheryl wanted to explain that Julie was driven to finish the book, and that not finishing it before she died would be terrible for her — far worse than trying to find happier things to do.

But she knew that to continue this conversation with her father might alienate them. She felt that she had lessened the gap between her father and herself with this visit. At least, he had opened up a little bit to her. She didn't want to undo any good that had come from it.

Another time, perhaps, she would try to help her father see that her mother was preparing for death the only way she knew how. There were no teachers to help her, no much-admired role models; this was something Julie had to do in her own way. Cheryl, knowing her mother perhaps as well as anyone, trusted she would even do that well.

She reached over and patted her father's hand. "We just have to have some faith, Dad. Faith that Mom knows what's best for her, how she should be spending her time. I know it isn't easy. Believe me, I know. But we can't live her life for her—" Her words choked, and she thought, *What's left of it, anyway.* She got to her feet. "I'll give her a call later."

He nodded, still staring into the bottom of his empty cup. He didn't look up even when she leaned over and kissed him goodbye.

Chapter Thirty

Monday, November 17

I'm becoming so weak. Each day I beg God to let me live long enough to complete my book. I usually stay up most of the night writing my love's feelings in my journal.

Oh, how often I think of little Matthew and all the times I will miss watching him grow up. I think of Cheryl and Robert and Tom, and the days we will never share. I ache inside with longing for the college degree I will never have. Life is so unfair for allowing me to come so close to something and then snatching it away with so little respect for me.

My heart cries when I think of Don, whom I have met too late in life, and with whom the moments I have shared were too few. It is the pain from my illness, and the pain from my heart's sorrow, that allows me to write.

Although death seems to be coming entirely too soon, my life has indeed been full. I have known the love of a very special man with whom I have shared twenty-five years of my life. I have known the beauty of seeing my daughter and my little grandson. So well I recall the love of being a woman in the arms of a lover.

My life has been a mixed basket of emotions. I know the true meaning of joy, the grandest joy, and of sorrow, the deepest sorrow, of all the emotions that only a woman about to lose it all could know. It is with that love as my guide that I write it down, in a way that only I can.

The book is almost finished. Daily, Don reads what I have written. He always makes welcomed suggestions. This book is a real dream come true for both of us. In a sense, it was bound by our love. Don has agreed to draw a picture of his gazebo for the cover, and to include the poem he has written for me, as well. He promised to make certain that when something does happen to me, he will do all in his power to see that the book is published....

Julie's health deteriorated rapidly over the next three weeks. The kidney dialysis was keeping her alive, but she developed an infection in her lungs in late November, and nothing Dr. Cole did seemed to help. Even shallow breathing was extremely painful. Finally, Dr. Cole told her and Robert that she would have to go into the hospital again for more intensive treatment.

"Is this it?" Julie asked as she and Robert sat in Dr. Cole's office. As difficult as it was to ask the question, she needed to know what to expect. "Will... will this be a one-way trip to the hospital for me?"

He averted his eyes. "We certainly would hope not, Julie—"

"Dr. Cole," she interrupted quietly. "We've been through a lot together." She took Robert's hand in hers. "All three of us. I want to know how you expect this to work out."

He drew in a breath, let it out in a soft sigh. "I'm afraid it doesn't look good, Julie. I've been throwing everything I can at this infection. The kidneys have continued to weaken, and I'm afraid your body just doesn't have the strength to fight anymore."

Beside Julie, Robert was sobbing quietly. Her own voice remained steady as she said, "I'll check in tomorrow afternoon. I have a few things to do first."

He nodded solemnly. "I understand, Julie."

Don had hand-waxed the old Plymouth, and the gold paint shown with new life. The interior had been vacuumed and the seats shampooed. The car had a clean, new smell. He'd even cleaned the dashboard with something that made it shine.

"I'm impressed!" Julie said with a smile as he helped her into the passenger side.

"Nothing's too good for my lady," Don said after he got in behind the wheel. "I was thinking about renting a limo, but decided to just turn this old dog into one, instead."

It was a bright, sunny day, and the ride down the country roads to the narrow footpath seemed especially beautiful. Julie knew it would be the last trip to the gazebo for her, but for some reason, she felt no sense of loss this time. She wanted only to enjoy this day as much as possible, not to imbue it with sadness. She had already told Don that she would be going into the hospital the next day.

After he parked the car beside the familiar row of mailboxes, Don took Julie's hand and they began walking slowly toward the gazebo. She leaned against him, taking the support of his arm. Without it, she would have fallen.

When they reached the clearing, she stopped and stared. A perfectly shaped, six-foot blue spruce had been placed on a stand next to the gazebo, and was festooned with strings of cranberries, popcorn chains, and paper cutouts of birds. As they got closer, she could hear Christmas music coming from small speakers Don had placed in the foliage around the gazebo.

"Oh, Don...." That was as far as she could go. She leaned against him, feeling the burn in her eyes but determined to keep the tears from spilling out.

Don led her forward past the tree and opened the door of the gazebo. He had spent several weekends working on the gazebo, and now it looked as good as the day he'd put the last coat of paint on it more than twenty years ago. The redwood deck and rails had been sanded down and re-stained, and the benches had thick, protective coatings of forest green paint. He had even trimmed the shrubbery around it.

He took Julie's hand and helped her up the steps. Don closed the door behind her, and she turned slowly, her eyes widening as she saw what he had done. The gazebo was decorated too, with strings of bulbs and colored paper draped from beams in the ceiling. She saw that he had placed a small heater under the seat, and even though the gazebo was open, the warm air was collecting under the ceiling and warming it nicely.

In the corner, Don had set up a small table that was draped with a Christmas tablecloth. Underneath, she could see a large wicker box.

"What's that?" she asked.

"You'll see. I have something for you. But first, we dance."

They danced gently, slowly, to "Silent Night" and "Silver Bells." Then Julie needed to rest, and he eased her down onto the new cushions he had brought to the gazebo several weeks ago.

"Just sit her and rest, doll," he told her. "I'll have everything ready in a minute."

She watched, speechless, as he pulled the box from under the table, opened it, and began taking out things which he set on the table. First was a small candle arrangement decorated with wax bells in red and green. He lit the candle, then reached into the box again and brought out covered plates, silverware, and napkins. He set the table, then brought out a bottle of nonalcoholic champaign and two crystal goblets.

This was almost too much for her. His thoughtfulness was so touching, and again she felt the tears threaten. She pushed them back with an act of will. She was not going to cry. Not this time. She was grateful that she'd had a few precious months to enjoy this place with Don. He had given her so much. During these final weeks of her life, he had showed her how to laugh even in the worst of times. Together, they had found a love unlike any either had known before. In a very special, beautiful way — indeed, a way that many people have lived a lifetime without doing — they had touched each others' hearts.

Finally, he stepped over to her and offered his arm. "Madam, dinner is served."

After pulling out one of the chairs and sitting her down at the table, he removed the covers over the plates, revealing thin slices of roast duck, mashed potatoes and gravy, and sweet corn.

"Fixed it all myself," he said.

Julie didn't know what to say. The food smelled wonderful, and the gesture was unbelievably sweet. But she had little appetite, and she knew she wouldn't be able to eat much.

Don must have seen the doubtful look on her face. "Eat whatever you want, doll," he said. "Or nothing, if you don't feel like it. This is for you. The last thing I want to do is push you into eating if you don't feel up to it."

"Thank you for all this," she whispered. "It's just wonderful, Don. Everything is perfect."

He sat down across from her, and she did manage to eat more than she'd expected to. "You really cooked all this?" she asked, lifting a skeptical eyebrow.

He nodded. "I used to be quite an accomplished cook. It's just one more thing I haven't done in a long time."

Don poured champagne, and they toasted to their love. Then Don helped her back over to the cushioned bench.

"This is all so wonderful, Don," she whispered.

He reached into the wicker box again and brought out a brightly wrapped present, which he handed to her. When she opened it, she found a photo album with photographs of the places they had been together: the lighthouse, the gazebo, the cabin, and some of the most beautiful spots along their various walks and drives.

On the cover of the album was a pencil sketch of the gazebo. She knew he had done it, and it was beautiful.

"Thank you, Don," she said softly, leaning into him as he gave her a hug. "This is the most wonderful thing anyone has ever done for me. Can we dance again?"

The Christmas music had ended, and Don reached under the bench to get the tape player started again.

"We don't need music," she said. "We've danced without it before."

"Right, you are." Don slipped his hands along her ribs and pulled her gently up under her arms until she was standing. She leaned against his body, and together they moved back and forth ever so slowly to a beautiful love song playing in their hearts that only the two of them could hear. Both of their hearts were playing the same song, *Please never let this end.*

After a while, Julie began leaning more heavily upon Don.

"I'm afraid we're going to have to stop," she said weakly. "God knows, I don't want to."

He kissed her gently on the lips, then helped her back to the bench.

He picked up the manuscript he had brought along. It was her book, her final gift of love to him, finished. He'd read it the night before.

Don held the book close to his heart and pressed his mouth against Julie's ear. "You've done it," he whispered. He pulled a neatly folded paper from between the pages. "Julie, this is my final gift to you... this poem and an eternity of love. I wrote it last night. Can I read it to you, love?"

Julie nodded. "Please do."

> "*My Forever Friend,*
>   *by Donald George Lipton.*
>
> *It was great to have a friend like you,*
>   *so nice to know you cared,*

I treasure all the happiness,
    that you and I have shared.
A shining dream at last came true,
    to know your wondrous worth,
the bit of Heaven sweet and dear,
    you brought me here on Earth.
It's nice to know you thought of me,
    that smiles have been our own,
that life was filled with tender warmth,
    that we never were alone.
To ever know the beautiful,
    the moon and stars on high,
while hand in hand we walked life's road,
    as hours and days sped by.
'Twas nice to share life's love with you,
    and know that you loved me.
Because you cared, it helped so much,
    how precious life can be.
Our sweetest dreams were sweeter still,
    since they were shared by two.
I pray this day, my trusted friend,
    I've made many dreams for you.
Some days, my life seems oh so short,
    yet your pain seems too long.
I lose myself in thoughts of death,
    and everything feels wrong.
Then like magic you appear,
    and lighten up my way,
with hugs and smiles, ever near,
    you know just what to say.
And when at last, your death does come,
    your earthly life is through,
I know I'll find the strength to live,
    in part, because of you.

> *And when you see God face to face,*
> *   and all pain has reached an end,*
> *I know He'll hold you gently,*
> *   I'll insist, my Forever Friend.*
> *Love, just know that when your body dies,*
> *   in my heart you will live on,*
> *that love forever lingers*
> *   even when the loved one's gone.*
> *I've loved you here your days on Earth,*
> *   I'll love you till the end.*
> *For all eternity, and more,*
> *   you'll be my Forever Friend."*

Julie had been holding tight rein on her emotions, but now she began to cry, warm tears that flowed down her cheeks. She hugged him fiercely, not caring that every muscle in her body cried out in pain. The future was later. Now the things she needed most were here in this sun washed gazebo.

That last time at the gazebo passed ever too quickly. Julie begged time to stop passing. "God," she pleaded, "make this moment last forever."

But time, merciless, stopped not at all. Julie realized that time was their most valuable, yet the most perishable of all their possessions, and Don agreed. Somewhere between the golden sunrise that morning and the now rapidly approaching sunset, with Don she had captured the time, their final hours together at the gazebo, and made them into a part of her very self that would become a lasting part of the universe.

Don held Julie close to his body, his tears blending with hers. In that way, they had become one.

"We'd better go," he said gently.

"In a minute," she murmured. She moved closer to him, feeling his strength, absorbing his love. She wondered if Heaven could be so sweet.

Chapter Thirty-One

Final Diary entry

I'm so weak and exhausted, so ready to give up. This, at last, is the final page of my story.... My mind is full of a million questions about life... and about death.... Although my heart is crushed knowing I must leave so much love behind, I'm not afraid to die. My life and the people in it have given me a glimpse of Heaven on Earth, just enough to make me yearn for the real thing.

The physical part of me is leaving, but the greatest part of me can't die. I truly believe that love is forever. Eternally, I will live on in the hearts and memories of those who have loved me....

Later, Don wondered if it was really just a coincidence that he was having such a pleasant dream when the call came from Cheryl. In the dream, he was surrounded by figures he could not quite see. They were like shifting, gauzy images. They moved about gracefully, touching him and whispering words he couldn't quite understand. Each light touch brought him a feeling of love and comfort unlike anything he'd ever felt before. These beings didn't have to speak to him to communicate the way they felt.

For a moment, he resisted the jangling, intruding sound. He wanted to stay in this place. He wanted to feel the soft touches and the energy of love and acceptance.

Finally, though, it broke up, and he realized the insistent sound was the telephone. He came awake instantly. His mind was already on Julie as he rolled over and reached for the bedside phone.

"Don?" came a frantic voice. "It's Cheryl."

Ten minutes later he was dressed and out the door, roaring toward the hospital in his faithful old Plymouth. Julie had been in the hospital for two days, and now Dr. Cole had told Cheryl that she was slipping away quickly.

God, he prayed, *let me get there before you take her.*

Don had paid long visits each day, and was there when Robert came in after work. They had met earlier, and Robert knew that Don had been Julie's instructor at college and had been helping with her book. He seemed to have no idea at all that their friendship went much deeper than that.

Don had been expecting and dreading this telephone call, knowing that the end wouldn't be long coming.

~

"Julie Hunter... let's see...." The receptionist tapped at her keyboard, then frowned slightly at what she saw on the screen. "Mrs. Hunter's doctors have ordered that only family members can visit." She looked up at Don. "Sorry, sir."

Don forced himself to remain calm even though he felt ready to explode from anxiety and impatience. "Mrs. Hunter's daughter called me just a little while ago and asked me to come. I'm a very close friend. Could you check and see if an exception can be made?"

"Well, I doubt...." The look on his face made her change her mind about what she had been about to say. "Let me call the nurses' station on that floor, sir."

Don drummed his fingers on the counter top while she made the call. He knew that only Cheryl would be with Julie now. Robert had gone to Seattle on a business trip the day before. Don thought he knew why Julie had insisted that Robert make this trip, even though he wanted to cancel. On several occasions, Julie had told Don about the difficulty Robert was having accepting her illness. He wondered now if she had insisted that he go on his trip so he would be spared the final painful hours with her.

On the phone, Cheryl told him she'd called her father, and that Robert was getting the first flight back.

The receptionist finally hung up and told him he could go up to Julie's room, and he took the elevator to the third floor. As he walked down the long hallway toward her room, he tried to gather the needed courage to go in to see her. He wouldn't let her see him cry.

Cheryl was there, sitting next to her mother. Julie's frail body looked tiny in the bed. The only movement was the heaving of her chest as she struggled for each breath. It was as if her body was begging for just one more moment of life.

Don knew there was no use trying to pretend that Julie would get better *someday*. God, how much they had shared, how often they had talked about this moment. Was one ever really prepared for this?

Julie was still conscious, but her voice was so weak he could barely hear her as she told Cheryl that she would like to be alone with him for a little while. Cheryl was reluctant to leave, but gave her mother a hug and went downstairs for some coffee, saying she would be back in an hour.

Don walked over to the bed and took Julie's hand. How little it looked lying inside his own. He softly rubbed the top of her hand with his thumb, and Julie opened her eyes again. He could see the slightest trace of a smile upon her lips. He leaned over and gave her a kiss on her cheek.

"There now, that isn't being too pushy is it?" Then, in a more serious voice, he whispered, "I love you, Julie."

Her eyes were flooded with tears as she nodded to show that she understood.

Don reached across the bed and seized a tissue from the box on the bedside table. As he gently wiped her eyes, he teased, "That will be fifty cents today, doll."

Julie's eyes held his for a long moment. Then her lips moved slightly, and he heard her whisper, "I love you, Don."

"I love you too, Julie," he said softly.

With a trembling hand, she reached to the bedside table and touched a folded piece of paper. "I wrote... something for you," she murmured. "That day we went to... the lighthouse...." Every word was costing her dearly. He tried to shush her, but she was determined to say it. "I wish... wish we could have gone back." She paused, closing her eyes for a moment as if to regather her strength. "In my mind, my love... we've gone back to the lighthouse... many times...." Her eyes went to the folded piece of paper.

He picked up the paper and opened it to find a handwritten poem:

Come Take a Walk With Me
by Julie Anne Hunter

My precious friend, my forever friend,
*   if you could only know,*
The millions of times we have walked in my head,
*   to this place that you love so...*
We smiled as we walked hand in hand on the beach,
*   as the waves cast a spray on our face,*
And sometimes we'd cry as we saw life pass by,
*   too quickly, it seemed like a race...*
Sometimes it was late, and together we'd wait,
*   to make a memory I'll never forget,*

You'd hold me so tight, and kiss me goodnight,
 as together we'd watch the sunset...
We lay on the beach, wrapped in each other's arms,
 at sunrise we'd watch a new day start,
My hands were hugging your body as
 your hand was embracing my heart...
Sometimes in my head our walks seem so real,
 I'm so thankful for each night with you,
I hope and I pray, before my final day,
 We can make all these moments come true.

He looked up, his eyes brimming despite the promise he'd made to himself that he wouldn't cry in front of her. They had never gone back to the lighthouse... at least, not physically. Now it was clear that she'd returned many times in her imagination.

In a choked voice, he said, "It's beautiful, Julie. God, how I wish...."

She gently squeezed his hand, and he saw a slight movement of her head. She didn't want to hear regrets now.

She drew a shallow breath and closed her eyes. Above her, the monitor beeped slowly, as if even it was exhausted from the effort of keeping track of her life signs. Every now and then, Julie opened her eyes and looked at him. He sensed her uneasiness and fear, but for once there was nothing he could do but stay close and love her. Occasionally, he sensed her squeezing his hand more tightly with her own. Somehow, he knew she was telling him never to let go. How often she had told him that as long as he was in her life, she would have a reason to live. He knew that this time his presence or love wouldn't be enough.

"It's okay, Julie, I'm here," he whispered. "I'm not going anywhere. We'll do this thing together. It will be okay... I promise."

But Don knew that at least for him, it would never be *okay* again. A very special lady, a beautiful part of his life, was about to disappear forever. She had found her way into his life, his very heart, a place no one else had dared to even come close to for many years. She had showed him how to live every day to the fullest, and now she was showing him how to die. She had taught him how to live and love again, and through her own writing she had helped him recapture his own love for it. She had set him free, had given him a second chance at life. Now he owed it to her to make the most of it.

Don talked about the short time they had been able to spend together, and about her book. He sensed that even with her eyes closed, she was listening and clinging to his every word. He had no doubt that her book would be a huge success. The depth of emotion, he told her, was truly amazing.

A young nurse came in and checked the monitor. After studying it for a moment, she pressed a button and the beeping stopped. She turned to Don. "A friend?"

Don looked at her and hesitated a moment before answering, "Ahh, yes... a friend." His voice broke. "A forever friend."

The nurse looked at Don as if she understood. "I'm sorry, sir. I wish I could help. I think it's time to tell Julie goodbye."

Don nodded. *Goodbye.* How she had always hated that word. They had promised each other, "never a goodbye."

For the final time, Don took Julie's hand in his own and willed all his love to travel through from his hand to hers. "God speed, my love. It's time for you to go. Someone who loves you even more than any of us here is waiting to hold you now. Remember what I told you, Julie. Heaven is a great big hug. I will never forget you, Julie. Your name is written on my heart."

Julie's hand squeezed his ever so slightly, then relaxed. Finally, the labored breathing stopped.

Cheryl returned a few moments later and found Don still seated beside the bed, holding Julie's hand.

"She's asleep?" Cheryl asked.

Don shook his head and whispered, "We've lost her."

Cheryl wiped away tears, then sat on the other side of the bed and stroked her mother's arm. "At least she isn't in pain anymore."

After a long time, Don got to his feet. He gently touched Julie's face for the final time, gave Cheryl a warm embrace, and left the room. He could see the young nurse headed that way with Robert, who was just arriving. Don couldn't force himself to stop and talk. What could he possibly say?

He took the elevator to the first floor, and realized that even elevators would never be the same. Many times on the way down to the first floor from his office, he and Julie had stolen moments on the elevator to hug and kiss.

He exited through the emergency room door. It took longer to get to the parking lot that way, but for the moment, time had stood still. He walked slowly to his car. When he turned the ignition to start the engine, the radio came on and, almost as if it had been planned, he heard their song: *Remember Me This Way.*

He put his head in his hands and cried like a baby.

Epilogue

Dearest Julie,

I have done some different and strange things in my lifetime, but this is probably the most unusual. Writing in someone else's journal is not something that I ever planned to do.

When you first gave me your journal, I knew it was full of your deepest feelings and inner thoughts, and I had no business knowing what went on in your heart and mind. But then I started to think back over the time we had known each other and decided to read your thoughts and try to understand your spirit — that which made you live through these last few months... with us together and yet apart.

When we first met, we didn't really know each other because I had a mask on... a mask that protected me from seeing the world. I put the mask on after the accident and kept it between me and everyone else.

All of a sudden, you were out there in the class, and you were a target — one that just kept coming back for more. At first I picked on you just to pick, but then I started to notice that there was something special in the things you wrote. This "something special" came from a still, small, and unused voice inside of you. I was the teacher, the professor, and I was the one with all the answers. You, on the other hand, were just another person to throw darts at. You were subject to whatever I dished out.

Someplace along the line, things started to change. My challenges of your writing were becoming good constructive criticism. Then the day came and you had done your research, such as any good writer should do. Then you became the teacher and I became the student. You were now the one with the challenges.

Little things started to happen, and the relationship developed, changed, whatever. I sure did not understand what was going on. The next thing I knew, we were forever friends, stealing precious moments together at every chance. Many times I have felt life coming back into me, a life that I never thought would be rekindled. As hacked as it might seem, the hourglass of time was running out of you and into me. I will never be able to write the way I did before, but maybe now I can write better because I have had your love in my life.

Now I have read your journal, the words that represent what was in your heart, but oh how those words fall short of what I saw in your eyes and felt in your arms. As this entry closes — this final entry in your journal — let me say this: You brought a life back into me, and I have no way to thank you other than to say, with words — words that are so limited — that I will do with the grains of life's sands what I can. Do what I can to hug the memories of the past while pushing to life in the present, so that sometime in the future I may be able to write well enough to express what has happened over the past few months, express these feelings in such a way as well as you have expressed your love in this journal.

Lots of love and huggggggggs.

Don

After signing his name below the final entry, Don closed

the journal and sat looking down at it for a long moment. Julie had put her heart and soul into this journal, and now he had put a little of himself into it, as well. He felt sure that she wouldn't mind. In a way, perhaps this was the final consummation of their love. Somewhere, somehow, she would read this and understand.

He became aware of movement to his left, and when he turned in that direction he saw a sparrow perched on the gazebo's railing, staring at him with beady eyes. For a moment they held each other's gaze, then the bird was gone with a flutter of wings.

He sighed heavily. His hands were gripping the journal so tightly that his muscles ached. It took him several heartbeats of effort to release them, and he lay it with the hardbound novel on the bench beside him.

As Don looked out at the forest surrounding the gazebo, he realized that he could at last think about Emily and Abby without pain. The poisons of guilt and regret were gone, and now he could cherish the good memories and relive them again.

If not for Julie, he knew that he would have lived his life to the end in bitterness. Now he had a future to look forward to. His own book of poetry would be published in a few months, and he was very pleased with a novel he was working on. He still felt that special bond with Julie. No matter what happened in his life, it would always be there — a part of her living inside him, helping him find the right words for a poem or to appreciate the simple beauty in a daisy.

Could he ever accomplish with his poetry what she had done as a writer? Could he ever hope to touch peoples' hearts the way she had? He wasn't sure. But he knew he would try. And with her help, he just might succeed.